CBSE Term II
2022

Geography

Class XI

- Complete Theory Covering NCERT
- Case Based Questions
- Short/Long Answer Type Questions
- 3 Practice Papers with Explanations

Author
Farah Sultan

ARIHANT PRAKASHAN (School Division Series)

ARIHANT PRAKASHAN (School Division Series)

© **Publisher**

No part of this publication may be re-produced, stored in a retrieval system or by any means, electronic, mechanical, photocopying, recording, scanning, web or otherwise without the written permission of the publisher. Arihant has obtained all the information in this book from the sources believed to be reliable and true. However, Arihant or its editors or authors or illustrators don't take any responsibility for the absolute accuracy of any information published and the damage or loss suffered thereupon.

All disputes subject to Meerut (UP) jurisdiction only.

卐 **Administrative & Production Offices**

Regd. Office
'Ramchhaya' 4577/15, Agarwal Road, Darya Ganj, New Delhi -110002
Tele: 011- 47630600, 43518550

卐 **Head Office**
Kalindi, TP Nagar, Meerut (UP) - 250002, Tel: 0121-7156203, 7156204

卐 **Sales & Support Offices**
Agra, Ahmedabad, Bengaluru, Bareilly, Chennai, Delhi, Guwahati,
Hyderabad, Jaipur, Jhansi, Kolkata, Lucknow, Nagpur & Pune.

卐 **ISBN :** 978-93-25796-83-6

卐 **PRICE :** ₹150.00

PO No : TXT-XX-XXXXXXX-X-XX

Published by Arihant Publications (India) Ltd.

For further information about the books published by Arihant, log on to
www.arihantbooks.com or e-mail at info@arihantbooks.com

Follow us on   

Contents

Syllabus CBSE Term II Class XI

PART A	FUNDAMENTALS OF PHYSICAL GEOGRAPHY	15 Marks
Unit IV	**Climate** • Atmosphere- composition and structure; elements of weather and climate • Insolation-angle of incidence and distribution; heat budget of the earth-heating and cooling of atmosphere (conduction, convection, terrestrial radiation and advection); temperature - factors controlling temperature; distribution of temperature - horizontal and vertical; inversion of temperature • Pressure-pressure belts; winds-planetary, seasonal and local; air masses and fronts; tropical and extra-tropical cyclones • Precipitation-evaporation; condensation-dew, frost, fog, mist and cloud; rainfall-types and world distribution	08
Unit V	**Water (Oceans)** • Movements of ocean water-waves, tides and currents; submarine reliefs • Ocean resources and pollution	04
Unit VI	**Life on the Earth** • Biosphere - importance of plants and other organisms; biodiversity and conservation.	04
PART B	**India - Physical Environment**	15 Marks
Unit III	**Climate, Vegetation and Soil** • Weather and climate - spatial and temporal distribution of temperature, pressure winds and rainfall, Indian monsoon: mechanism, onset and withdrawal, variability of rainfalls: spatial and temporal; use of weather charts • Natural vegetation-forest types and distribution; wild life; conservation; biosphere reserves • Soils - major types (ICAR's classification) and their distribution, soil degradation and conservation	15
	Map work on identification/ interpolation of features based on the units on the outline Physical/Political map of the world/ India	05 Marks

CBSE Circular

Acad – 51/2021, 05 July 2021

Exam Scheme Term I & II

केन्द्रीय माध्यमिक शिक्षा बोर्ड

(शिक्षा मंत्रालय, भारत सरकार के अधीन एक स्वायत संगठन)

CENTRAL BOARD OF SECONDARY EDUCATION

(An Autonomous Organisation under the Ministryof Education, Govt. of India)

Term I Examinations:

- At the end of the first term, the Board will organize **Term I Examination** in a flexible schedule to be conducted between November-December 2021 with a window period of 4-8 weeks for schools situated in different parts of country and abroad. Dates for conduct of examinations will be notified subsequently.
- The Question Paper will have Multiple Choice Questions (MCQ) including case-based MCQs and MCQs on assertion-reasoning type. Duration of test will be **90 minutes** and it will cover only the rationalized syllabus of **Term I only** (i.e. approx. 50% of the entire syllabus).
- Question Papers will be sent by the CBSE to schools along with marking scheme.
- The exams will be conducted under the supervision of the External Center Superintendents and Observers appointed by CBSE.
- The responses of students will be captured on OMR sheets which, after scanning may be directly uploaded at CBSE portal or alternatively may be evaluated and marks obtained will be uploaded by the school on the very same day. The final direction in this regard will be conveyed to schools by the Examination Unit of the Board.
- Marks of the **Term I** Examination will contribute to the final overall score of students.

Term II Examination/ Year-end Examination:

- At the end of the second term, the Board would organize **Term II or Year-end Examination** based on the rationalized syllabus of Term II only (i.e. approximately 50% of the entire syllabus).
- This examination would be held around **March-April 2022** at the examination centres fixed by the Board.
- The paper will be of **2 hours duration** and have questions of different formats (case-based/ situation based, open ended- short answer/ long answer type).
- In case the situation is not conducive for normal descriptive examination **a 90 minute MCQ based exam** will be conducted at the end of the Term II also.
- Marks of the Term II Examination would contribute to the final overall score.

केन्द्रीय माध्यमिक शिक्षा बोर्ड

(शिक्षा मंत्रालय, भारत सरकार के अधीन एक स्वायत संगठन)

CENTRAL BOARD OF SECONDARY EDUCATION

(An Autonomous Organisation under the Ministryof Education, Govt. of India)

Assessment / Examination as per different situations

A. **In case the situation of the pandemic improves and students are able to come to schools or centres for taking the exams.**

Board would conduct Term I and Term II examinations at schools/centres and the theory marks will be distributed equally between the two exams.

B. **In case the situation of the pandemic forces complete closure of schools during November-December 2021, but Term II exams are held at schools or centres.**

Term I MCQ based examination would be done by students online/offline from home - in this case, the weightage of this exam for the final score would be reduced, and weightage of Term II exams will be increased for declaration of final result.

C. **In case the situation of the pandemic forces complete closure of schools during March-April 2022, but Term I exams are held at schools or centres.**

Results would be based on the performance of students on Term I MCQ based examination and internal assessments. The weightage of marks of Term I examination conducted by the Board will be increased to provide year end results of candidates.

D. **In case the situation of the pandemic forces complete closure of schools and Board conducted Term I and II exams are taken by the candidates from home in the session 2021-22.**

Results would be computed on the basis of the Internal Assessment/Practical/Project Work and Theory marks of Term-I and II exams taken by the candidate from home in Class X / XII subject to the moderation or other measures to ensure validity and reliability of the assessment.

In all the above cases, data analysis of marks of students will be undertaken to ensure the integrity of internal assessments and home based exams.

Dr. Joseph Emmanuel
Director (Academics)

CHAPTER 01

Composition and Structure of Atmosphere

In this Chapter...

- Composition of the Atmosphere
- Structure of the Atmosphere
- Elements of Weather and Climate

Air is essential for the survival of all the organisms. Human beings may survive for sometime without food and water but can't survive even a few minutes without breathing air. That is why atmosphere is a very essential part for human as well as for other living organisms. Atmosphere is a mixture of different gases and it envelopes the earth all round. It contains life-giving gases like oxygen for human and animals and carbon dioxide for plants. The air is the integral part of the earth's mass and 99% of the total mass of the atmosphere is confined to the height of 32 km from the earth's surface. The air is colourless and odourless and can be felt only when it blows as wind.

Composition of the Atmosphere

The atmosphere is composed of gases, water vapour and dust particles. The proportion of the gases, changes in the higher layers of the atmosphere in such a way that oxygen will be almost in negligible quantity at the height of 120 km. Similarly, carbon dioxide and water vapour are found only upto 90 km from the surface of the earth.

Gases

Atmosphere consists of a number of gases with different composition. Among all permanent gases, Nitrogen contributes maximum percentage i.e. 78.08 % in the atmosphere. Other permanent gases are Oxygen (20.95%), Argon (0.93%), Carbon dioxide (0.036%), Neon (0.002%), etc.

Carbon Dioxide (CO_2)

Apart from the useful gases, carbon dioxide (CO_2) is meteorologically a very important gas, as it is transparent to the incoming radiation of the sun but opaque to the outgoing terrestrial radiation. It absorbs a part of terrestrial radiation and reflects back some part of it towards the earth's surface.

CO_2 is largely responsible for the **greenhouse effect**. The volume of other gases is constant but the volume of CO_2 has been rising in the past few decades mainly because of burning of fossil fuels which resulted into increase in earth's temperature.

Ozone

It is another important component of the atmosphere found between 10 and 50 km above the earth's surface and acts as a filter and absorbs the ultraviolet rays radiating from the sun. It prevents them from reaching the surface of the earth.

Water Vapour

It is a variable gas in the atmosphere which decreases with altitude. In the warm and wet tropics, it accounts for 4% of the air by volume, while in the dry and cold areas of desert and polar regions, it may be less than 1% of the air.

Water vapour also decreases from the **equator**[1] towards the poles. It absorbs parts of the insolation from the sun and preserves the earth's radiated heat. Thus, it acts like a blanket allowing the earth neither to become too cold nor too hot. It also contributes to the stability and instability in the air.

Dust Particles

Atmosphere has a sufficient capacity to keep small solid particles, which originate from different sources and include sea salts, fine soil, smoke soot, ash, pollen, dust and disintegrated particles of meteors. Dust particles are generally concentrated in the lower layers of the atmosphere but convectional air currents may transport them to great heights.

In sub-tropical and temperate region, concentration of dust particles is higher due to dry winds in comparison to equatorial and polar region. Dust and salt particles act as hygroscopic nuclei around which water vapour condenses to produce clouds.

Structure of the Atmosphere

The atmosphere consists of different layers with varying density and temperature. Density is highest near the surface of the earth and decreases with increasing altitude.

The column of atmosphere is divided into five different layers depending upon the temperature condition. These are explained in detail below:

Troposphere

It is the lowermost layer of the atmosphere. Its average height is 13 km and extends roughly to a height of 8 km near the poles and 18 km at the equator.

Thickness of the troposphere is greatest at the equator because heat is transported to great heights by strong convectional currents. This layer contains dust particles and water vapour. All changes in climate and weather take place in this layer. Temperature in this layer decreases at the rate of 1° C for every 165 m of height. It is the most important layer for all biological activity.

The zone separating the troposphere from stratosphere is called as **tropopause**. The air temperature at the tropopause is about minus 80° C over the equator and about minus 45° C over the poles. Temperature in this layer is nearly constant that is why it is known as tropopause.

Stratosphere

Stratosphere is found above the tropopause and extends up to a height of 50 km. Important feature of the stratosphere is location of ozone layer which absorbs ultraviolet radiation and shields life on the earth from intense, harmful form of energy.

Mesosphere

It lies above the stratosphere which extends up to a height of 80 km. Temperature decreases with increase in altitude and reaches up to minus 100° C at the height of 80 km. The upper limit of mesosphere is known as the **mesopause.**

Ionosphere

It is located between 80 and 400 km above the mesopause. It contains electrically charged particles known as **ions**[2], that is why it is known as Ionosphere. Radio waves transmitted from the earth are reflected back to the earth by this layer. Temperature here starts increasing with height. That's the reason the layer is also called as **thermosphere.**

Exosphere

The uppermost layer of the atmosphere above the thermosphere or ionosphere is known as the exosphere. Geographers do not know much about this layer and its contents. It is the highest layer and it gradually merges with the outer space. Although, all layers of the atmosphere must be exercising influence on human beings, geographers are concerned with the first two layers of the atmosphere.

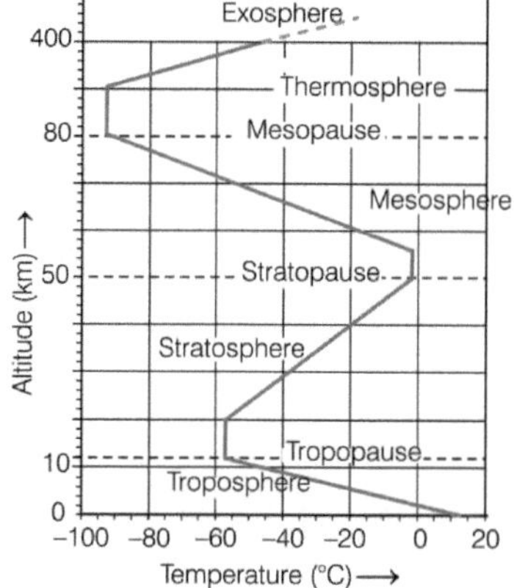

Structure of Thermosphere

Elements of Weather and Climate

The main elements of atmosphere which are subject to change and which influence human life on the earth are temperature, pressure, winds, humidity, clouds and precipitation.

---

1 **Equator** It is an imaginary line around the middle of the earth at an equal distance from the North pole and the South pole.
2 **Ions** It is an atom or molecule with a net electric charge due to the loss or gain of one or more electrons. It is present in ionosphere.

Chapter Practice

Objective Questions

• **Multiple Choice Questions**

1. Which atmospheric gas is transparent to incoming solar radiation but opaque to outgoing terrestrial radiation?
(a) Oxygen   (b) Water Vapour
(c) Carbon Dioxide   (d) Krypto.

Ans. (c) Carbon dioxide is transparent to solar radiation but opaque to outgoing terrestrial radiation.

2. Which of the following constituents of the atmosphere decrease from the equator towards the poles?
(a) Dust Particles   (b) Water Vapour
(c) Argon   (d) Neon

Ans. (b) Water vapour decreases from the equator towards the poles.

3. Disintegrated particles of meteors are associated with which of the following?
(a) Gases   (b) Solid particles
(c) Helium   (d) Water vapour

Ans. (b) Disintegrated particles of meteors, like soot, ash , pollen etc are associated with solid particles and the atmosphere has the capacity to retain them.

4. Where is a higher concentration of dust particles found?
(a) Subtropical and temperate regions
(b) Only temperate regions
(c) Polar regions
(d) Only subtropical regions.

Ans. (a) The higher concentration of dust particles is found in subtropical and temperate regions due to dry winds in comparison to equatorial and polar regions.

5. In which layer of the atmosphere does changes in climate and weather take place?
(a) Troposphere   (b) Stratosphere
(c) Mesopause   (d) Exosphere

Ans. (a) Most rising and sinking of air takes place in the troposphere which also contains water vapour and dust particles, hence contributing to all climate and weather phenomena taking place in this layer.

6. Which atmospheric layer is found above the tropopause?
(a) Mesopause
(b) Mesosphere
(c) Stratosphere
(d) Ionosphere

Ans. (c) The stratosphere is found above the tropopause and extends upto a height of 50 km.

7. Which layer helps in the transmission of radio waves?
(a) Mesosphere
(b) Troposphere
(c) Stratosphere
(d) Ionosphere

Ans. (d) Ionosphere contains electrically charged particles called ions which helps in the transmission of radio waves.

8. Choose the correctly matched pair about the atmosphere.

(a)	Dust Particles	–	Fine soil
(b)	Ozone	–	Exosphere
(c)	Nitrogen	–	Greenhouse gas
(d)	Ions	–	Tropopause

Ans. (a) Fine soil, comes under the category of dust particles or small solid particles that is retained by the atmosphere.

9. Match the items in List I with their correct pairs in List II.

	List I		List II
A.	Troposphere	1.	upto 80 kms
B.	Mesosphere	2.	upto 50 kms
C.	Stratosphere	3.	Between 80-400 kms
D.	Ionosphere	4.	8-18 kms

Codes

	A	B	C	D
(a)	1	2	3	4
(b)	2	1	3	4
(c)	4	2	3	1
(d)	4	1	2	3

Ans. (d)

10. Match the items in list I with their correct pairs in list II.

List I		List II
A. Troposphere	1.	Dust particles
B. Exosphere	2.	Electrically charged particles
C. Stratosphere	3.	Extremely rarified contents
D. Ionosphere	4.	Ozone

Codes

	A	B	C	D			A	B	C	D
(a)	2	3	4	1		(b)	2	1	3	4
(c)	1	3	4	2		(d)	4	1	2	3

Ans. (c)

11. Consider the following statements and choose the correct option.

  I. Dust particles are only concentrated in the lower layers of the atmosphere.

  II. Dust and salt particles act as hygroscopic nuclei around which water vapour condenses to produce clouds.

(a) Statement I is correct but statement II is incorrect.
(b) Statement I is incorrect but statement II is correct.
(c) Both statements I and II are correct.
(d) Both statements I and II are incorrect.

Ans. (b) Statement II is correct. Statement I is incorrect because dust particles are generally concentrated in the lower layers of the atmosphere but conventional air currents may transfer them to great heights.

12. Which of the following statements about the earth's atmosphere are incorrect? Choose the right option.

  I. The atmosphere consists of different layers with varying density but same temperature

  II. Density of atmosphere is highest near the surface of the earth.

(a) Statement I is incorrect but statement II is correct.
(b) Statement I is correct but statement II is incorrect.
(c) Both statements I and II are correct.
(d) Both statements I and II are incorrect.

Ans. (a) Statement I is incorrect because the atmosphere consists of different layers of varying density and also varying temperature. For example, the temperature in the troposphere decreases at the rate of 1 degree Celsius for every 165 m of height.

13. Consider the following statements and choose the correct option.

  I. The troposphere is the lowermost layer of the atmosphere.

  II. This is the important layer for all biological activity.

(a) Statement I is correct but statement II is incorrect.
(b) Statement I is incorrect but statement II is correct.
(c) Both statements I and II are correct.
(d) Both statements I and II are incorrect.

Ans. (c) Both the statements are correct.

14. Arrange the following layers of the atmosphere in an increasing order of height from the earth's surface.

  I. Stratopause   II. Mesosphere
  III. Mesopause   IV. Stratosphere

Codes
(a) IV, III, II, I   (b) IV, II, III, I
(c) IV, I, II, III   (d) I, II, III, IV

Ans. (c) The correct order is stratosphere, stratopause, mesosphere and mesopause. Stratosphere extends upto a height of 10-50 km. Stratopause is found above the Stratosphere at 50 km. Mesosphere is found above the Stratopause and extends from 50-80 km. Mesopause is found above Mesosphere, at a height of 80 km from the earth's surface.

15. Arrange the following elements in an increasing order of the percentage by volume that they occupy in the composition of air.

  I. Xenon

  II. Helium

  III. Hydrogen

Codes
(a) III, I, II   (b) II, III, I
(c) I, II, III   (d) III, II, I

Ans. (a) The correct order is hydrogen, xenon and helium. Hydrogen comprises of 0.00005 % of the air, xenon comprises of 0.00009 % and helium comprises of 0.0005% of the air.

• Case Based MCQs

16. Read the case/source given and answer the questions that follow by choosing the correct option.

Carbon dioxide is meteorologically a very important gas as it is transparent to the incoming solar radiation but opaque to the outgoing terrestrial radiation. It absorbs a part of terrestrial radiation and reflects back some part of it towards the earth's surface. It is largely responsible for the Greenhouse effect.

The volume of other gases is constant but the volume of carbon dioxide has been rising in the past few decades mainly because of the burning of fossil fuels. This has also increased the temperature of the air.

Ozone is another important component of the atmosphere found between 10 and 50 km above the earth's surface and acts as a filter and abosorbs the ultra-violet rays radiating from the sun and prevents them from reaching the surface of the earth.

(i) Which of the following options given below is absorbed by carbon dioxide?
(a) Incoming solar radiation
(b) Water vapour
(c) Outgoing terrestrial radiation
(d) Surface convection

Ans. (c) The outgoing terrestrial radiation is absorbed by carbon dioxide.

(ii) Burning of fossil fuels can result in ....
(a) increase in volume of ozone
(b) decrease in volume of carbon dioxide
(c) increase in volume of carbon dioxide
(d) None of the above

Ans. (c) Burning of fossil fuels results in the release of carbon dioxide into the atmosphere thereby increasing its volume.

(iii) Ozone layer is found in which layer of atmosphere?
(a) Troposphere
(b) Stratosphere
(c) Ionosphere
(d) Thermosphere

Ans. (b) Ozone layer is found in the stratosphere which is located at a height of 10- 50km.

(iv) Which of the following gases is opaque to the outgoing terrestrial radiation?
(a) Nitrogen
(b) Oxygen
(c) CO_2
(d) Argon

Ans. (c) CO_2 is opaque to the outgoing terrestrial radiation.

17. Study the following graph and answer the questions that follow by choosing the correct options.

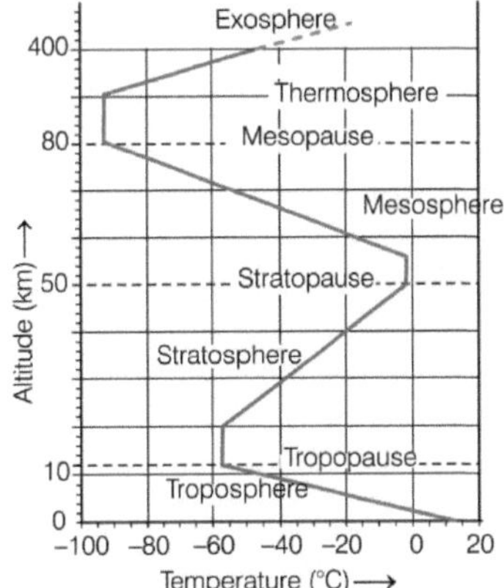

(i) Which layer of atmosphere has the lowest temperature?
(a) Stratopause   (b) Mesopause
(c) Troposphere   (d) Thermosphere

Ans. (b) Mesopause has the lowest temperature.

(ii) The temperature increases with altitude in which of the following layers?
(a) Mesosphere   (b) Stratosphere
(c) Troposphere   (d) All of these

Ans. (b) The temperature increases with altitude in Stratosphere.

(iii) Which of the following layers of atmosphere is most suitable for airplanes?
(a) Troposphere   (b) Exosphere
(c) Stratosphere   (d) Mesosphere

Ans. (c) Stratosphere is most suitable for airplanes.

(iv) The Atmosphere of Earth is bound to its surface by which of the following force?
(a) Gravitational Force   (b) Magnetic Force
(c) Tidal Force   (d) Gravity

Ans. (d) The Atmosphere of Earth is bound to its surface by gravity.

PART 2
Subjective Questions

• Short Answer (SA) Type Questions

1. Discuss the role of carbon dioxide in the atmosphere.

Ans. The role of carbon dioxide in the atmosphere is
- The carbon dioxide is meteorologically a very important gas, as it is transparent to the incoming solar radiation but opaque to the outgoing terrestrial radiation.
- Carbon dioxide absorbs a part of terrestrial radiation and reflects back some part of it towards the earth's surface. CO_2 is largely responsible for the greenhouse effect.
- The volume of other gases in the atmosphere is constant but the volume of carbon dioxide is increasing in the past few decades mainly because of the burning of fossil fuels. Carbon dioxide contributes maximum in increasing the temperature of air.

2. How water vapour contributes to the stability and instability in the air?

Ans. Water vapour contributes to the stability and instability in the air in the following ways

- Water vapour is a variable gas in the atmosphere. It decreases with altitude. In the warm and humid region, it accounts for 4% of the air by volume but only 1% in dry and polar regions.
- Water vapour also decreases from the equator toward the poles. It absorbs part of the insolation from the sun and preserves the earth's radiated heat.
- Water vapour acts like a blanket allowing the earth neither to become too cold nor too hot.

3. Describe the concentration of the vapours and dust particles in the atmosphere and how they are important variables of weather and climate?

Ans. There is sufficient amount of water vapour and dust particles in the atmosphere. But, their density varies region to region and with altitude. Water vapours are present maximum in hot and humid region and dust particles are found generally concentrated in lower layers of the earth.

Both water vapour and dust particles are important variables of weather and climate as they are the source of all forms of condensation and main absorbers of heat received from the sun or radiated from the earth. Dust particles and salt particles act as hygroscopic nuclei around which water vapour condenses to produce cloud.

4. Which layer is combinedly called as Homosphere? Discuss.

Ans. Troposphere, stratosphere, and mesosphere combinedly called as homosphere. Homosphere extends from the earth's surface upto an altitude of 80 km. Even though the atmosphere rapidly decreases in density with increasing altitude, the blend of gases is nearly uniform throughout the homosphere.

The only exception is the concentration of ozone in the stratosphere from 19 to 50 km, and the variation in water vapour and pollutants in the lowest portion of the atmosphere near the earth's surface. The stable mixture of gases throughout the homosphere has evolved slowly.

5. Why is the troposphere the most important of all the layer of the atmosphere?

Ans. Troposphere is the lowermost layer of the atmosphere. It is the most important layer due to its following features

- Its average height is 13 km.
- Troposphere contains dust particles and water vapours.
- All changes in climate and weather take place in this layer.
- Temperature in this layer decreases at the rate of 1°C for every 165 m of height.
- All phenomena which are important for existence of life like precipitation, clouds, etc occur only in this layer.

6. Describe the main characteristics of stratosphere.

Ans. The main characteristics of stratosphere are

- Stratosphere lies above the tropopause.
- The stratosphere ranges from about 19 to 50 km above the earth's surface.
- The temperature of the stratosphere varies from 57°C at the tropopause to 0°C at the stratopause. Thus, there is increase in temperature with increase in height.
- This sphere is known for the aviation activities.
- The sphere is characterised by the presence of ozone layer.

7. Differentiate between mesosphere and ionosphere.

Ans. Differences between mesosphere and ionosphere are

Mesosphere	Ionosphere
The mesosphere lies above the stratosphere.	Ionosphere lies above the mesosphere.
It extends upto the 80 km.	It is the thinner layer which starts at a height of 80 km.
In this layer, the temperature starts decreasing with increase in height.	The temperature increases with increase in height.
It is the coldest portion of the atmosphere.	It contains ions that acquire electrical charges when they absorb cosmic rays.
The upper limit of mesosphere is mesopause.	In this layer, radiowaves transmitted from the earth are reflected back to the earth.

8. "Humans may survive for sometimes without food and water but can't survive even a few minutes without breathing air". Point out the factors which are responsible for polluting air. Also discuss the ways which need to adopt for making the air breathable.

Ans. Responsible factors for air pollution are

- Consumption of fossil fuel in the form of coal, petroleum, etc.
- Growing industrialisation without any safety measures for environment.
- Burning of agriculture residue in the farms.

Ways which are needed to be adopted for making the air breathable are

- We should shift towards renewable source of energy which is eco-friendly and cheap for consumption.
- Appropriate technology should be developed to absorb carbon and other harmful gases from industries.
- Proper guidelines and strict regulation is required to prevent air pollution.
- Sufficient carbon sink should be developed in the form of forestation.

• Long Answer (LA) Type Questions

1. Give an account of atmosphere. Also explain its characteristics.

Ans. The atmosphere is the thin envelop of gases surrounding the earth that forms a protective boundary between the outer space and the biosphere. The atmosphere of the earth is formed by gases from the crust and interior and the exhalations of all life over the time.

Characteristics of atmosphere are

- The uniqueness of earth's atmosphere is that it supports life. The composition is so unique that it doesn't cause any combustion in the atmosphere.
- Atmosphere is composed of balanced amount of life giving gases such as oxygen for human and animal and carbon dioxide for plants.
- Atmosphere works as a protective boundary between the outer space and the biosphere.
- It also has water vapour and dust particles. Water vapour absorbs parts of the insolation from the sun and preserves the earth's radiated heat. Thus, acts like a blanket allowing the earth neither to become too hot nor too cold.

2. Explain the properties of the prominent constituent gases of the atmosphere.

Ans. The atmosphere is the composition of various significant gases like nitrogen, oxygen, carbon dioxide, ozone, etc. The quantity of these gases is not uniform but their contribution in the atmosphere is significant.

Some of the gases and their properties are

- **Nitrogen** It is the maximum available gas which contributes 78.08 % in the earth's atmosphere. Nitrogen does not easily enter the chemical union without substances but gets fixed into soil and hence, it is useful for nitrogen fixation and increases productivity of soil. Nitrogen regulates the combustion, as it is not inflammable.
- **Oxygen** It is the biggest source of respiration for human and animals. It is the only source of life and a salient feature of this planet. Oxygen is the most combustible gas and it contributes 20.95% in the earth's atmosphere.
- **Carbon dioxide** It is meteorologically very important gas, as it is transparent to the incoming radiation but opaque to the outgoing terrestrial radiation. Carbon dioxide is the life giving gas for plants and trees, as it is the biggest source of photosynthesis. Carbon dioxide is largely responsible for the greenhouse effect.
- **Ozone** It is highly reactive oxygen molecule made up of three oxygen atoms. It is found in stratosphere. Ozone absorbs wavelengths of ultraviolet light. Through this process, the most harmful ultraviolet radiation is effectively 'filtered' from the incoming solar radiation, safeguarding the earth's surface.

3. Describe the composition of the atmosphere.

Ans. The atmosphere is composed of gases, water vapour and dust particles. Nitrogen constitutes 78.08%, oxygen contributes 20.94% and argon constitutes 0.93% in the atmosphere. Other gases include carbon dioxide, helium, ozone, methane, hydrogen, krypton, xenon, neon, etc. Nitrogen and oxygen together constitute 99% of the atmosphere. Neon, krypton, xenon are scarce gases.

The proportion of gases changes in the higher layers of the atmosphere in such a way that oxygen will be almost in negligible quantity at the height of 120 km. Similarly, carbon dioxide and water vapour are found only up to 90 km from the surface of the earth. Carbon dioxide is meteorologically a very important gas, as it is transparent to the incoming solar radiation but opaque to the outgoing terrestrial radiation and reflects back some part of it towards the earth's surface.

It is largely responsible for the greenhouse effect. Ozone is another important component of the atmosphere. It is found between 10 and 50 km above the earth's surface and acts as a filter. It absorbs the ultra-violet rays, radiating from the sun. It prevents them from reaching the surface of the earth.

4. Discuss about the structure of atmosphere.

Ans. The structure of atmosphere is composed of five different layers depending upon the temperature condition. These layers are

- (i) **Troposphere** It is the lowermost layer of the atmosphere. Its average height is 13 km. The thickness of the troposphere is greatest at the equator because heat is transported to great heights by strong convectional currents. All weather and climate related prominent incidents occur in this layer.
- (ii) **Stratosphere** It is found above the tropopause and extends up to a height of 50 km. This layer is characterised by the presence of ozone layer which protects us from the ultraviolet rays coming from the sun.
- (iii) **Mesosphere** It lies above the stratosphere which extends upto a height of 80 km. Temperature decreases with increases in altitude and reaches upto minus 100°C at the height of 80 km.
- (iv) **Ionosphere** It is located in between 80 km and 400 km. It contains electrically charged particles known as Ions, that is why it is called Ionosphere. The temperature here starts increasing with height due to which it is also known as thermosphere.
- (v) **Exosphere** The uppermost layer of the atmosphere above the thermosphere is known as the exosphere. It is the highest layer and gradually merges with the outer space.

• Case Based Questions

1. Read the case/source given and answer the following questions.

The troposphere is the lowermost layer of the atmosphere. Its average height is 13 km and extends roughly to a height of 8 km near the poles and about 18 km at the equator. Thickness of the troposphere is greatest at the equator because heat is transported to great heights by strong convectional currents. This layer contains dust particles and water vapour. All changes in climate and weather take place in this layer. The temperature in this layer decreases at the rate of 1°C for every 165m of height. This is the most important layer for all biological activity.

The zone separating the tropsophere from stratosphere is known as the tropopause. The air temperature at the tropopause is about minus 80°C over the equator and about minus 45°C over the poles. The temperature here is nearly constant and hence, it is called the tropopause. The stratosphere is found above the tropopause and extends up to a height of 50 km. One important feature of the stratosphere is that it contains the ozone layer. This layer absorbs ultra-violet radiation and shields life on the earth from intense, harmful form of energy.

(i) Explain why the troposphere is considered to be the most important layer of the atmosphere.

Ans. The troposphere is considered to be the most important layer of the atmosphere because all changes in climate and weather take place in this layer which is the lowermost layer of the atmosphere. All biological activity takes place in this layer making it conducive for the survival of all living organisms.

(ii) Identify one distinguishing feature of the stratosphere and explain its importance.

Ans. One distinguishing feature of stratosphere is that this layer contains ozone gas which makes this layer significant among all other atmospheric layers.

The importance of stratosphere is that the ozone gas present in this layer absorbs ultraviolet radiation coming from the sun. This layer shields life on the earth from the UV rays which are intense and harmful form of energy.

(iii) Define tropopause.

Ans. Tropopause is the zone in the atmosphere that separates the troposphere from the stratosphere.

The air temperature at the tropopause is about minus 80 degree Celsius over the equator and about minus 45 degree Celsius over the poles. The temperature in this zone is nearly constant and hence it is known as the tropopause.

2. Read the case/source given and answer the following questions.

Carbon dioxide is meteorologically a very important gas as it is transparent to the incoming solar radiation but opaque to the outgoing terrestrial radiation. It absorbs a part of terrestrial radiation and reflects back some part of it towards the earth's surface. It is largely responsible for the Greenhouse effect. The volume of other gases is constant but the volume of carbon dioxide has been rising in the past few decades mainly because of the burning of fossil fuels. This has also increased the temperature of the air. Ozone is another important component of the atmosphere found between 10 and 50 km above the earth's surface and acts as a filter and absorbs the ultra-violet rays radiating from the sun and prevents them from reaching the surface of the earth.

(i) Explain the Greenhouse effect.

Ans. The warming of the earth's surface due to the trapping of the sun's heat by greenhouse gases like carbon dioxide is known as greenhouse effect. It is a natural process that keeps the earth warm.

(ii) Identify and describe any human activity that is impacting the greenhouse effect.

Ans. Human activities like the burning of fossil fuels (coal, oil etc.) increases the volume of carbon dioxide in the atmosphere. This increase in the volume of carbon dioxide in the air while the volume of other gases is constant causing the atmosphere to trap more heat thereby abnormally warming up the earth's surface.

(iii) How carbon dioxide is a significant gas?

Ans. Carbon dioxide is meteorologically a very significant gas as it is transparent to the incoming solar radiation but opaque to the outgoing terrestrial radiation. Therefore, it is largely responsible for the greenhouse effect as it absorbs a part of the terrestrial radiation and reflects some part of it towards the earth's surface.

Objective Questions

1. Around 99% of the total mass of the atmosphere is confined at what height?

(a) 15 km
(b) 13 km
(c) 25 km
(d) 32 km

2. The atmosphere is composed of gases, ... and dust particles.

(a) clouds
(b) precipitation
(c) sun
(d) water vapour

3. Ozone layer is found between .... above the earth's surface.

(a) 3 to 5 km
(b) 10 to 50 km
(c) 12 to 30 km
(d) 30 to 60 km

4. Consider the following statements and choose the correct option

I. Air is essential for the survival of all the organisms.

II. Atmosphere is a mixture of different gases.

Codes

(a) Only I is correct
(b) Only II is correct
(c) Both statements are incorrect
(d) Both statements are correct

Short Answer Type Questions

5. What is the significance of dust and vapour for the climatic conditions?

6. Discuss the properties of nitrogen gas.

7. What is the importance of carbon dioxide on the earth?

8. How are mesosphere and ionosphere different from each other? State any three points.

9. Discuss the process of formation of atmosphere.

Long Answer Type Questions

10. Distinguish between troposphere and stratosphere.

11. Define atmosphere. Explain its importance for human life.

Answers

1. (d) 32 km   **2.** (d) water vapour   **3.** (b) 10 to 50 km   **4.** (d) Both statements are correct

CHAPTER 02

Solar Radiation, Heat Balance and Temperature

In this Chapter...

- Solar Radiation
- Insolation
- Heating and Cooling of Atmosphere
- Heat Budget
- Temperature

Solar Radiation

The earth receives almost all its energy from the sun in short wavelengths which is radiated back to space by the earth. As a result, the earth neither warms up, nor does it get cooled over a period of time.

The amount of heat received by different parts of the earth is not same which causes pressure differences in the atmosphere. This leads to transfer of heat from one region to the other by wind. As the earth is a **geoid** resembling a sphere, the sun rays fall obliquely at the top of the atmosphere and the earth intercepts a very small portion of the sun's energy. On an average, the earth receives 1.94 calories per sq cm per minute at the top of its atmosphere.

Aphelion

The solar output received at the top of the atmosphere varies slightly in a year due to the variations in the distance between the earth and the sun.

During its revolution around the sun, the earth is farthest from the sun (152 million km) on 4th July. This position of the earth is known as aphelion.

Perihelion

On 3rd January, the earth is the nearest to the sun (147 million km) which is known as perihelion. Therefore, the annual insolation received by the earth on 3rd January is slightly more than the amount received on 4th July. However, the effect of this variation in the solar output is marked by other factors like the distribution of land and sea and the atmospheric circulation.

Thus, this variation in the solar output does not have great effect on daily weather changes on the surface of the earth.

Insolation

The energy received by the earth is known as incoming solar radiation which in short termed as insolation. The surface of the earth receives most of its energy in short wave lengths.

Variability of Insolation at the Surface of the Earth

The amount and the intensity of insolation vary during a day, in a season and in a year. This variation in insolation is marked by a number of factors such as

(i) The rotation of the earth on its axis.

(ii) The angle of inclination of the Sun's rays.

(iii) The length of the day.

(iv) The transparency of the atmosphere.

(v) The configuration of land in terms of its aspect.

The last two however, have less influence.

The Rotation of the Earth on its Axis

The earth's axis makes an angle of   – with the plane of its orbit round the sun which has a greater influence on the amount of insolation received at different latitudes.

The Angle of Inclination of the Sun's Rays

It depends upon the **latitude**[1] of a place. The higher the latitude the less is the angle they make with the surface of the earth resulting in slant sun rays.

The area covered by vertical rays is always less than the slant rays. If more area is covered, the energy gets distributed and the net energy receive per unit area decreases. Moreover, the slant rays are required to pass through greater depth of the atmosphere resulting in more absorption, **scattering**[2] and diffusion.

The Passage of Solar Radiation through the Atmosphere

The atmosphere is largely transparent to short wave solar radiation. The incoming solar radiation passes through the atmosphere before striking the earth's surface. Within the troposphere, water vapour, ozone and other gases absorb much of the near infrared radiation.

Scattering

Very small suspended particles in the troposphere scatter visible spectrum both to the space and towards the earth's surface. This process adds colour to the sky. The red colour of the rising and setting of the sun and the blue colour of the sky are the result of scattering of light within the atmosphere.

Spatial Distribution of Insolation at the Earth's Surface

The insolation received at the surface varies from about 320 watt/m^2 in the tropics to about 70 watt/m^2 in the poles.

Maximum insolation is received over the sub-tropical deserts where the cloudiness is the least. Equator receives comparatively less insolation than the tropics.

Generally, at the same latitude the insolation is more over the continent than over the oceans. In winter, the middle and higher latitudes receive less radiation than in summer.

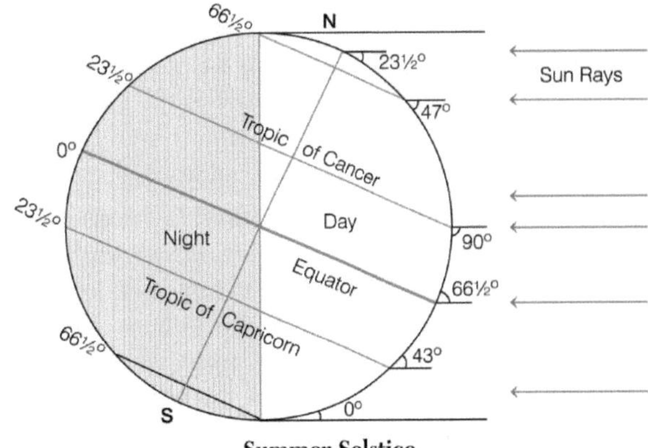

Summer Solstice

Heating and Cooling of Atmosphere

The ways of heating and cooling of the atmosphere are

Conduction

After heating, the earth transmits the heat to the atmospheric layers near to the earth, in long wave form. The air in contact with the land gets heated slowly and the upper layers in contact with the lower layers also get heated. This process is called conduction.

Conduction takes place when two bodies of unequal temperature are in contact with one another, there is a flow of energy from the warmer to cooler body. The transfer of heat continues until both the bodies attain the same temperature or the contact is broken. Conduction is important in heating the lower layers of the atmosphere.

Convection

The air in contact with the earth rises vertically on heating in the form of currents and further transmits the heat to the atmosphere. This process of vertical heating of the atmosphere is known as convection. This process occurs only in **troposphere**.

Advection

The transfer of heat through horizontal movement of air is called advection. The horizontal movement of air is relatively more important than the vertical movement. In middle latitudes, most of dirunal (day and night) variations in daily weather are caused by advection. In tropical regions, particularly in Northern India during summer season, local winds called **loo** is the outcome of advection process.

---

1 **Latitude** Distance from north and south of the equator measured in degrees upto 90 degree.

2 **Scattering** The process in which radiation or particles are deflected or diffused.

Terrestrial Radiation

Insolation comes in short wave forms and heats up the earth's surface. The earth after being heated itself becomes a radiating body and it radiates energy to the atmosphere in long wave form which heats up the atmosphere from below. This process is known as terrestrial radiation.

By this process, the long wave **radiation**[3] is absorbed by the atmospheric gases particular by carbon dioxide and the other green house gases. The atmosphere in turn radiates and transmits heat to the space. Finally, the amount of heat received from the sun is returned to space, thereby maintaining constant temperature at the earth's surface and in the atmosphere.

Heat Budget of the Earth

A heat budget is the perfect balance between incoming heat absorbed by the earth and outgoing heat escaping it in the form of radiation. If the balance is disturbed, then earth would get progressively warmer or cooler with each passing year.

The earth as a whole does not accumulate or loose heat. It maintains its temperature through terrestrial radiation. This can happen only if the amount of heat received in the form of insolation equals the amount lost by the earth through terrestrial radiation. The heat budget of the earth can be understood through the following facts

Albedo of the Earth

Out of 100 units of heat received, while passing through the atmosphere some amount of energy is reflected, scattered and absorbed. Only the remaining part reaches the earth surface. Roughly 35 units are reflected back to space even before reaching the earth's surface.

Of these, 27 units are reflected back from the top of the clouds and 2 units from the snow and ice-covered areas of the earth. The amount of radiation reflected back by various sources is known as albedo of the earth.

Estimation of Radiation

The remaining 65 units are absorbed, 14 units within the atmosphere and 51 units by the earth's surface. The earth radiates back 51 units in the form of terrestrial radiation. Of these 17 units are radiated to space directly and remaining 34 units are absorbed by the atmosphere.

Within the 34 units of the atmosphere, 6 units absorbed directly by the atmosphere, 9 units through convection and turbulence and 19 units through latent heat of **condensation**[4].

48 units absorbed by the atmosphere (14 units from insolation +34 units from terrestrial radiation) are also radiated back into space.

Thus, the total radiation returning from the earth and the atmosphere respectively is $17 + 48 = 65$ units which balance the total of 65 units received from the sun. This whole process of huge transfer of heat is termed as heat balance of the earth. This explains, why the earth neither warms up nor cools down despite the huge transfer of heat that takes place.

Variation in the Net Heat Budget at the Earth's Surface

There are variations in the amount of radiation received at the earth's surface. Some part of the earth has surplus radiation balance, while the other part has deficit, e.g. there is a surplus of net radiation balance between 40° N and S and the region near the poles have a deficit.

The surplus heat energy from the tropics is redistributed pole wards. As a result, the tropics do not get progressively heated up due to accumulation of excess heat or the high latitudes get permanently frozen due to excess deficit.

Temperature

The interaction of insolation with the atmosphere and the earth's surface creates heat which is measured in terms of temperature. While heat represents the molecular movement of particles comprising a substance, the temperature is the measurement in degrees of hotness or coldness of a thing (or a place).

Factors Controlling Temperature Distribution

The factors are responsible to influence the temperature at any place are

The Latitude The temperature of a place depends on the insolation received. The insolation varies according to the latitude, hence, the temperature also varies accordingly.

The Altitude The atmosphere is indirectly heated by terrestrial radiation from below. Therefore, the places near the sea-level record higher temperature than the places situated at higher elevations. In other words, the temperature generally decreases with increasing height. The rate of decrease of temperature with height is termed as normal lapse rate. It is 6.5° C per 1,000 m.

Distance from Sea The temperature is influenced by the location of a place with respect to the sea. Compared to land, the sea gets heated slowly and loses heat slowly. Land heats up and cools down quickly.

---

3 Radiation The emission of energy in the form of rays or waves.
4 Condensation The conversion of a vapour or gas to a liquid.

Therefore, the variation in temperature over the sea is less compared to land. The places situated near the sea come under the moderating influence of the sea and land breezes which moderate the temperature.

Air Mass and Ocean Currents Passage of air masses also affects the temperature. The places which come under the influence of warm air masses experience higher temperature and the places that come under the influence of cold air masses experience low temperature. Similarly, the places located on the coast where the warm ocean currents flow record higher temperature than the places located on the coast, where the cold current flows.

Distribution of Temperature

The global distribution of temperature can well be understood by studying the temperature distribution in January and July. The distribution of temperature is generally shown through **isotherms**. Isotherms are lines joining places having equal temperature. Generally, isotherms are parallel to the latitude. The deviation from this general trend is more seen in January than in July especially in Northern Hemisphere.

In Northern Hemisphere, the land surface area is much larger than in the Southern Hemisphere, hence, the effects of landmass and the ocean current are well pronounced.

Temporal Distribution

- In January, the isotherms deviate to the North over the ocean and to the South over the continent. This can be seen on the North Atlantic Ocean. The Northern Atlantic Ocean becomes warmer and the isotherms bend towards the North in the presence of warm currents i.e. Gulf stream and North Atlantic drift.

- Over the land, the temperature decreases sharply and the isotherms bend towards South in Europe. In Siberian plain, it is much pronounced.

- The mean January temperature along 60° E longitude is − 20° C both at 80° N and 50° N latitudes.

- The mean monthly temperature for January is over 27°C in equatorial oceans, over 24°C in the tropic, 2°C − 0°C in the middle latitudes and − 18°C to − 48°C in the Eurasian continental interior.

- In the Southern Hemisphere the effect of ocean is well pronounced. The isotherms here are more or less parallel to the latitudes and the variation in temperature is more gradual than in the Northern Hemisphere. The isotherm of

20°C, 10°C and 0°C runs parallel to 35°S, 45°S and 60°S latitudes, respectively.

- In July, the isotherms generally run parallel to the latitude. The equatorial oceans record warmer temperature more than 27°C. Over the land, more than 30° C is noticed in the sub-tropical continental region of Asia along the 30° N latitude.

- Along the 40° N runs the isotherm of 10°C and along the 40°S the temperature is 10°C.

- If we see the range of temperature between January and July, the highest range of temperature is more than 60°C over the North-Eastern part of Eurasian continent. This is due to continentality.

- The least range of temperature is 3°C which is found between 20°S and 15° N latitudes.

Inversion of Temperature

Normally, temperature decreases with increase in elevation which is known as normal lapse rate. At times, the situations is reversed and the normal lapse rate is inverted. It is called inversion of temperature. Inversion is usually of short duration. A long winter night with clear skies and still air is ideal situation for inversion. The heat of the day is radiated off during night, and in early morning, earth is cooler than the air above.

Over polar areas, temperature inversion is normal throughout the year. Surface inversion promotes stability in the lower layers of the atmosphere. Smoke and dust particles get collected beneath the inversion layer and spread horizontally to fill the lower strata of the atmosphere. Dense fogs in mornings are common occurrences especially during winter season. This inversion commonly lasts for few hours until the sun comes up and beings to warm the earth.

The inversion takes place in hills and mountains due to air drainage. Cold air at the hills and mountains produced during night, flows under the influence of gravity. Being heavy and dense, the cold air moves down the slope like water to pile up deeply in valley bottoms with warm air above. This is called **air drainage** which protects plants from frost damages.

Plank's Law and Specific Heat

Plank's Law states that if a body is hotter, then it will radiate more energy and wavelength of that radiation will be shorter. Specific heat is the energy needed to raise the temperature of one gram of substance by one Celsius.

Chapter Practice

Objective Questions

• Multiple Choice Questions

1. On an average, the earth receives .... calories per sq per minute at the top of its atmosphere.
(a) 1.94
(b) 1.56
(c) 1.99
(d) 0.94

Ans. (a) The earth receives 1.94 calories per sq per minute at the top of its atmosphere.

2. The surface of the earth receives most of its energy in the form of ....
(a) longwave lengths
(b) shortwave lengths
(c) mediumwave lengths
(d) None of the above

Ans. (b) The surface ofthe earth receives most of its energy in the form of short wave lengths.

3. On which of the following days Aphelion is observed?
(a) 31st December
(b) 30th June
(c) 4th July
(d) 1st August

Ans. (c) Aphelion is observed on 4th July. During earth's revolution around the sun, it is farthest from the sun (152 million km) on 4th July. This position of the earth is known as aphelion.

4. Within the troposphere which of the following absorbs much of the near infrared radiation?
(a) Water Vapour
(b) Ozone
(c) Gases
(d) All of these

Ans. (d) Within the troposphere, water vapour, ozone and other gases absorb much of the near infrared radiation.

5. The red colour of the rising and the setting of the sun and the blue colour of the sky are the result of ....
(a) scattering
(b) reflection
(c) refraction
(d) absorption

Ans. (a) The red colour of the rising and the setting of the sun and the blue colour of the sky are the result of scattering.

6. The earth maintains its temperature through ......
(a) terrestrial radiation
(b) conduction
(c) convection
(d) absorption

Ans. (a) The earth maintains its temperature through terrestrial radiation.

7. Which among the following pair is correctly matched?
(a) Aphelion — 4th June
(b) Perihelion — 3rd January
(c) Summer Solstice — 23rd September
(d) Winter Solstice — 22nd February

Ans. (b) Perihelion is observed on 3rd January. On this date, the earth is nearest to the sun (147 million km). Aphelion is observed on 4th July, Summer Solstice is observed on 21st June and Winter Solstice is observed on 21st December.

8. Which among the following pairs is incorrectly matched?
(a) The insolation received in the tropics – 320 watt/
(b) The insolation received in the poles – 70 watt/
(c) During Aphelion the distance from the Earth to the Sun – 156 million km
(d) During Perihelion the distance from the Earth to the Sun – 147 million km

Ans. (c) During Aphelion the distance from the Earth to the Sun is 152 million km.

9. Match the following.

List I	List II
A. Latitude	1. Distance from North and South of the equator measured in degrees upto 90 degree
B. Radiation	2. The emission of energy in the form of rays or waves
C. Scattering	3. The process in which radiation or particles are deflected or diffused
D. Isotherm	4. The line which joins the places having equal temperature

Codes

	A	B	C	D			A	B	C	D
(a)	1	2	3	4		(b)	2	3	1	4
(c)	3	2	1	4		(d)	2	4	3	1

Ans. (a)

10. Match the following.

	List I (Terms)		List II (Meaning)
A.	Conduction	1.	Radiant energy emitted by the sun from a nuclear fusion reaction that creates electromagnetic energy.
B.	Insolation	2.	The transfer of heat through contact
C.	Solar Radiation	3.	The amount of radiation reflected back by various sources
D.	Terrestrial Radiation	4.	The solar radiation that reaches the earth's surface
E.	Heat Budget	5.	The perfect balance between incoming heat absorbed by the earth and outgoing heat escaping it in the form of radiation
F.	Albedo	6.	The earth after being heated itself becomes a radiating body and it radiates energy to the atmosphere in long wave form which heats up the atmosphere from below

Codes

	A	B	C	D	E	F
(a)	2	4	1	6	5	3
(b)	6	3	2	4	1	5
(c)	1	5	6	3	2	4
(d)	2	1	4	6	3	5

Ans. (a)

11. Consider the following statements and choose the correct option from the given options

I. Maximum insolation is received over the sub tropical deserts.

II. Cloudiness is the least in the sub-tropical deserts.

Codes

(a) Only I is correct

(b) Only II is correct

(c) Both statements are incorrect

(d) Both statements are correct and statement II correctly explains statement I.

Ans. (d) Maximum insolation is received over the sub-tropical deserts where the cloudiness is the least.

12. Arrange the following as per their date of occurrence.

I. Aphelion   II. Perihelion

III. Summer Solstice   IV. Winter Solstice

Codes

(a) IV, II, I, III   (b) II, III, I, IV

(c) I, IV, III, II   (d) I, II, III, IV

Ans. (b) The date of occurrence of Perihelion is 3rd January, Summer Solstice is 21st June, Aphelion is 4th July and Winter Solstice is 22nd December.

• Case Based MCQs

13. Read the given case/source and answer the questions that follow by choosing the correct option.

There are different ways of heating and cooling of the atmosphere. The earth after being heated by insolation transmits the heat to the atmospheric layers near to the earth in long wave form. The air in contact with the land gets heated slowly and the upper layers in contact with the lower layers also get heated. This process is called conduction. Conduction takes place when two bodies of unequal temperature are in contact with one another, there is a flow of energy from the warmer to cooler body. The transfer of heat continues until both the bodies attain the same temperature or the contact is broken. Conduction is important in heating the lower layers of the atmosphere. The air in contact with the earth rises vertically on heating in the form of currents and further transmits the heat of the atmosphere. This process of vertical heating of the atmosphere is known as convection. The convective transfer of energy is confined only to the troposphere. The transfer of heat through horizontal movement of air is called advection.

Horizontal movement of the air is relatively more important than the vertical movement. In middle latitudes, most of dirunal (day and night) variation in daily weather are caused by advection alone. In tropical regions particularly in Northern India during summer season local winds called 'loo' is the outcome of advection process.

The insolation received by the earth is in short waves forms and heats up its surface. The earth after being heated itself becomes a radiating body and it radiates energy to the atmosphere in long wave form. This energy heats up the atmosphere from below. This process is known as terrestrial radiation.

(i) Which process is significant when transfer of heat takes place between land and lower layers of atmosphere?

(a) Insolation   (b) Terrestrial radiation
(c) Convection   (d) Conduction

Ans. (d) Conduction process is significant when transfer of heat takes place between land and lower layers of atmosphere.

(ii) Convection could not occur beyond the height of .... from the Earth's surface.

(a) 18 to 20 kms   (b) 6 to 20 kms
(c) 16 to 25 kms   (d) 6 to 25 kms

Ans. (b) Convection could not occur beyond the height of 6 to 20 kms.

(iii) Which of the following phenomena is the result of advection process?

(a) Norwesters   (b) South-west monsoon
(c) Loo   (d) Mango showers

Ans. (c) 'Loo' is a phenomena which is the result of advection process.

(iv) Which is the most important process involved in transfer of heat between upper atmosphere and outer space?

(a) Conduction
(b) Convection
(c) Radiation
(d) None of the above

Ans. (c) Radiation is involved in transfer of heat between upper atmosphere and outer space.

14. Study the following graphs and answer the questions that follow by choosing the correct option.

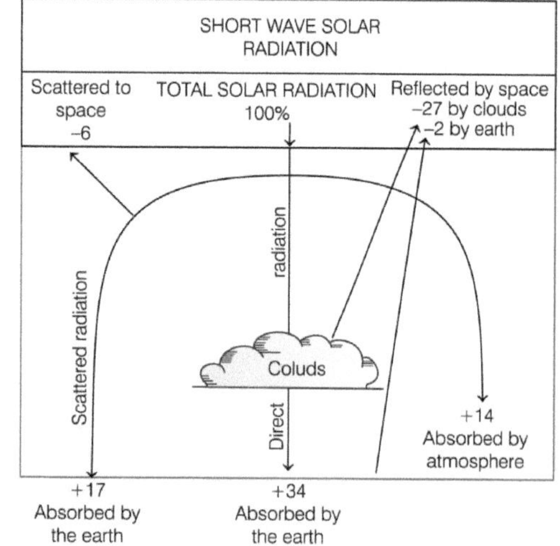

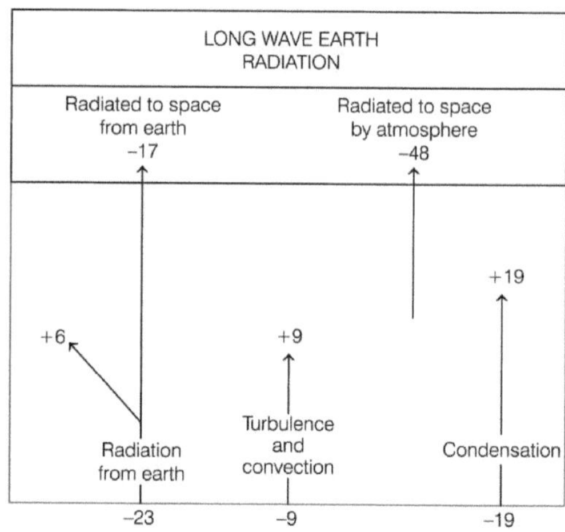

(i) What amount of radiation is reflected back to outer space directly without reaching the surface?

(a) 50 units
(b) 35 units
(c) 22 units
(d) 10 units

Ans. (d) 35 units are reflected back to space even before reaching the earth's surface.

(ii) What is the total amount of terrestrial radiation originating from the surface of earth?

(a) 51 units   (b) 22 units
(c) 19 units   (d) 9 units

Ans. (a) The earth radiates back 51 units in the form of terrestrial radiation.

(iii) What is the total amount of energy that passes through the earth's atmosphere?

(a) 35 units
(b) 100 units
(c) 65 units
(d) 51 units

Ans. (c) The total radiation returning from the earth and the atmosphere respectively is 17 + 48 = 65 units.

(iv) How much solar insolation is directly absorbed by the atmosphere?

(a) 34 units
(b) 12 units
(c) 51 units
(d) 19 units

Ans. (a) The earth radiates back 51 units in the form of terrestrial radiation. Of these 17 units are radiated to space directly and remaining 34 units are absorbed by the atmosphere.

Subjective Questions

• Short Answer (SA) Type Questions

1. List the factors which are responsible for the variability of insolation at the earth's surface.

Ans. The factors responsible for the variability of insolation at the earth's surface are
  - **The Rotation of the Earth on its Axis** The earth's axis makes an angle of – with the plane of its orbit round the sun which has a greater influence on the amount of insolation received at different latitudes.
  - **The Angle of Inclination of the Sun's Rays** It depends upon the latitude of a place. The higher the latitude the less is the angle they make with the surface of the earth resulting in slant sun rays.
  - **Duration/Length of the Day** Duration of the day varies from place to place and season to season. It decides the amount of insolation received on the earth's surface
  - **Transparency of the Atmosphere** The transparency of the atmosphere depends upon the cloud cover and its thickness, dust particles, water vapour, etc. They reflect, absorb or transmit insolation.

2. How scattering takes place? Explain.

Ans. Scattering is the process in which radiation or particles are deflected or diffused. In the troposphere, there are different gases, water vapours and dust particles. These very small suspended particles in the troposphere scatter visible spectrum both to the space and towards the earth's surface. This process adds colour to the sky which is called scattering.

The red colour of the rising and the setting sun and the blue colour of the sky are the result of scattering of light within the atmosphere.

3. Discuss the spatial distribution of insolation at the earth's surface.

Ans. The spatial distribution of insolation at the earth's surface is
  - The insolation received at the surface of the earth varies from 320 watt/m^2 in the tropics to about 70 watt/m^2 in the poles. The maximum insolation is received by the subtropical deserts where the formation of cloud is least.
  - Equatorial regions receive comparatively less insolation than the tropics as in equatorial region, there is more evaporation and more condensation. Generally, at the same latitude the insolation is more over the continents than over the oceans.
  - In winter, the middle and higher latitudes receive less radiation than in summer.

4. Distinguish between conduction and convection.

Ans. Differences between conduction and convection are

Conduction	Convection
It takes place when bodies of different temperatures are in contact with one another.	In convection, there is transfer of heat vertically in the form of current.
In conduction, the air in contact with the land gets heated slowly and further heat is transferred to another layer.	In convection, the heat is transmitted layer by layer in atmosphere through air.
The transfer of heat continues until both the bodies attain the same temperature.	The convection transfer of energy is confined only to the lower layer i.e., troposhere.

5. The terrestrial radiation is important to maintain constant temperature on the earth's surface. Explain in brief.

Ans. Terrestrial radiation is the long wave electromagnetic radiation originating from the earth and its atmosphere. It is important as it returned the amount of heat received from the sun to space and maintains constant temperature on the earth's surface.

The insolation received by the earth is in short wave form which heats up the surface. The earth after being heated itself becomes a radiating body and it radiates energy to the atmosphere in long wave form which heats up the atmosphere from below. This process is known as terrestrial radiation.

The long wave radiation is absorbed by the atmospheric gases and thus, the atmosphere is indirectly heated by the earth's radiation. The atmosphere in turn radiates and transmits heat into the space. Finally, the amount of heat received from the sun is returned to space.

6. Differentiate between insolation and terrestrial radiation.

Ans. Differences between insolation and terrestrial radiation are

Insolation	Terrestrial Radiation
It is the incoming solar radiation.	It is the radiation of energy from the earth's surface into the atmosphere.
The earth surface receives insolation in short wave length.	It radiates energy to the atmosphere in long wave form.
It does not cause heating up of the atmosphere.	The atmosphere is heated by the earth's radiation.

Insolation	Terrestrial Radiation
The main source of insolation is the sun rays.	Solar radiation is the source of terrestrial radiation.
It is only received in day time.	It continues to radiate both during day as well as at night.

7. Describe the variation in the net heat budget of the earth's surface.

Ans. There are variations in the amount of radiation received at the earth's surface which are

- Some part of the earth has surplus radiation balance, while the other part has deficit, e.g. there is a surplus of net radiation balance between 40° N and S and the region near the poles have a deficit.
- The surplus heat energy from the tropics is redistributed pole wards. As a result, the tropics do not get progressively heated up due to accumulation of excess heat or the high latitudes get permanently frozen due to excess deficit.

8. Explain the significance of location of a place near sea in distribution of temperature.

Ans. The location of a place with respect to sea is a significant factor that influences the temperature. For example

- As compared to land, the sea gets heated slowly and loses heat slowly.
- Land heats up and cools down quickly. Therefore, the variation in temperature over the sea is less in comparison to land.
- The place situated near the sea comes under the moderating influence of the sea and land breezes which moderate the temperature.

9. What are the factors that control temperature distribution on the surface of the earth?

Ans. The factors controlling temperature distribution are

The Latitude The temperature of a place depends on the insolation received. The insolation varies according to the latitude, hence, the temperature also varies accordingly.

The Altitude The atmosphere is indirectly heated by terrestrial radiation from below. Therefore, the places near the sea-level record higher temperature than the places situated at higher elevations.

Distance from Sea The temperature is influenced by the location of a place with respect to the sea. Compared to land, the sea gets heated slowly and loses heat slowly. Land heats up and cools down quickly.

Air Mass and Ocean Currents Passage of air masses also affects the temperature. The places which come under the influence of warm air masses experience higher temperature and the places that come under the influence of cold air masses experience low temperature. Similarly, the places located on the coast where the warm ocean currents flow record higher temperature than the places located on the coast, where the cold current flows.

10. There is differential heating of land and sea at the same latitude. Elucidate with examples.

Ans. There is differential heating of land and sea at the same latitude because the sun rays on land can penetrate only upto a depth of one metre, while they penetrate much deeper in water. The two places situated at the same latitude i.e. one along the sea coast and the other in the interior away from the coast will record different temperatures.

For example, Mumbai and Nizamabad (Telangana) are situated almost at the same latitude, but because of differential heating of sea-coast and the interior land, there is a marked difference in their mean annual range of temperature. The annual range of temperature at Mumbai is only about 6° C, while at Nizamabad it is about 20° C.

11. In India, why is the day temperature maximum in May and why not after the summer solstice?

Ans. In India, the sun reaches on the Tropic of Cancer on 21st June but May is accounted as the hottest month because

- Before summer solstice, the sun covers a large portion of Indian peninsula and the sunrays are perpendicular to that region.
- At that time due to high amount of heat, evaporation is very high.
- Condensation process is not able to happen which causes high temperature in whole part of India.
- From 1st June onwards Monsoon reaches to Indian sub continent and with sufficient amount of rainfall and cloud, temperature is not able to increase.

● Long Answer (LA) Type Questions

1. How do the latitude and the tilt in the axis of rotation of the earth affect the amount of radiation received at the earth's surface?

Ans. The rotation of the earth on the tilted axis and the angle of inclination of the sun rays i.e. latitudinal difference affect the amount of radiation received at the earth's surface in the following ways

Latitude The angle of inclination of the sun's rays depends on the latitude of a place. The higher the latitude, the less is the angle they make with the surface of the earth. This results in slant sun rays. Slant sun rays cover more area hence, the energy gets distributed and the net energy received per unit area decreases. Since angle of incidence is always higher between the Tropic of Cancer and Capricorn, hence temperature is high.

Rotation of the Earth The earth rotates on the tilted axis and the earth's axis makes an angle of $66\frac{1}{2}°$ with the plane of its orbit round the sun.

It has a greater influence on the amount of insolation received at different latitudes. This tilted axis causes movement of the sun from the Tropic of Cancer to the Tropic of Capricorn.

When the sun comes at the Tropic of Cancer on 21st June, it is called summer solstice. At this situation, sun rays cover maximum area of the Northern Hemisphere hence, the Northern Hemisphere is warm in comparision to the Southern Hemisphere.

In same way, when the sun reaches on the Tropic of Capricorn, it is known as winter solstice. At this situation, the Southern Hemisphere is more warm than the Northern Hemisphere.

2. Discuss the processes through which the earth atmospheric system maintains heat balance.

Ans. The processes through which earth's atmosphere succeed to maintain the heat balance are.

Terrestrial Radiation The insolation received by the earth is in short wave form and heats up its surface. Later, earth radiates its energy to the atmosphere in long wave form which heats up the atmosphere from below. The long wave radiation is absorbed by the atmospheric gases particularly by carbon dioxide. The atmosphere in turn radiates and transmits heat to the space i.e. the amount of heat received from the sun is returned to space. This process is responsible for maintaining constant temperature at the earth and in the atmosphere.

Process of Conduction The earth transmits the heat to the atmospheric layers near to the earth in long wave form. The air in contact with the land gets heated slowly and the upper layers in contact with the lower layers also get heated. This process of conduction is important in heating the lower layers of the atmosphere.

Process of Convection The air in contact with the earth rises vertically on heating in the form of currents and further transmits the heat of the atmosphere through the process of convection.

Process of Advection Advection is the transfer of heat through horizontal movement of air which is more important than vertical movement.

3. Explain in brief the heat budget of the earth.

Ans. A heat budget is the perfect balance between incoming heat absorbed by the earth and outgoing heat escaping it in the form of radiation. If the balance is disturbed, then earth would get progressively warmer or cooler with each passing year.

The earth as a whole does not accumulate or loose heat. It maintains its temperature through terrestrial radiation. This can happen only if the amount of heat received in the form of insolation equals the amount lost by the earth through terrestrial radiation.

The heat budget of the earth can be understood through the following facts

- **Albedo of the Earth** Out of 100 units of heat received, while passing through the atmosphere some amount of energy is reflected, scattered and absorbed. The amount of radiation reflected back by various sources is known as albedo of the earth.
- **Estimation of Radiation** Roughly 35 units of radiation out of 100 units are reflected back to space even before reaching the earth's surface. The remaining 65 units are absorbed, 14 units within the atmosphere and 51 units by the earth's surface. The earth radiates back 51 units in the form of terrestrial radiation.

Thus, the total radiation returning from the earth and the atmosphere respectively is $17+48 = 65$ units which balance the total of 65 units received from the sun. This whole process of huge transfer of heat is termed as heat balance of the earth.

This explains, why the earth neither warms up nor cools down despite the huge transfer of heat that takes place.

4. Explain the distribution of temperature in brief.

Ans. The distribution of temperature is generally shown through isotherms.

The distribution of temperature is

- In January, the isotherms deviate to the North over the ocean and to the South over the continent. This can be seen on the North Atlantic Ocean. The Northern Atlantic Ocean becomes warmer and the isotherms bend towards the North in the presence of warm currents i.e. Gulf stream and North Atlantic drift.
- Over the land, the temperature decreases sharply and the isotherms bend towards South in Europe. In Siberian plain, it is much pronounced.
- The mean January temperature along 60° E longitude is–20° C both at 80° N and 50° N latitudes.
- The mean monthly temperature for January is over 27°C in equatorial oceans, over 24°C in the tropic, 2°C-0°C in the middle latitudes and – 18°C to -48°C in the Eurasian continental interior.
- In the Southern Hemisphere the effect of ocean is well pronounced. The isotherms here are more or less parallel to the latitudes and the variation in temperature is more gradual than in the Northern Hemisphere. The isotherm of 20°C, 10°C and 0°C runs parallel to 35°S, 45°S and 60°S latitudes, respectively.
- In July, the isotherms generally run parallel to the latitude. The equatorial oceans record warmer temperature more than 27°C. Over the land, more than 30° C is noticed in the sub-tropical continental region of Asia along the 30° N latitude.

- Along the 40° N runs the isotherm of 10°C and along the 40°S the temperature is 10°C.
- If we see the range of temperature between January and July, the highest range of temperature is more than 60°C over the North-Eastern part of Eurasian continent. This is due to continentality.
- The least range of temperature is 3°C which is found between 20°S and 15° N latitudes.

5. Compare the global distribution of temperature in January over the Northern and the Southern hemisphere of the earth.

Ans. The comparison of the global distribution of temperature in January over the Northern and Southern Hemisphere of the earth is

Northern Hemisphere	Southern Hemisphere
The effect of land is well observed in this region.	The effect of ocean is well observed in this region. Isotherms are more or less parallel to the latitudes.
In the month of January, the deviation in isotherm line is more seen comparatively. Due to larger land surface area, the isotherms deviate to the North over the ocean and to the South over the continent.	Since, continental part is less in the Southern Hemisphere, so deviation of isotherm line is less.
In the month of January, temperature decreases sharply over the continental part of the Northern Hemisphere. Although in North Atlantic ocean, the presence of warm ocean currents, Gulf Stream, North Atlantic drift make the oceans warmer.	The variation of temperature is less in comparison to the Northern Hemisphere.
In the Siberian region, the mean January temperature is minus 20°C due to continental temperate climate. Whereas the mean montly temperature for Januray over tropics is 24°C and 2°C-0°C in middle latitudes.	In the month of January, the isotherms of 20°C, 10°C and 0°C runs parallel to 35°S 45°S and 60°S latitude, respectively.

6. Describe the inversion of temperature.

Ans. If there is an increase of air temperature with increase in height, it is known as inversion of temperature. It is also called as negative lapse rate. The inversion of temperature occurs near the earth's surface, or at greater height in the troposphere.

Over polar areas, temperature inversion is normal throughout the year. Surface inversion promotes stability in the lower layers of the atmosphere. Smoke and dust particles get collected beneath the inversion layer and spread horizontally to fill the lower strata of the atmosphere. Dense fogs in mornings are common occurrences especially during winter season. This inversion commonly lasts for few hours until the sun comes up and beings to warm the earth.

The inversion takes place in hills and mountains due to air drainage. Cold air at the hills and mountains produced during night, flows under the influence of gravity. Being heavy and dense, the cold air moves down the slope like water to pile up deeply in valley bottoms with warm air above. This is called air drainage which protects plants from frost damages.

• Case Based Questions

1. Read the case/source given and answer the following questions.

We inhale and exhale but we feel the air when it is in motion. It means air in motion is wind. You have already learnt about the fact that earth is surrounded by air all around. This envelop of air is atmosphere which is composed of numerous gases. These gases support life over the earth's surface.

The earth receives almost all of its energy from the sun. The earth in turn radiates back to space the energy received from the sun. As a result, the earth neither warms up nor does it get cooled over a period of time. Thus, the amount of heat received by different parts of the earth is not the same. This variation causes pressure differences in the atmosphere. This leads to transfer of heat from one region to the other by winds. This chapter explains the process of heating and cooling of the atmosphere and the resultant temperature distribution over the earth's surface.

The earth's surface receives most of its energy in short wavelengths. The energy received by the earth is known as incoming solar radiation which in short is termed as insolation. As the earth is a geoid resembling a sphere, the sun's rays fall obliquely at the top of the atmosphere and the earth intercepts a very small portion of the sun's energy. On an average the earth receives 1.94 calories per sq. cm per minute at the top of its atmosphere.

(i) What is the position of the earth on 4th July and 3rd January?

Ans. During its revolution around the sun, the earth is farthest from the sun (152 million km) on 4th July. This position of the earth is called aphelion. On 3rd January, the earth is the nearest to the sun (147 million km). This position is called perihelion. Therefore, the annual insolation received by the earth on 3rd January is slightly more than the amount received on 4th July

(ii) Explain about the incoming solar radiation.

Ans. The earth's surface receives most of its energy in short wavelengths. The energy received by the earth is known as incoming solar radiation which in short is termed as insolation. On an average the earth receives 1.94 calories per sq. cm per minute at the top of its atmosphere.

(iii) What are the different factors that cause variations in insolation?

Ans. The factors that cause these variations in insolation are the rotation of earth on its axis, the angle of inclination of the sun's rays, the length of the day, the transparency of the atmosphere and the configuration of land in terms of its aspect.

2. Read the case/source given and answer the following questions.

Normally, temperature decreases with increase in elevation. It is called normal lapse rate. At times, the situation is reversed and the normal lapse rate is inverted. It is called Inversion of temperature. Inversion is usually of short duration but quite common nonetheless. A long winter night with clear skies and still air is ideal situation forbinversion. The heat of the day is radiated off during the night, and by early morning hours, the earth is cooler than the air above. Over polar areas, temperature inversion is normal throughout the year. Surface inversion promotes stability in the lower layers of the atmosphere. Smoke and dust particles get collected beneath the inversion layer and spread horizontally to fill the lower strata of the atmosphere. Dense fogs in mornings are common occurrences especially during winter season. This inversion commonly lasts for few hours until the sun comes up and beings to warm the earth.

(i) What is Air Drainage type inversion?

Ans. The inversion takes place in hills and mountains due to air drainage. Cold air at the hills and mountains, produced during night, flows under the influence of gravity. Being heavy and dense, the cold air acts almost like water and moves down the slope to pile up deeply in pockets and valley bottoms with warm air above. This is called air drainage. It protects plants from frost damages.

(ii) Over polar areas, temperature inversion is normal throughout the year. Why?

Ans. Over poler areas, temperature inversion is normal throughout the year because the earth has curved geoid shape because of which the sun rays can't reach on the surface of the poles and it makes solar vertex which is above the surface. Due to this circumstance, temperature increases with increase in height.

(iii) What are the different factors responsible for the ground surface inversion?

Ans. The ground surface inversion occurs under the following geographical conditions

- Long winter nights
- Cloudless clear sky
- Dry air and low relative humidity
- Calm atmosphere
- Snow covered surface

• Map Based Questions

1. On the map of the world given below, the distribution of surface air temperature in the month of January is shown by lines as (i), (ii), (iii), (iv) and (v). Identify the temperature shown over these lines.

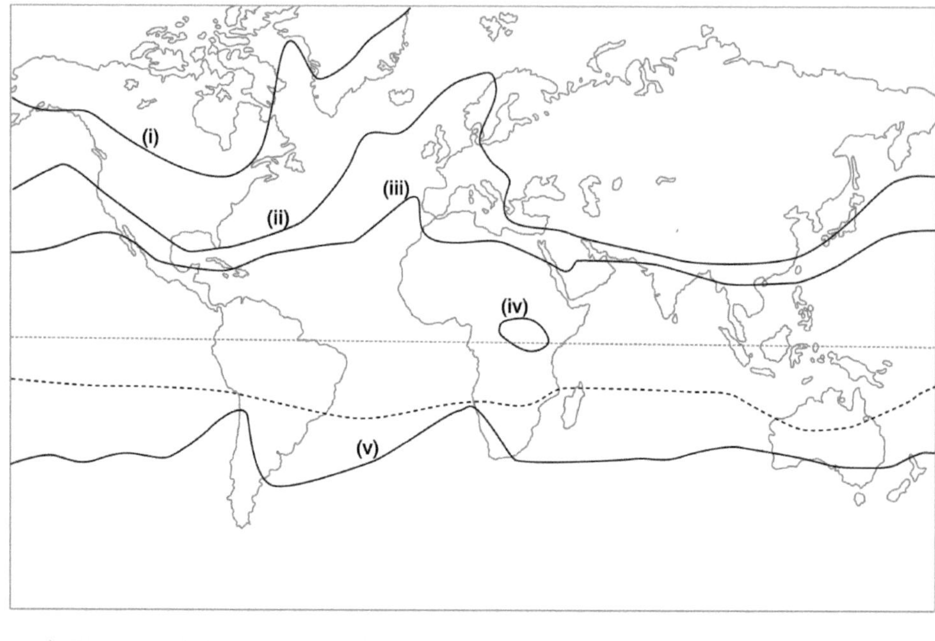

Ans. (i) –25°C   ii) 0°C   (iii) 10°C   (iv) 30°C   (v) 20°C

2. On the map of the world given below, the distribution of surface air temperature in the month of July is shown by lines as (i), (ii), (iii), (iv) and (v). Identify the temperature shown over these lines.

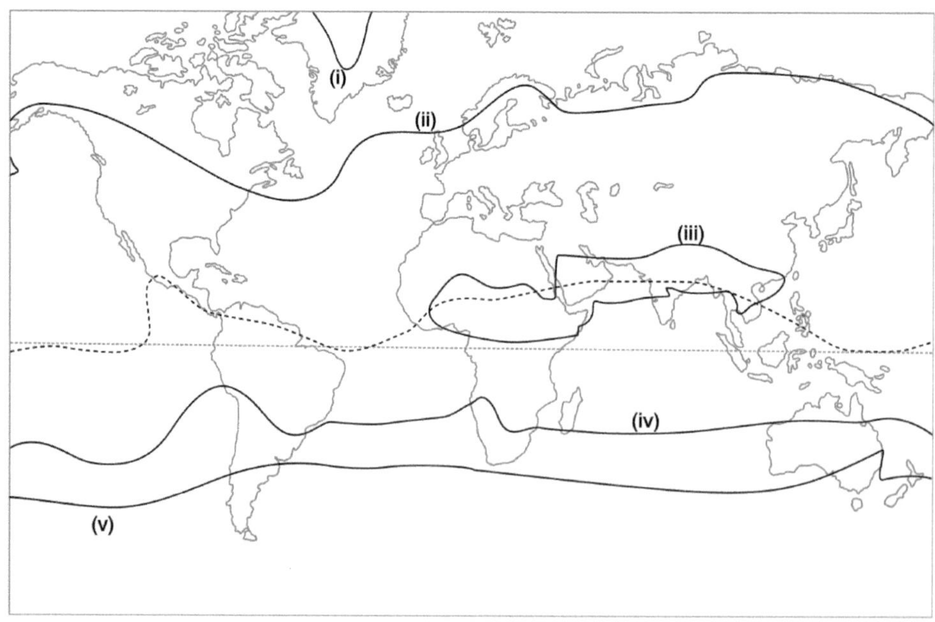

Ans. (i) 0°C   (ii) 10°C   (iii) 30°C   (iv) 20°C   (v) 10°C

Chapter Test

Objective Questions

1. Incoming solar radiation is also known as
    (a) Conduction   (b) Convection
    (c) Advection   (d) Insolation

2. Out of 100 units of heat received, roughly how much units are reflected back to space even before reaching the earth's surface?
    (a) 15 Units   (b) 30 Units
    (c) 35 Units   (d) 50 Units

3. The Earth is farthest from the sun on ....
    (a) 1st August   (b) 2nd October
    (c) 4th July   (d) 3rd January

4. The atmosphere is largely transparent to ....
    (a) long waves   (b) short waves
    (c) medium waves   (d) micro waves

5. Consider the following statements and choose the correct option from the given options

    I. The Sun rays fall obliquely at the top of the atmosphere and the earth intercepts a veny small portion of the Sun's energy.

    II. The earth is a geoid resembling a sphere.

    Codes
    (a) Only (I) is correct   (b) Only (II) is correct
    (c) Both statements are incorrect   (d) Both statements are correct

Short Answer Type Questions

6. Discuss the variations in the distribution of insolation over the earth's surface.

7. What is the role played by prevailing winds in temperature modification?

8. Explain why the angle of the sun rays fall variably on different latitudes.

9. Explain how the ocean currents influence the temperature distribution over the earth's surface.

10. Differentiate between advection and convection.

Long Answer Type Questions

11. Explain the reasons why isotherm bend polewards on continents and the equator towards on oceans.

12. Describe the various conditions for inversion of temperature.

13. How is atmosphere heated? Discuss the role of terrestrial radiation in this process.

Answers

1. (d) Insolation   **2.** (c) 35 Units   **3.** (c) 4th July

4. (b) short waves   **5.** (d) Both statements are correct

CHAPTER 03

Atmospheric Circulation and Weather Systems

In this Chapter...

- Atmospheric Pressure
- General Circulation of the Atmosphere
- Cyclonic and Anti-cyclonic Circulation

Atmospheric Pressure

The weight of a column of air contained in a unit area from the mean sea level to the top of the atmosphere is called atmospheric pressure. The atmospheric pressure is expressed in units of Millibar (mb) and Pascals or Kilopascal (kPa). At sea level, the average atmospheric pressure is 1,013.2 mb.

Due to gravity, the air at the surface is denser and hence, has higher pressure. Air pressure is measured with the help of a **mercury barometer** or the **aneroid barometer**. The pressure decreases with height.

At any elevation it varies from place to place and its variation is the primary cause of air motion, i.e. wind (horizontal motion of air) which moves from high pressure areas to low pressure areas.

Vertical Variation of Pressure

In the lower atmosphere, the pressure decreases rapidly with height. The decrease amounts to about 1 mb for each 10 m height but it does not always decrease with the same rate. Vertical pressure gradient force is much larger than the horizontal pressure gradient. But, it is generally balanced by a nearly equal but opposite gravitational force. Hence, we do not experience strong upward winds.

Standard Temperature and Pressure at Selected Levels

Level	Pressure in mb	Temperature °C
Sea level	1,013. 25	15.2
1 km	898.76	8.7
5 km	540.48	-17.3
10 km	265.00	-49.7

Horizontal Distribution of Pressure

Small differences in pressure are highly significant in terms of the wind direction and velocity. Horizontal distribution of pressure is studied by drawing isobars at constant levels. **Isobars** are lines connecting places having equal pressure. In order to eliminate the effect of altitude on pressure, it is measured at any station after being reduced to sea level for purposes of comparison. The sea level pressure distribution is shown on **weather maps**.

World Distribution of Sea Level Pressure

Near the equator, the sea level pressure is low and the area is known as **equatorial low**. The high-pressure areas known as the **sub-tropical highs** are found along 30°N and 30°S. Further pole wards along 60°N and 60°S, the low pressure belts are termed as the **sub-polar lows**.

Near the poles the pressure is high and it is known as the **polar high**. These pressure belts are not permanent in nature. They oscillate with the apparent movement of the sun. In the Northern hemisphere in winter, they move Southwards and in the summer, they move Northwards.

Forces Affecting the Velocity and Direction of Winds

The air is set in motions due to the differences in atmospheric pressure. The air in horizontal motion is called **wind**. The wind blows from high pressure to low pressure. The wind at the surface experiences **friction**[1] and rotation of the earth also affects the wind movement. The horizontal winds near the earth surface respond to the combined effect of three forces. In addition, the gravitational force acts downward. The three forces are

(i) **Pressure Gradient Force** The differences in atmospheric pressure produce a force. The rate of change of pressure with respect to distance is the pressure gradient. The pressure gradient is strong where the isobars are close to each other and is weak where the isobars are apart.

(ii) **Frictional Force** It affects the speed of wind. Its influence generally extends upto an elevation of 1-3 km. Over the sea surface, the friction is minimal and at the land surface it is greatest.

(iii) **Coriolis Force** The force exerted by the rotation of the earth is known as the coriolis force.

It is named after the French physicist who described it in 1844. Coriolis force deflects the wind to the right direction in the Northern hemisphere and to the left in the Southern hemisphere. The deflection is more when the wind velocity is high.

It is directly proportional to the angle of latitude. It is maximum at the poles and absent at the equator. The coriolis force acts perpendicular to the pressure gradient force. The pressure gradient force is perpendicular to an isobar. The higher the pressure gradient force, the more is the velocity of the wind and the larger is the deflection in the direction of wind. As a result of these two forces operating perpendicular to each other, in the low-pressure areas the wind blows around it.

At the equator, the coriolis force is zero and the wind blows perpendicular to the isobars due to which the low pressure gets filled instead of getting intensified. This is the reason due to which tropical cyclones are not formed near the equator.

Pressure and Wind

The velocity and direction of the wind are the net results of the wind generating forces. The winds in the upper atmosphere about 2-3 km above the surface, are free from frictional effect of the surface and are controlled by the pressure gradient and the Coriolis force.

When isobars are straight and when there is no friction, the pressure gradient force is balanced by Coriolis force and the resultant wind blows parallel to the isobars which is known as **geostrophic wind**.

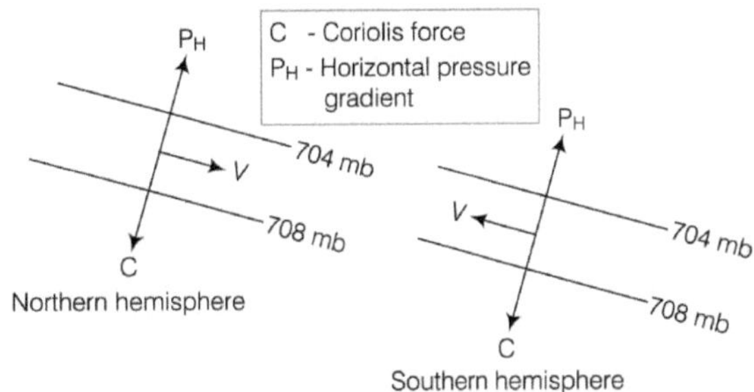

Geostrophic Wind

General Circulation of the Atmosphere

The pattern of the movement of the planetary winds is called the general circulation of the atmosphere. The general circulation of the atmosphere also sets in motion the ocean water circulation which influences the earth's climate.

Planetary Winds

The pattern of planetary winds largely depends on

- Latitudinal variation of atmospheric heating.
- Emergence of pressure belts.
- The migration of belts following apparent path of the sun.
- The distribution of continents and oceans.
- The rotation of the earth.

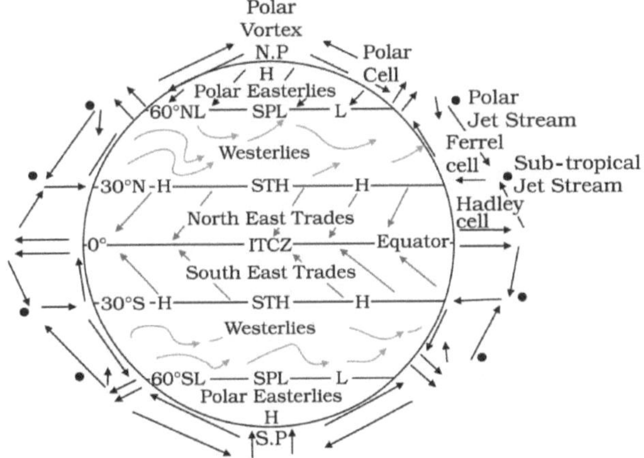

Simplified General Circulation of the Atmosphere

---

1 Friction It is the force which resists the relative motion of solid surfaces, fluid layers and material elements sliding against each other.

Convection Cells

The general circulation of the air at the Inter Tropical Convergence Zone (**ITCZ**)[2] rises because of convection caused by high insolation and a low pressure. The winds from the tropics converge at this low pressure zone. The converged air rises along with the convective cell. It reaches the top of the troposphere up to an altitude of 14 km and moves towards the poles.

This causes accumulation of air at about 30°N and S. Part of the accumulated air sinks to the ground and forms a sub-tropical high.

Another reason for sinking is the cooling of air when it reaches 30°N and S latitudes. Down below near the land surface, the air flows towards the equator as the easterlies. The easterlies from either side of the equator converge in the Inter-Tropical Convergence Zone (ITCZ).

The circulations of wind from the surface upwards and *vice-versa* are called cells. There are three cells found in the atmosphere.

(i) **Hadley Cell** It originates by the rising air from the equator which sinks near sub-tropics. On the surface, this **air mass**[3] bifurcates into two parts i.e. towards the equator and towards the poles.

(ii) **Ferrel Cell** In the middle latitudes, the circulation is created by sinking cold air coming from the poles and rising warm air that blows from the sub-tropical high. At the surface, these winds are called **Westerlies** and the cell is known as Ferrel cell.

(iii) **Polar Cell** At polar latitudes, the cold dense air subsides near the poles and blows towards middle latitudes as the polar Easterlies. This cell is called polar cell.

These three cells set the pattern for general circulation of the atmosphere. The transfer of heat energy from lower latitudes to higher latitudes maintains the general circulation.

The general circulation of the atmosphere also affects the oceans. The large-scale winds of the atmosphere initiate large and slow moving currents of the ocean. Oceans in turn provide input of energy and water vapour into the air. These interactions take place rather slowly over a large part of the ocean.

General Atmospheric Circulation and its Effects on Oceans

Warming and cooling of the Pacific Ocean is most important in terms of general atmospheric circulation. The warm water of the central Pacific Ocean slowly drifts towards South American coast and replaces the cool Peruvian current. Such appearance of warm water off the coast of Peru is known as the **El Nino**.

The El Nino event is closely associated with the pressure changes in the Central Pacific and Australia. This change in pressure condition over Pacific is known as the **Southern Oscillation**. The combined phenomenon of southern oscillation and El Nino is known as ENSO (EL Nino Southern Oscillation).

In the years when the ENSO is strong, large-scale variations in weather occur over the world. The arid West-coast of South America receives heavy rainfall, drought occurs in Australia and sometimes in India and floods in China. This phenomenon is closely monitored and is used for long range forecasting in major parts of the world.

Seasonal Wind

The pattern of wind circulation is modified in different seasons due to shifting of regions of maximum heating, pressure and wind belts. The effect of such shift is noticed in the monsoons, especially over South-East Asia.

Local Winds

Differences in the heating and cooling of the earth surfaces and the cycles those develop daily or annually can create several common, regional winds which are called **local winds**.

Land and Sea Breezes

The land and sea absorb and transfer heat differently. During the day, the land heats up faster and become warmer than the sea. Therefore, over the land the air rises giving rise to a low pressure area, whereas the sea is relatively cool and pressure over sea is relatively high. Thus, pressure gradient from sea to land is created and the wind blows from sea to land as sea breeze. In the night, the reversal of this condition takes place. The land loses heat faster and is cooler than the sea. The pressure gradient is from land to the sea and hence, land breeze results.

Mountain and Valley Winds

In mountainous regions, during the day the slopes get heated up and air moves to upslope and to fill the resulting gap, the air blows up the valley. This wind is known as the **valley breeze**.

During night, the slopes get cooled and the dense air descends into the valley as the **mountain wind**. The cool air of the high plateaus and ice fields draining into the valley is called katabatic wind.

Another type of warm wind occurs on the leeward side of the mountain ranges. The moisture in these winds, while crossing the

---

2 ITCZ Near the equator, from about 5° North and 5° South, the North-East trade winds and South-East trade winds converge in a low-pressure zone known as the Inter Tropical Convergence Zone or ITCZ.

3 Air Mass A body of air with horizontally uniform levels of temperature, humidity and pressure.

mountain ranges condense and precipitate. When it descends down the leeward side of the slope, the dry air gets warmed up by **adiabatic process**. This dry air can melt the snow in a short time.

Air Masses

The air with distinctive characteristics in terms of temperature and humidity is called an air mass. It is defined as large body of air having little horizontal variation in temperature and moisture.

Source Regions of Air Mass

When the air remains over a homogenous area for a sufficiently longer time, it acquires the characteristics of the area. The air masses are formed on the homogenous surfaces that can be the vast ocean surface or vast plains, these homogenous surfaces are called the source regions. Tropical air masses are warm and polar air masses are cold.

The air masses are classified according to source regions. There are five major source regions which are

(i) Warm tropical and sub-tropical oceans.

(ii) The sub-tropical hot deserts.

(iii) The relatively cold high latitude oceans.

(iv) The very cold snow covered continents in high latitudes.

(v) Permanently ice covered continents in the Arctic and Antarctica.

According to these, following types of air masses are recognised

- Maritime tropical (mT)
- Continental tropical (cT)
- Maritime polar (mP)
- Continental polar (cP)
- Continental arctic (cA)

Fronts

When two different air masses meet, the boundary zone between them is called a front. The process of formation of the front is known as **Frontogenesis**.

There are four types of fronts

(i) **Stationary** When the front remains stationary, it is called a stationary front.

(ii) **Cold** When the cold air mass moves towards the warm air mass, its contact zone is called the cold front.

(iii) **Warm** If the warm air mass moves towards the cold air mass, the contact zone is called the warm front.

(iv) **Occluded** If an air mass is fully lifted above the land surface, it is called occluded front. The fornts occur in middle latitudes and characterised by steep gradient in temperature and pressure. Fronts bring abrupt changes in temperature and cause the air to rise to form clouds and cause precipitation.

Cyclonic and Anti-cyclonic Circulation

The wind circulation around a low pressure area is called cyclonic circulation. Around a high, it is called anti-cyclonic circulation. The direction of winds around such systems changes according to their location in different hemispheres.

The wind circulation at the earth's surface around low and high on many occasions is closely related to the wind circulation at higher level. Generally, over low pressure area the air will converge and rise. Over high pressure area, the air will subside from above and diverge at the surface. Apart from convergence, some eddies, convection currents, orographic uplift and uplift along fronts cause the rising of air, which is essential for the formation of clouds and precipitation. These circulations sometimes give rise to extra tropical cyclones, tropical cyclones, thunderstorms, tornadoes, etc.

Patterns of Wind Direction in Cyclone and Anti-cyclone

Pressure System	Pressure Condition at the Centre	Pattern of Wind Direction	
		Northern Hemisphere	Southern Hemisphere
Cyclone	Low	Anti-clockwise	Clockwise
Anti-cyclone	High	Clockwise	Anti-clockwise

Extra-Tropical Cyclone

The system developing in the mid and high latitude, beyond the tropics are called the **middle latitude** or extra tropical cyclones. The passage of front causes abrupt changes in the weather conditions over the area in the middle and high latitudes.

Formation of Extra-Tropical Cyclone

Extra-tropical cyclones form along the polar front. Initially, the front is stationary. In the Northern hemisphere, warm air blows from the South and cold air from the North of the front. When the pressure drops along the front, the warm air moves Northwards and the cold air moves towards South which causes anti-clockwise cyclonic circulation.

This cyclonic circulation leads to a well-developed extra tropical cyclone, with a warm and cold front. There are pockets of warm air or warm sector wedged between the forward and the rear cold air or cold sector. The warm air glides over the cold air and a sequence of cloud appears over the sky ahead of the warm front which cause precipitation.

The cold front approaches the warm air from behind and pushes the warm air up. As a result, cumulus clouds develop along the cold front. The cold front moves faster than the warm front ultimately overtaking the warm front. By this, the warm air is completely lifted up and the front is occluded and the cyclone dissipates (vanish).

The processes of wind circulation both at the surface and aloft are closely interlinked.

Tropical Cyclones

These are violent storms that originate over oceans in tropical areas and move over to the coastal areas. They bring large scale destruction caused by violent winds, heavy rainfall and storm surges. They are known as **Cyclones** in Indian Oceans, **Hurricanes** in the Atlantic, **Typhoons** in the Western Pacific and South China Sea and **Willy-willies** in the Western Australia.

The tropical cyclones originate and intensify over warm tropical oceans. The favorable condition for the formation and intensification of tropical cyclones are

- Large sea surface with temperature higher than 27°C.
- Presence of the Coriolis force.
- Small variations in the vertical wind speed.
- A pre-existing weak-low pressure area of low level cyclonic circulations.
- Upper divergence above the sea level system.

Process of Development of Tropical Cyclones

The energy that intensifies the storm, comes from the condensation process in the towering cumulonimbus (a dark cloud of great vertical extent charged with electricity) clouds, surrounding the centre of the storm. With continuous supply of moisture from the sea, the storm is further strengthened.

On reaching the land, the moisture supply is cut off and the storm dissipates. The place where a tropical cyclone crosses the coast is called the **land fall of the cyclone**.

Characteristics of Tropical Cyclones

- A mature tropical cyclone is characterised by the strong, spirally circulating wind around the centre called the **eye**.
- The diameter of the circulating system can vary between 150 and 250 km.
- The eye is a region of calm with subsiding air. Around the eye is the eye wall, where there is a strong spiralling ascent of air to greater height, reaching the tropopause. The wind reaches maximum velocity in this region reaching as high as 250 km per hour.
- They give torrential rainfall.
- From the eye wall, rain bands may radiate and trains of cumulus and cumulonimbus clouds may drift into the outer region.
- They are destructive causing great damage to life and property.

- The cyclones, which cross 20°N latitude generally, recurve and they are more destructive in nature.
- Over the Bay of Bengal, Arabian sea and Indian ocean, the diameter of the storm is between 600-1200 km.
- The system moves slowly about 300-500 km per day.
- The cyclone creates storm surges and they inundate the coastal low lands. The storm weakens the land.

Differences between Extra-Tropical Cyclone and Tropical Cyclone

- The extra-tropical cyclones have a clear frontal system which is not present in the tropical cyclones.
- Extra-tropical cyclones cover a larger area and can originate over the land and sea. Whereas the tropical cyclones originate only over the seas and on reaching the land they dissipate.
- The extra-tropical cyclones affect a much larger area as compared to the tropical cyclone. The wind velocity in a tropical cyclone is much higher and it is more destructive.
- The extra-tropical cyclones move from West to East. But the tropical cyclones move from East to West.

Thunderstorms and Tornadoes

Thunderstorms and tornadoes are of short duration, occurring over a small area but are violent.

Thunderstorms

These are caused by intense convection on moist hot days. A thunderstorm is well grown cumulonimbus cloud producing thunder and lightening. When the clouds extend to heights where sub-zero temperature prevails, hails are formed and they come down as hailstorm.

If there is insufficient moisture, a thunderstorm can generate dust storms. A thunderstorm is characterised by intense updraft of rising warm air, which causes the clouds to grow bigger and rise to greater height which causes precipitation. Later, downdraft brings down to earth the cool air and the rain.

Tornadoes

Sometimes spiralling wind from severe thunderstorms, descends like a trunk of an elephant with great force, with very low pressure at the centre and cause massive destruction on its way. This phenomenon is called a tornado. It generally occurs in middle latitudes. The tornado over the sea is called **water spouts**.

These violent storms are the manifestation of the atmosphere's adjustments to varying energy distribution. The potential and heat energies are converted into kinetic energy in these storms and the restless atmosphere again returns to its stable state.

Chapter Practice

Objective Questions

• Multiple Choice Questions

1. The force exerted by the rotation of the earth is known as ....
   (a) Coriolis force   (b) Frictional force
   (c) Gravitational force   (d) None of these

Ans. (a) The force exerted by the rotation of the earth is known as the coriolis force.

2. ITCZ stands for
   (a) Intra Tropical Convergence Zone
   (b) Inter Tropical Convergence Zone
   (c) Inter Temperate Convergence Zone
   (d) None of the above

Ans. (b) ITCZ stands for Inter Tropical Convergence Zone. This zone is found in the equatorial latitudes characterised by low pressure.

3. When two different air masses meet, the boundary zone between them is called a ....
   (a) ITCZ   (b) Cell
   (c) Front   (d) None of these

Ans. (c) When two different air masses meet, the boundary zone between them is called a front.

4. Where does tropical cyclone originate and intensify?
   (a) Warm tropical oceans
   (b) Tropical landmass
   (c) All oceans
   (d) None of the above

Ans. (a) Tropical cyclones are violent storms that originate and intensify over oceans in tropical areas/warm tropical oceans.

5. A thunderstorm is a well-grown .... cloud producing thunder and lightening.
   (a) Cumulus   (b) Cumulonimbus
   (c) Stratocumulus   (d) Nimbus

Ans. (b) A thunderstorm is a well-grown cumulonimbus cloud producing thunder and lightening.

6. Choose the correctly matched pair.
   (a) Cyclones   – Indian Ocean
   (b) Typhoons   – Atlantic
   (c) Hurricanes   – Western pacific
   (d) Cyclones   – Western pacific and South China Sea

Ans. (a) Tropical cyclones are known as cyclones in the Indian Ocean, Hurricanes in the Atlantic, Typhoons in the Western Pacific and South China Sea.

7. Choose the incorrectly matched pair.

(a)	Stationary front –	When the front remains stationary
(b)	Cold front –	When the warm air moves towards the cold air mass
(c)	Warm front –	When warm air mass moves towards the cold air mass
(d)	Occluded front –	When the air mass is fully lifted above the land surface

Ans. (b) When cold air mass moves towards the warm air mass (not cold air mass), its contact zone is known as the cold front.

8. Match the following terms List I with their associated statements on List II.

	List I		List II
A.	Atmospheric pressure	1.	The differences in atmospheric pressure produces a force
B.	Pressure gradient force	2.	The weight of a column of air contained in a unit area from the mean sea level to the top of the atmosphere.
C.	Frictional force	3.	When isobars are straight and when there is no friction.
D.	Geostrophic winds	4.	It is greatest at the surface and its influence generally extends upto an elevation of 1-3 km

Codes

	A	B	C	D			A	B	C	D
(a)	2	1	4	3		(b)	2	1	3	4
(c)	1	3	4	2		(d)	4	1	2	3

Ans. (a)

9. Match the following terms List I with their associated statements on List II.

List I		List II
A.	Cyclonic circulation	1.	The systems develop in the mid and high latitude beyond the tropics.
B.	Extra tropical cyclones	2.	Violent storms that originate over oceans in tropical areas.
C.	Anti-cyclonic circulation	3.	The wind circulation around a high.
D.	Tropical cyclones	4.	The wind circulation around a low.

Codes

	A	B	C	D			A	B	C	D
(a)	2	1	4	3		(b)	4	1	3	2
(c)	1	3	4	2		(d)	4	1	2	3

Ans. (b)

10. Consider the following statements and choose the correct option

   I. The vertical pressure gradient force is much larger than that of the horizontal pressure gradient.

   II. It is generally balanced by a nearly equal but opposite gravitational force.

(a) Statement I is correct, but statement II is incorrect.

(b) Statement I is incorrect, but statement II is correct.

(c) Both the statements I and II are correct.

(d) Both the statements I and II are incorrect.

Ans. (c) Both the statements I and II are correct.

11. Consider the following statements and choose the correct option

   (i) Thunderstorms are caused by intense convection on moist hot days.

   (ii) A thunderstorm is characterised by intense updraft of rising warm air.

(a) Statement (i) is correct, but statement, (ii) is incorrect.

(b) Statement (i) is incorrect, but statement (ii) is correct.

(c) Both the statements (i) and (ii) are correct.

(d) Both the statements (i) and (ii) are incorrect.

Ans. (c) Both the statements I and II are correct.

12. Arrange the following in the correct order moving from the equator towards the poles.

   I. Polar cell

   II. Hadley cell

   III. Ferrel cell

Codes

(a) I, III, II   (b) II, III, I

(c) II, I, III   (d) III, II, I

Ans. (b) The correct order of the given cells moving from the equator towards the poles is Hadley cell, Ferrel cell and Polar cell.

• Case Based MCQs

13. Read the case/source given and answer the questions that follow by choosing the correct option.

General Atmospheric Circulation and Its Effects on Oceans

Warming and cooling of the Pacific Ocan is most important in terms of general atmospheric circulation. The warm water of the central Pacific Ocean slowly drifts towards South American coast and replaces the cool Peruvian current. Such appearance of warm water off the coast of Peru is known as the EI Nino. The EI Nino event is closely associated with the pressure changes in the Central Pacific and Australia. This change in pressure condition over Pacific is known as the Southern oscillation. The combined phenomenon of Southern oscillation and EI Nino is known as ENSO. In the years when the ENSO is strong, large-scale variations in weather occur over the world. The arid West coast of South America receives heavy rainfall, drought occurs in Australia and sometimes in India and floods in China. This phenomenon is closely monitored and is used for long range forecasting in major parts of the world.

(i) Warm water of Central Pacific Ocean replaces which oceanic current near South American Coast?

(a) Peruvian current

(b) Gulf stream

(c) North Equatorial current

(d) South Equatorial current

Ans. (a) The warm water of Central Pacific ocean slowly drifts towards South American coast and replaces the cool Peruvian current.

(ii) Drifting of warm water from Central Pacific to the coast of Peru results in a phenomenon known as

(a) El Nino   (b) La Nina

(c) Southern oscillation   (d) Polar cell

Ans. (a) Drifting of warm water from Central Pacific to the coast of Peru results in a phenomenon known as El Nino. El Nino is closely associated with the pressure changes in the Central Pacific and Australia.

(iii) Strong ENSO results in

(a) heavy rainfall in East Coast of North America, drought in Australia, flooding in Japan

(b) heavy rainfall on West South American coast, drought in Australia, flooding in China

(c) heavy rainfall in Australia, flooding in China, drought in West South American coast

(d) None of the above

Ans. (b) Strong ENSO results in heavy rainfall on West South American coast, drought in Australia and flooding in China.

(iv) Change in pressure conditions over Pacific due to El Nino is known as ....
(a) Northern Oscillation
(b) Trade winds
(c) Southern Oscillation
(d) Tropical cyclones

Ans. (c) Change in pressure conditions over Pacific due to El Nino is known as Southern Oscillation.

20. Study the given diagram and answer the questions that follow by choosing the correct option.

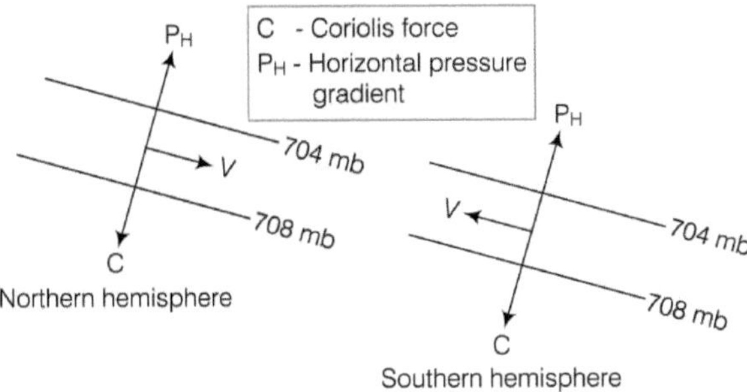

(i) What type of wind is shown by the Symbol V?
(a) Easterly wind
(b) Sea breeze
(c) Geostrophic wind
(d) Jet stream

Ans. (c) Geostrophic wind is shown by the Symbol V.

(ii) Which of the following forces determines the velocity of a wind?
(a) Corialis force
(b) Pressure gradient force
(c) Gravitational force
(d) Magnetic force

Ans. (b) Pressure gradient force determines the velocity of a wind.

(iii) The corialis force is zero in which of the following regions?
(a) Polar region
(b) Mountains
(c) Equatorial region
(d) Temperate region

Ans. (c) The corialis force is zero in equatorial region.

(iv) The effect of frictional force on the wind is minimum over which of the following areas?
(a) Mountains
(b) Grasslands
(c) Oceans
(d) Plains

Ans. (c) The effect of frictional force on the wind is minimum over oceans.

PART 2
Subjective Questions

• Short Answer (SA) Type Questions

1. The wind redistribute the heat and moisture across the planet. Discuss.

Ans. The wind redistribute the heat and moisture across the planet in the following ways
- The wind is the horizontal movement of air. Air moves from high pressure to low pressure. When the heat or temperature of any area increases, it causes low pressure zone and air starts to move from high pressure to low pressure. The earth's atmospheric circulation is an important transfer mechanism for both energy and mass.
- The transfer of heat energy from lower latitude to higher latitude is done in general circulation. It reduces the imbalance between equatorial energy surplus and polar energy deficit.

2. Discuss the factors affecting the speed and direction of wind.   **(NCERT)**

Ans. The factors affecting the speed and direction of wind are
- **The Pressure Gradient Force** The differences in atmospheric pressure produces a force. The rate of change of pressure with respect to distance is the pressure gradient. The pressure gradient is the driving force as wind moves from high pressure to low pressure.
- **Frictional Force** It affects the speed of wind. It is the greatest at the surface and its influence generally extends upto an elevation of 1-3 km. Over the sea surface, the friction is minimal.
- **Coriolis Force** The force exerted by the rotation of the earth is known as the coriolis force. It is named after the French physicist who described it in 1844. Coriolis force deflects the wind to the right direction in the Northern hemisphere and to the left in the Southern hemisphere. Coriolis force is directly proportional to the angle of latitude. It is maximum at the poles and is absent at the equator.

3. What are the factors which determine the pattern of planetary wind?

Ans. The pattern of planetary wind largely depends upon following factors
- Latitudinal variation of atmospheric heating.
- Emergence of pressure belt.
- The migration of belts following apparent path of the sun.
- The distribution of continents and oceans.
- The rotation of the earth.

4. The winds are the horizontal movement of air which are classified into major groups. Explain.

Ans. The winds are the horizontal movement of air. They are classified into four major groups

(i) **Permanent Winds** The trade winds, anti-trade winds and polar winds are known as the permanent winds.

(ii) **Periodic or Seasonal Winds** Seasonal winds change their direction with change to season. Monsoon is a seasonal wind. In the monsoon climate, there is a complete reversal of wind direction after every six months.

(iii) **Local Winds** Daily variations in atmospheric pressure develop in many parts of the world lead to distinctive local wind patterns. These variations in pressure result from moving air caused by changing surface temperature throughout the day. They result in daily changes in wind direction and velocity.

(iv) **Variable Winds** The winds which change their direction after every few hours are known as variable winds. These include cyclones and anti-cyclones.

5. Air masses are classified according to the source regions. Explain the source region. Also mention major source regions.

Ans. The air masses are formed on the homogenous surfaces that can be vast ocean surface or vast plains. These homogenous surfaces are called the source regions.

The five major source regions are

(i) Warm tropical and sub-tropical oceans.

(ii) The sub-tropical hot deserts.

(iii) The relatively cold high latitude ocean.

(iv) The very cold snow covered continents in high latitude.

(v) Permanently ice covered continents in the Arctic and Antarctica.

6. Front is the boundary zone between two air masses. Discuss its various types.

Ans. When two different air masses meet, the boundary zone between them is called a front. Fronts may be classified into four types

(i) **Stationary Front** When the front remain stationary, it is called stationary front.

(ii) **Cold Front** When the cold air mass moves towards the warm air mass, its contact zone is called the cold front.

(iii) **Warm Front** If the warm air mass moves towards the cold air mass, the contact zone is called warm front.

(iv) **Occluded Front** If an air mass is fully lifted above the land surface, it is called the occluded front.

7. Describe the process of formation of extra-tropical cyclone.

Ans. Extra tropical cyclones form along the polar front. Initially, the front is stationary. In the Northern hemisphere, warm air blows from the South and cold air from the North of the front. When the pressure drops along the front, the warm air moves Northwards and the cold air moves towards South which causes anti-clockwise cyclonic circulation.

This cyclonic circulation leads to a well-developed extra tropical cyclone, with a warm and cold front. There are pockets of warm air or warm sector wedged between the forward and the rear cold air or cold sector. The warm air glides over the cold air and a sequrence of cloud appears over the sky ahead of the warm front which cause precipitation.

8. Extra-tropical cyclones have many important characteristics. Identify them.

Ans. The important characteristics of extra-tropical cyclones are

- These cyclones have a clear frontal system.
- They cover a large area and can originate over the land and sea.
- They affect a much larger area as compared to tropical cyclone.
- The extra-tropical cyclone moves from West to East but tropical cyclones move from East to West.
- They are less destructive and causes light showers.

9. Tropical cyclones have many important features. Identify them.

Ans. Important features of tropical cyclones are

- A mature tropical cyclone is characterised by the strong, spirally circulating wind around the centre called the eye.
- The diameter of the circulating system can vary between 150 and 250 km.
- The eye is a region of calm with subsiding air. Around the eye is the eyewall, where there is a strong spiralling ascent of air to greater height, reaching the tropopause. The wind reaches maximum velocity in this region reaching as high as 250 km per hour.
- They give torrential rainfall.
- They are destructive causing great damage to life and property.

10. Differentiate between tropical cyclones and temperate cyclones. Discuss.

Ans. Differences between tropical cyclones and temperate cyclones are

Extra-Tropical	Cyclone Tropical
The extra-tropical cyclones have a clear frontal system.	The tropical cyclones does not have a clear frontal system.
Extra-tropical cyclones cover a larger area and can originate over the land and sea.	The tropical cyclones originate only over the seas and on reaching the land they dissipate.
The extra-tropical cyclones affect a much larger area as compared to the tropical cyclone.	The wind velocity in a tropical cyclone is much higher and it is more destructive.
The extra-tropical cyclones move from West to East.	The tropical cyclones move from East to West.

11. Thunderstorms are local storms which are of short duration but are violent. Elucidate.

Ans. Thunderstorms are local storms that are of short duration, occuring over a small area but are violent. Thunderstorms are caused by intense convection on moist hot days. A thunderstorm is a well-grown cumulonimbus clouds producing thunder and lightening. When the clouds extend to heights where sub-zero temperature prevails, hails are formed and they come down as hail storm.

A thunderstorm is characterised by intense updraft of rising warm air, which causes the clouds to grow bigger and rise to greater height which cause precipitation.

12. "Tornadoes are the violent storms which cause massive destruction on its way". Discuss its impact on human life. Also suggest some important measures to mitigate this disaster.

Ans. Tornadoes are the strong circular moving storm which generally occur in middle latitudes. Hence, this region specially Eastern parts of continent is highly vulnerable to tornadoes. Tornado occurs on landmass, therefore, it causes huge loss of mass, man and material and affect the whole human life i.e. education, bussiness, hospital facilities, infrastructure etc.

To mitigate its effect on the human life, following measures should be adopted

- The tornado sensitive areas should be identified.
- Regional planning must be adopted for mitigation on particular region.
- Proper alternatives should be developed to assist the human life.
- Fundamental services should be well protected from any storms and calamities.

• Long Answer (LA) Type Questions

1. Discuss the effect of general circulation of atmosphere.

Ans. The effects of general circulation of atmosphere are

- **Resolve Imbalances** Earth's atmospheric circulation is an important transfer mechanism for both energy and mass. In this process, the imbalances between equatorial energy surplus and polar energy deficit is partly resolved, Earth's weather patterns are generated and ocean currents are produced.
- **Effect on Oceans** The general circulation of the atmosphere also affects the oceans. The large scale winds of the atmosphere initiate large and slow moving currents on the ocean. Ocean in turn provides input of energy and water vapours into the air. For example, warming and cooling of the Pacific Ocean is the most important in terms of general atmospheric circulation. The warm water of the central Pacific ocean slowly drift towards South American coast and replaces the cold Perunian current which is known as El-Nino. The El-Nino event is closely associated with the pressure changes in the central Pacific and Australia which is called Southern Oscillation.
  The combination of both El-Nino and Southern Oscillation is known as ENSO. In the years where the ENSO is strong, the large scale variations in weather occur over the world.

2. "The extra-tropical cyclone has greater significance in the region it occurs." Give arguments in support of this statement.

Ans. The extra-tropical cyclone occurs in mid-latitude of Southern hemisphere which are born along the polar front. The temperate cyclone covers around 1000 km wide area. These cyclones move at a gentle pace of 5 to 25 km per hour.

The significance extra-tropical cyclone for this region are

- Extra tropical cyclone gives light shower which are highly beneficial for the agriculture.
- It causes snowfall in the region which causes attraction for tourism. The snowfall becomes the fresh source of water for rivers.
- Since the movement of wind is low, it does not cause any harm to life and property.
- Extra-tropical cyclones do not require so much disaster management machinery due to their less violent nature.

3. Tropical cyclones are violent storms that originate over oceans in tropical areas and move over to the coastal areas. Explain.

Ans. Tropical cyclones are violent storms that originate over oceans in tropical areas and move over to the coastal areas. They bring large scale destruction caused by violent winds, heavy rainfall and storm surges.

They are known as Cyclones in Indian Oceans, Hurricanes in the Atlantic, Typhoons in the Western Pacific and South China Sea and Willy-willies in the Western Australia.

The tropical cyclones originate and intensify over warm tropical oceans. The favorable condition of the formation and intensification of tropical cyclones are

- Large sea surface with temperature higher than 27°C.
- Presence of the Coriolis force.
- Small variations in the vertical wind speed.
- A pre-existing weak-low pressure area of low level cyclonic circulations.
- Upper divergence above the sea level system.

Process of Development of Tropical Cyclones

The energy that intensifies the storm, comes from the condensation process in the towering cumulonimbus (a dark cloud of great vertical extent charged with electricity) clouds, surrounding the centre of the storm.

With continuous supply of moisture from the sea, the storm is further strengthened. On reaching the land, the moisture supply is cut off and the storm dissipates. The place where a tropical cyclone crosses the coast is called the land fall of the cyclone.

4. Why does the tropical cyclone originate over the seas? In which part of the tropical cyclones do torrential rain and high velocity winds blow and why?

Ans. The tropical cyclone originates over the seas because latent heat of condensation is the main source of energy for tropical cyclones. This condition is available in the tropical oceanic part. A tropical cyclone usually develops from a small tropical depression. Condensation begins in the ascending air and the tropical cyclone takes shape.

Thus, the tropical cyclones form within one warm, humid air mass between 10° and 25° in both the hemispheres.

Torrential rains and high velocity wind blows in the area of eyewall. The area around the eye is eyewall. There is a strong spiralling ascent of air to greater height reaching the tropopause. The central part of the tropical cyclone is surrounded by the walls of cumulonimbus clouds.

The maximum wind velocity are always recorded adjacent to the centre of tropical cyclone. The winds slow down at uniform rate from the eye wall to the centre, where rain practically ceases.

• Case Based Questions

1. Read the case/source given and answer the following questions.

Do you realise that our body is subjected to a lot of air pressure. As one moves up the air gets varified and one feels breathless. The weight of a column of air contained in a unit area from the mean sea level to the top of the atmosphere is called the atmospheric pressure. The atmospheric pressure is expressed in units of milibar. At sea level the average atmospheric pressure is 1,013.2 milibar. Due to gravity the air at the surface is denser and hence has higher pressure.

Air pressure is measured with the help of a mercury barometer or the aneroid barometer. The pressure decreases with height. At any elevation it varies from place to place and its variation is the primary cause of air motion, i.e. wind which moves from high pressure areas to low pressure areas.

(i) Define Atmospheric pressure. What is the average atmospheric pressure at sea level?

Ans. The atmospheric pressure is defined as the weight of a column of air contained in a unit area from the mean sea level to the top of the atmosphere.

The average atmospheric pressure at sea level is 1,013.2 milibar.

(ii) How is atmospheric pressure measured and what is the unit of measurement?

Ans. A mercury barometer or the aneroid barometer is used for measuring the atmospheric pressure.

The unit of measurement for atmospheric pressure is milibar.

(iii) What is the relation of pressure and height? How is motion in air dependent on pressure?

Ans. The relution of pressure and height is such that the atmospheric pressure decreases with increasing height.

Motion in air is dependent on pressure as different locations have different atmospheric pressure, and this difference in pressure results in movement of air from high to low pressure areas.

2. Read the case/source given and answer the following questions.

Horizontal Distribution of Pressure

Small differences in pressure are highly significant in terms of the wind direction and velocity. Horizontal distribution of pressure is studied by drawing isobars at constant levels. Isobars are lines connecting places having equal pressure. In order to eliminate the effect of altitude on pressure, it is measured at any station after being reduced to sea level for purposes of comparison.

The sea level pressure distribution is shown on weather maps. Lowpressure system is enclosed by one or more isobars with the lowest pressure in the centre. High-pressure system is also enclosed by one or more isobars with the highest pressure in the centre.

World Distribution of Sea Level Pressure

Near the equator the sea level pressure is low and the area is known as equatorial low. Along 30° N and 30o S are found the high-pressure areas known as the subtropical highs. Further pole wards along 60o N and 60o S, the low-pressure belts are termed as the sub polar lows. Near the poles the pressure is high and it is known as the polar high. These pressure belts are not permanent.

(i) What is an Isobar?

Ans. Isobars are lines that connects places with equal atmospheric pressure in a weather map. The isobars are used to study the horizontal distribution of atmospheric pressure.

(ii) What does 'Low' and 'High' represent on weather map and how are these related to isobars?

Ans. 'High' and 'low' on the weather map represent high and low pressure systems. Area marked as 'High' will be enclosed in isobars with highest pressure in the centre and 'Low' will be enclosed in isobar with lowest pressure in centre.

(iii) State two high pressure and two low pressure regions according to latitudinal locations.

Ans. Regions located near 30° N and 30° S and poles are high pressure regions. Whereas, regions near the equator, and 60° N and 60° S latitudes are low pressure regions.

3. Read the case/source given below and answer the following questions.

Forces Affecting the Velocity and Direction of Wind

You already know that the air is set in motion due to the differences in atmospheric pressure. The air in motion is called wind. The wind blows from high pressure to low pressure. The wind at the surface experiences friction. In addition, rotation of the earth also affects the wind movement.

The force exerted by the rotation of the earth is known as the Coriolis force. Thus, the horizontal winds near the earth surface respond to the combined effect of three forces – the pressure gradient force, the frictional force and the Coriolis force. In addition, the gravitational force acts downward.

Pressure Gradient Force The differences in atmospheric pressure produces a force. The rate of change of pressure with respect to distance is the pressure gradient. The pressure gradient is strong where the isobars are close to each other and is weak where the isobars are apart.

Frictional Force It affects the speed of the wind. It is greatest at the surface and its influence generally extends upto an elevation of 1 - 3 km. Over the sea surface the friction is minimal.

Coriolis Force The rotation of the earth about its axis affects the direction of the wind. This force is called the Coriolis force after the French physicist who described it in 1844. It deflects the wind to the right direction in the Northern hemisphere.

(i) What are the forces affecting velocity and direction of wind? How does pressure determine the wind direction?

Ans. The three forces affecting the velocity and direction of wind are pressure gradient force, frictional force and coriolis force.

The wind flows from high pressure system to low pressure system and hence determines the direction of the wind.

(ii) Where is the highest frictional force experienced and till what elevation?

Ans. The frictional force is highest at the surface and its effects generally influence wind till an elevation of 1-3 kms from the earth's surface.

(iii) How is Coriolis force generated and how does it affect the wind direction in Northern hemisphere?

Ans. The rotation of earth about its axis generates the coriolis force. It affects the wind direction by deflecting the wind to the right direction in the Northern hemisphere.

• Map Based Questions

1. Identify the distribution of pressure (in millibars) in January shown by the lines marked as (i), (ii), (iii), (iv) and (v) on the map of the world given below

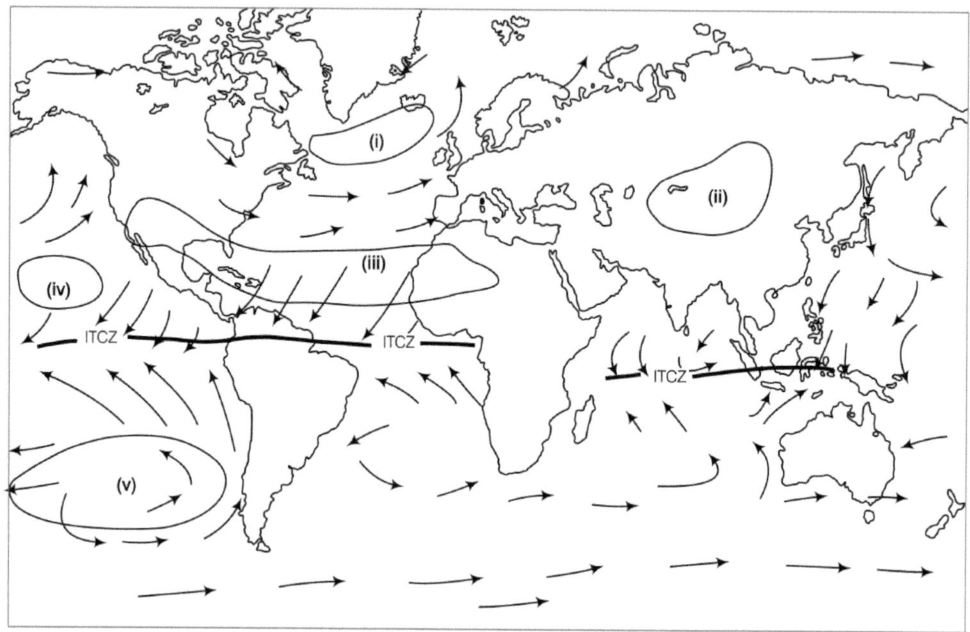

Ans. (i) Low Pressure - 1000 mb   (ii) High Pressure - 1030 mb   (iii) High Pressure - 1020 mb
(iv) High Pressure - 1020 mb   (v) High Pressure - 1015 mb

2. Identify the distribution of pressure (in millibars) in July shown by the lines marked as (i), (ii), (iii), (iv) and (v) on the map of the world given below.

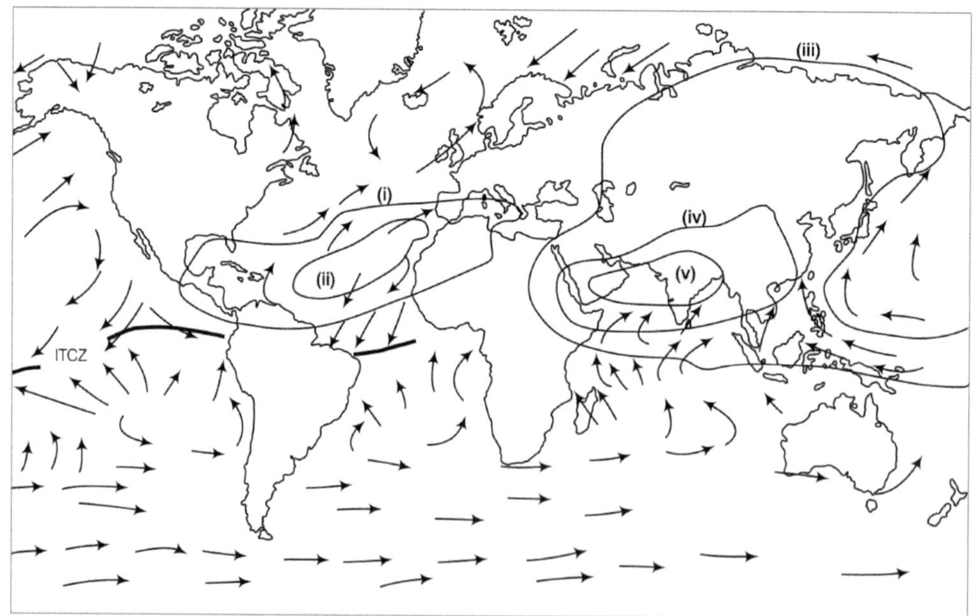

Ans. (i) High Pressure - 1015 mb   (ii) High Pressure - 1020 mb   (iii) Low Pressure - 1010 mb
(iv) Low Pressure - 1005 mb   (v) Low Pressure - 1000 mb

Chapter Test

Objective Questions

1. Which of following redistributes the heat and moisture across the Planet?

    (a) Wind   (b) Cloud   (c) Cyclones   (d) Tornadoes

2. In the lower atmosphere, the pressure decreases to about 1 mb for each .... height.

    (a) 5m   (b) 10m   (c) 15m   (d) 20m

3. The cool air of the high plateaus and ice fields draining into the valley is called ....

    (a) Mountain wind   (b) Katabatic wind

    (c) Valley breeze   (d) None of these

4. Warming and cooling of which of the following oceans is most important in terms of general atmospheric circulation?

    (a) Arctic Ocean   (b) Atlantic Ocean

    (c) Pacific Ocean   (d) Indian Ocean

5. Consider the following statements and choose the correct option.

    I. The pattern of the movement of the planetary winds is called the general circulation of the atmosphere.

    II. The general circulation of the atmosphere also sets in motion the ocean water circulation which influences the   earth's climate.

    (a) Only I is correct   (b) Only II is correct

    (c) Both statements are incorrect   (d) Both statements are correct

Short Answer Type Questions

6. How do air pressure and wind influence the weather?

7. What is Coriolis force and who discovered it first?

8. Explain Ferrel's law.

9. Explain the importance of ITCZ.

10. What do you understand by horse latitude?

11. Write the importance of air mass.

Long Answer Type Questions

12. Describe the global pattern of the distribution of pressure.

13. Discuss the seasonal variations in the pressure distribution over the earth's surface.

14. Describe the thunderstorm and tornado.

Answers

1. (a) Wind   **2.** (b) 10 m   **3.** (b) Katabatic wind

4. (c) Pacific Ocean   **5.** (d) Both statements are correct

CHAPTER 04

Water in the Atmosphere

In this Chapter...

- Water Vapour and Humidity
- Evaporation
- Condensation
- Precipitation

`Water is a very important life giving resource which is essential for all living beings. There is a continuous exchange of water between the atmosphere, the Oceans and the continents through the process of evaporation, condensation and precipitation. In this chapter, we will study these processes and also the world distribution of rainfall.

Water Vapour and Humidity

Air contains water vapour which varies from zero to four per cent by volume of the atmosphere. Water plays an important role in the weather phenomena. The moisture in the atmosphere is derived from the water bodies through evaporation and from plants through **transpiration**[1].

Water vapour present in the air is known as **humidity**. It is present in three forms i.e solid, liquid and gaseous. Humidity is expressed quantitatively in different ways. These ways are discussed below:

Absolute Humidity

The actual amount of the water vapour present in the atmosphere is known as the absolute humidity. It is the weight of water per unit volume of air. It is expressed in grams per cubic metre.

The ability of the air to hold water vapour depends entirely on its temperature. The absolute humidity differs from place to place on the earth's surface.

Relative Humidity

The percentage of moisture present in the atmosphere as compared to its full capacity at a given temperature is known as relative humidity. With the change of air temperature, the capacity to retain moisture increases or decreases and the relative humidity is also affected. It is greater over the oceans and least over the continents. The air containing moisture to its full capacity at a given temperature is said to be **saturated**.

---

1   **Transpiration** It is the process by which moisture is carried through plants from roots to small pores on the underside of leaves, where it changes to vapour and is released to the atmosphere. Transpiration is essentially the evaporation of water from plant leaves.

It means that the air at the given temperature is incapable of holding any additional amount of moisture at that stage. The temperature at which saturation occurs in a given sample of air is known as **dew point**.

Evaporation

It is a process by which water is transformed from liquid to gaseous state. This process increases the amount of water vapour in the atmosphere. Heat is the main cause for evaporation. The temperature at which the water starts evaporating is referred to as the latent heat of vapourisation.

Increase in temperature increases water absorption and retention capacity of the given parcel of air. Similarly, if the moisture content is low, air has a potentiality of absorbing and retaining moisture. Movement of air replaces the saturated layer with the unsaturated layer. Hence, the greater the movement of air, the greater is the evaporation.

Condensation

The transformation of water vapour into water is called condensation. This process withdraws the amount of water vapour from the atmosphere. It is caused by the loss of heat. When moist air is cooled, it may reach a level when its capacity to hold water vapour ceases. Then, the excess water vapour condenses into liquid form. If the excess water vapour directly condenses into solid form, it is known as sublimation.

In free air, condensation which results from cooling around very small particles is termed as **hygroscopic condensation nuclei**. Particles of dust, smoke and salt from the ocean are particularly good nuclei because they absorb water. Condensation also takes place when the moist air comes in contact with some colder object and it may also take place when the temperature is close to the dew point.

Conditions for Condensation

Condensation depends upon the amount of cooling and the relative humidity of air. Condensation is influenced by the volume of air, temperature, pressure and humidity. The favourable conditions due to which condesation takes place are

- When the temperature of the air is reduced to dew point with its volume remaining constant.
- When both the volume and temperature are reduced.
- When moisture is added to the air through evaporation. However, the most favourable condition for condensation is the decrease in air temperature.

Forms of Condensation

After condensation, the water vapour in the atmosphere takes one of the following forms—dew, frost, fog and clouds. Condensation takes place when the dew point is lower than the freezing point as well as higher than the freezing point.

Forms of condensation can be classified on the basis of temperature and location

Dew

When the moisture is deposited in the form of water droplets on cooler surfaces of solid objects (rather than nuclei in air above the surface) such as stone, grass blades and plant leaves, it is known as dew. The ideal condition for its formation is clear sky, calm air, high relative humidity and cold and long nights. Dew point must be above freezing point for the formation of dew.

Frost

It forms on cold surface when condensation takes place below freezing point (0° C) i.e. dew point is at or below the freezing point. The excess moisture is deposited in the form of minute ice crystals instead of water droplets. Air temperature must be at or below the freezing point for the formation of white frost. Besides, the ideal conditions for its formation are the same as those for the formation of dew.

Fog and Mist

When the temperature of an air mass containing a large quantity of water vapour falls all of a sudden, condensation takes place within itself on fine dust particles. So, the fog is a cloud with its base near the ground. In urban and industrial centres, smoke provides plenty of nuclei which help in the formation of fog and mist. Fog and mist reduce the visibility to zero. When fog is mixed with smoke it is called as **smog**. The only difference between mist and fog is that mist contains more moisture than fog.

Mists are frequent over mountains as the rising warm air up the slopes meets a cold surface and each nuclei of mist contains thicker layer of moisture. Fogs are drier than mists and they are prevalent where warm currents of air come in contact with cold currents. Fogs are mini clouds in which condensation takes place around nuclei provided by the dust, smoke and the salt particles.

Clouds

Cloud is a mass of minute water droplets or tiny crystals of ice formed by the condensation of the water vapour in free air at considerable elevations. As the clouds are formed at some height over the surface of the earth, they take various shapes.

According to the height, expanse, density and transparency of clouds, they are grouped under four types

(i) **Cirrus** These clouds are formed at high altitudes (8,000-12,000 m). They are the thin and detatched clouds having a feathery appearence. They are always white in colour.

(ii) **Cumulus** These clouds look like cotton wool. They are generally formed at a height of 4000 m-7000 m. They exist in patches and can be seen scattered here and there and have a flat base.

(iii) **Stratus** They are layered clouds covering large portions of the sky. These clouds are generally formed either due to loss of heat or the mixing of air masses with different temperatures.

(iv) **Nimbus** These clouds are black or dark grey. They form at middle levels or very near to the surface of the earth. Sometimes, the clouds are so low that they seem to touch the ground.

These are extremely dense and opaque to the rays of the sun. They are shapeless masses of thick vapour.

Categories of Clouds

A combination of these four basic types can give rise to the following types of clouds:

(i) **High Cloud** cirrus, **cirrostratus[2]**, **cirrocumulus[3]**.

(ii) **Middle Cloud** Altostratus and altocumulus.

(iii) **Low Cloud** Stratocumulus and nimbostratus.

(iv) **Cumulus and Cumulonimbus[4]** are clouds with extensive vertical development.

Precipitation

The process of continuous condensation in free air helps the condensed particles to grow in size. When the resistance of the air fails to hold them against the force of gravity, they fall onto the earth's surface. So, after the condensation of water vapour, the release of moisture is known as precipitation. This may take place in liquid or solid forms.

Forms of Precipitation

The precipitation in the form of water is called rainfall and when the temperature is lower than 0° C, then the precipitation takes place in the form of fine flakes of snow which is called **snowfall**.

Moisture is released in the form of hexagonal crystals. These crystals form flakes of snow.

Besides rain and snow, other forms of precipitation are **sleet** and **hail[5]**, though the latter are limited in occurrence and are sporadic in both time and space.

Sleet are frozen raindrops and refrozen melted snow-water. When a layer of air with the temperature above freezing point overlies a sub-freezing layer near the ground, precipitation takes place in the form of sleet. Raindrops, which leave the warmer air, encounter the colder air below. As a result, they solidify and reach the ground as small pellets of ice not bigger than the raindrops from which they are formed.

Sometimes, drops of rain after being released by the clouds become solidified into small rounded solid pieces of ice and reach the surface of the earth which are called **hailstones**. These are formed by the rainwater passing through the colder layers. Hailstones have several concentric layers of ice one over the other.

Types of Rainfall

On the basis of origin, rainfall may be classified into three main types

Convectional Rain

The air on being heated, becomes light and rises up in convection currents. As it rises, it expands and loses heat and consequently, condensation takes place and cumulous clouds are formed which causes conventional rain with thunder and lightening. Heavy rainfall takes place but this does not last long. Convectional rain is common in the summer or in the hotter part of the day and in equatorial regions and interior parts of continents, mainly in the Northern Hemisphere.

Orographic Rain

When the **saturated air[6]** mass comes across a mountain, it is forced to ascend and as it rises, it expands, the temperature falls and the moisture is condensed which causes orographic rain.

Windward slope receives greater rainfall. After giving rain on the windward side, when these winds reach the other slope, they descend and their temperature rises and their capacity to take in moisture increases. Hence, the leeward slopes remain rainless and dry.

---

2 **Cirrostratus Clouds** High altitude sheet like clouds composed of ice crystals. These clouds are thin and often cover the entire sky.

3 **Cirrocumulus Clouds** Patchy white high altitude clouds composed of ice crystals, found at high altitude range from 5,000-18,000 m.

4 **Cumulonimbus Clouds** A well-developed vertical cloud that often has top shaped like an anvil.

5 **Hail** It is a type of precipitation received in the form of ice pellets or hailstones. The size of hailstones can be between 5 and 190 mm in diameter.

6 **Saturated Air** Air that contains the maximum amount of water vapour that is possible at the given temperature and pressure .i.e. air in which the relative humidity is 100%, is known as ''saturated air''.

The area situated on the leeward side which gets less rainfall is known as **rain shadow area**. Orographic rain is also known as the **relief rain**.

Cyclonic Rain

The rainfall which occurs after temperate and tropical cyclone is called cyclonic rain.

World Distribution of Rainfall

Different places on the earth's surface receive different amount of rainfall in a year and that too in different seasons. Rainfall decreases steadily when moves upward i.e. from the equator to poles. The coastal areas of the world receive greater amount of rainfall than the interior of the continents. The rainfall is more over the oceans than on the landmasses as being the great source of water.

Between the latitude 35° and 40°N and S of the equator, the rain is heavier on the Eastern coast and goes on decreasing towards the West. But between 45° and 65° N and S of the equator, due to westerlies, the rainfall is first received on the Western margins of the continents and then it goes on decreasing towards the East.

Wherever mountins run parallel to the coast, the rain is greater on the coastal plain, on the windward side and it decreases towards the leeward side.

On the basis of the total amount of annual precipitation, major precipitation regimes of the world are identified as

- **Receive more than 200 cm per annum of Rainfall** The equatorial belt, the windward slope of mountains along the Western coasts in the cool temperate zone and the coastal area of monsoon land receive heavy rainfall.

- **Receive 100-200 cm per annum of Rainfall** Interior continental areas and coastal areas of continents receive moderate rainfall.

- **Receive 50-100 cm per annum of Rainfall** Central parts of the tropical land and the Eastern and interior parts of the temperate land.

- **Receive less than 50 cm per annum of Rainfall** Areas lying in the rain shadow zone of the interior continents and areas of high latitudes receive very low rainfall.
  Seasonal distribution of rainfall provides an important aspect to judge its effectiveness. In some of the regions, rainfall distributed evenly throughout the year i.e. in equatorial and in Western parts of cool temperate regions.

Chapter Practice

Objective Questions

- **Multiple Choice Questions**

1. The transformation of water vapour into water is called ....
(a) Vapourisation
(b) Sublimation
(c) Condensation
(d) Humidity

Ans. (c) The transformation of water vapour into water is called condensation which is caused by the loss of heat.

2. Condensation is influenced by
(a) volume of air
(b) temperature
(c) Both (a) and (b)
(d) None of these

Ans. (c) Condensation is influenced by the volume of air, temperature, pressure and humidity.

3. The ideal conditions for the formation of dew are
(a) high relative humidity
(b) warm nights
(c) Both (a) and (b)
(d) None of these

Ans. (a) The ideal conditions for the formation of dew are clear sky, calm air, high relative humidity and cold and long nights.

4. Frost forms when condensation takes place
(a) below the freezing point
(b) above the freezing point
(c) Both (a) and (b)
(d) None of the above

Ans. (a) Frost forms on cold surfaces when condensation takes place below the freezing point, 0 degree Celsius. The excess moisture is deposited in the form of minute ice crystals instead of water droplets.

5. What is smog ?
(a) Condition when fog is mixed with dew
(b) Condition when fog is mixed with salt particles
(c) Condition when smoke is mixed with water vapour
(d) Condition when fog is mixed with smoke.

Ans. (d) When fog is mixed with smoke, it is described as smog.

6. Mass of minute water droplets formed by the condensation of water vapour in free air at considerable height are known as
(a) Clouds
(b) Dew
(c) Smog
(d) Rainfall

Ans. (a) Cloud is a mass of minute water droplets or tiny crystals of ice formed by the condensation of the water vapour in free air at considerable elevations.

7. On the basis of origin rainfall is classified into how many types?
(a) 5
(b) 7
(c) 2
(d) 3

Ans. (d) Based on origin, rainfall may be classified into three main types i.e. convectional rainfall, orographic or relief rainfall and the cyclonic or frontal rainfall.

8. Choose the incorrectly matched pair.
(a) The actual amount of water vapour present in the atmosphere – Absolute humidity
(b) The percentage of moisture present in the atmosphere as compared to its full capacity at a given temperature – Relative humidity
(c) The air containing moisture to its full capacity at a given temperature – Saturated
(d) The temperature at which saturation occurs in a given sample of air – Sublimation

Ans. (d) When the water vapour is directly condensed into solid form, it is known as sublimation.

9. Choose the correctly matched pair.
(a) Middle clouds   – Altostratus
(b) High clouds   – Altocumulus
(c) Low clouds   – Cirrus
(d) High clouds   – Nimbostratus

Ans. (a) Altostratus and Altocumulus are middle clouds, cirrus are high clouds and nimbostratus are low clouds.

10. Match the following terms List I with their associated statements on List II.

	List I		List II
A.	Cirrus clouds	1.	Scattered
B.	Cumuls	2.	Layered clouds
C.	Stratus	3.	Black or dark gray
D.	Nimbus	4.	Feathery appearance

Codes

	A	B	C	D			A	B	C	D
(a)	2	1	4	3		(b)	2	1	3	4
(c)	1	3	4	2		(d)	4	1	2	3

Ans. (d)

11. Match the following terms List I with their associated statements on List II.

	List I		List II
A.	Equatorial belt	1.	100-200 cm rainfall per annum
B.	Inter-continental areas	2.	Less than 50 cm rainfall per annum
C.	High latitude areas	3.	Over 200 cm rainfall per annum
D.	Interior parts of temperate lands	4.	50-100 cm rainfall per annum

Codes

	A	B	C	D
(a)	2	1	4	3
(b)	3	1	2	4
(c)	1	3	4	2
(d)	4	1	2	3

Ans. (b)

12. Consider the following statements and choose the correct option

   I. The air containing moisture to its full capacity at a given temperature is said to be saturated.

   II. It means that the air at the given temperature can hold any additional amount of moisture at that stage.

(a) Statement I is correct, but statement II is incorrect.

(b) Statement I is incorrect, but statement II is correct.

(c) Both the statements I and II are correct.

(d) Both the statements I and II are incorrect.

Ans. (a) Statement I is correct. Statement II is incorrect as the air containing moisture to its full capacity at a given temperature is said to be saturated, means that the air at the given temperature is incapable of holding any additional amount of moisture.

13. Consider the following statements and choose the correct option

   I. Evaporation is a process by which water is transformed from a gaseous state to a liquid state.

   II. Heat is the main cause of evaporation.

(a) Statement I is correct, but statement II is incorrect.

(b) Statement I is incorrect, but statement II is correct.

(c) Both the statements I and II are correct.

(d) Both the statements I and II are incorrect.

Ans. (b) Statement II is correct. Statement I is incorrect as evaporation is a process by which water is transformed from liquid to gaseous state caused by heating.

14. Consider the following statements and choose the correct option

   I. Movement of air replaces the saturated layer with the unsaturated layer.

   II. Hence the greater the movement of air, the greater is the evaporation.

(a) Statement I is correct, but statement II is incorrect.

(b) Statement I is incorrect, but statement II is correct.

(c) Both statements I and II are correct.

(d) Both statements I and II are incorrect.

Ans. (c) Both the statements I and II are correct.

15. Arrange the following in the correct order moving from lowest altitude to highest altitude.

   I. Altocumulus II. Cirrus   III. Stratus

Codes

(a) I, II, III   (b) II, I, III

(c) III, II, I   (d) III, I, II

Ans. (d) Stratus clouds are low cloud, altocumulus are middle clouds and cirrus are high clouds.

• Case Base MCQs

16. Read the case/source given and answer the questions that follow by choosing the correct option.

World Distribution of Rainfall

Different places on the earth's surface receive different amounts of rainfall in a year and that too in different seasons.

In general, as we proceed from the equator towards the poles, rainfall goes on decreasing steadily. The coastal areas of the world receive greater amounts of rainfall than the interior of the continents. The rainfall is more over the oceans than on the landmasses of the world because of being great sources of water. Between the latitudes 35° and 40° N and S of the equator, the rain is heavier on the eastern coasts and goes on decreasing towards the west. But, between 45° and 65° N and S of equator, due to the westerlies, the rainfall is first received on the western margins of the continents and it goes on decreasing towards the east.

Wherever mountains run parallel to the coast, the rain is greater on the coastal plain, on the windward side and it decreases towards the leeward side.

(i) The amount of rainfall from equator towards the poles

(a) decreases towards the poles

(b) increases towards the poles

(c) remains the same   (d) None of these

Ans. (a) The amount of rainfall decreases as one proceeds from the equator towards the poles.

(ii) The amount of rainfall is higher over
    (a) oceans
    (b) landmasses
    (c) Both (a) and (b) receive equal amount of rainfall
    (d) None of the above

Ans. (a) The amount of rainfall is higher over oceans because oceans provide greater source of water for evaporation to take place.

(iii) Which side receives greater rainfall where a mountain runs parallel to the coast?
    (a) Leeward side   (b) Windward side
    (c) Both (a) and (b)   (d) None of these

Ans. (b) The windward side receives greater rainfall where a mountain runs parallel to the coast. The windward side refers to the side of the mountain towards which the wind is approaching, hence it receives more rainfall as compared to the leeward or opposite side.

(iv) The rain is intensive between which latitudes?
    (a) 45 and 65 degrees North and South of the equator
    (b) 35 and 40 degrees North and South of the equator
    (c) 40 and 65 degrees North and South of the equator
    (d) None of the above

Ans. (b) The rain is heavier on the eastern coast between 35-40 degrees latitude both North and South of the equator.

PART 2
Subjective Questions

• Short Answer (SA) Type Questions

1. What do you understand by evaporation? Give a brief account of it.

Ans. Evaporation is the process by which water is transformed from liquid to gaseous state.

This process increases the amount of water vapour in the atmosphere. Heat is the main cause for evaporation. The temperature at which the water starts evaporating is referred to as the latent heat of vapourisation.

Increase in temperature increases water absorption and retention capacity of the given parcel of air. Similarly, if the moisture content is low, air has a potentiality of absorbing and retaining moisture. Movement of air replaces the saturated layer with the unsaturated layer. Hence, the greater the movement of air, the greater is the evaporation.

2. Differentiate between absolute and relative humidity. State any four points.

Ans. Differences between absolute and relative humidity are

Absolute Humidity	Relative Humidity
It is the actual amount of water vapour present in the atmosphere.	It is the percentage of moisture present in the atmosphere as compared to its full capacity.
It is the weight of water vapour per unit volume of air.	It is the ratio between actual amount of water vapour and the capacity to hold moisture.
It is expressed in gram per cubic metre.	It is expressed in percentage by hygrometer.
It remains constant with the increase or decrease of temperature of the air.	It is the amount of heat required to raise the temperature.

3. Enlist the favourable conditions due to which condensation take place in the atmosphere.

Ans. Condensation depends upon the amount of cooling and the relative humidity of air. It is influenced by volume of air, temperature, pressure and humidity. The favourable conditions due to which condensation take place in the atmosphere are

- When the temperature of the air is reduced to dew point with its volume remaining constant.
- When both the volume and temperature are reduced.
- When moisture is added to the air through evaporation.

4. "Dew is not formed on the cloudy nights." Give reason for the specification of statement.

Ans. Dew is not formed on the cloudy nights because

- The ideal conditions for the formation of dew are clear sky, calm air, cold and long night and high relative humidity.
- Dew is formed when objects radiate heat thoroughly so that the moist air coming into contact with them may be sufficiently cooled down and the water vapour condenses into water droplets.
- The cloud acts as a blanket for the earth's surface. In the condition of cloudy night, cloud checks the radiation of heat, so it does not radiate heat thoroughly. Hence, dew is not formed on the cloudy nights.

5. What do you understand by the term fog? Also explain how fog affects the normal life of people?

Ans. Fog is a kind of cloud that touches the ground. Fog forms when the air near the ground is colds enough to turn its water vapour into liquid water or ice.

Fog becomes harmful for human life when it mixes with smoke and forms smog. Its effects are

- Fog reduces the visibility due to which road and train accidents occur.
- Smog is made up of a combination of air pollutants that can compromise human health, harm the environment and even cause property damage.
- Smog can cause or aggravate health problems such as asthma, emphysenra, chronic bronchitis and other respiratory problems.
- It also causes eye irritation and reduces resistence to colds and lung infections.
- The ozone in smog also inhibits plant growth and can cause widespread damage to crops and forests.

6. "Smog severely harms the health of human beings". Discuss the measures to mitigate this hazard.

Ans. Smog is a form of air pollution that is particularly hazardous on hot days. According to experts, it can be dangerous to breathe in too much smog.

Smog is mainly a mixture of smoke and fog, but it also contains some harmful gases which affect the health of human beings. Measures to mitigate the effect of smog are

- Avoid exercising near places with heavy traffic, especially during peak hours.
- Avoid outdoor activities when smog level is high.
- Ride bicycle or use public transportation system instead of car, whenever possible to reduce smoke.

7. There are different types of clouds according to their height, expanse, density and transparency. Explain different types of clouds.

Ans. The different types of clouds according to their height, expanse, density and transparency are

- **Cirrus** These clouds are formed at high altitudes (8,000-12,000 m). They are the thin and detatched clouds having a feathery appeerence. They are always white in colour.
- **Cumulus** These clouds look like cotton wool. They are generally formed at a height of 4000 m-7000 m. They exist in patches and can be seen scattered here and there and have a flat base.
- **Stratus** They are layered clouds covering large portions of the sky. These clouds are generally formed either due to loss of heat or the mixing of air masses with different temperatures.
- **Nimbus** These clouds are black or dark grey. They form at middle levels or very near to the surface of the earth. Sometimes, the clouds are so low that they seem to touch the ground. These are extremely dense and opaque to the rays of the sun. They are shapeless masses of thick vapour.

8. Sleet is frozen raindrops and refrozen melted snow water. Explain how does it occur? Also explain the occurrence of hailstones.

Ans. Sleet is frozen raindrops and refrozen melted snow water. When a layer of air with the temperature above freezing point overlies a sub freezing layer near the ground, precipitation takes place in the form of sleet. Raindrops which leave the warmer air, encounter the colder air below. As a result, they solidify and reach the ground as small pellets of ice not bigger than the raindrops from which they are formed.

9. "Excess evaporation and less precipitation is the main reason behind the dry climate." Discuss the economic activities which are important for human being in such climate.

Ans. It is correct that excess evaporation and less precipitation is the main reason behind the dry climate." Some parts of the world experience less precipitation in comparison to evaporation. Due to excess evaporation, desertification or dry zones are developed. In such regions, due to scarcity of water and fertile land, agriculture is not a good option for livelihood.

In such areas, the economic activities on which human beings depend are trade and transport activity. Merchants and sellers are prominent professionals of these areas. Apart from that with the help of dry farming, some adaptable crops could be cultivated. Date palm is a famous product in these regions which could be easily grown.

10. Write a short note on convectional rainfall.

Ans. Convectional rainfall occur when the air on being heated becomes light and rises up in convection currents. As it rises, it expands and loses heat and consequently, condensation takes place and cumulus clouds are formed which causes this type of rainfall. With thunder and lightening, heavy rainfall takes place but this does not last long.

Features of convectional rainfall are

- Such rain is common in the summer or in the hotter part of the day.
- This type of rainfall is very common in equatorial regions, where rainfall occurs daily.
- In the interior part of the continents particularly in the Northern hemisphere, convectional rainfall occurs prior to monsoon.

11. What do you understand by orographic and cylonic rainfall? Expain in brief.

Ans. Orographic rainfall occur when the saturated air mass comes across a mountain and it is forced to ascend. As it rises, it expands, the temperature falls and the moisture is condensed which causes this type of rainfall. Windward slope receives greater rainfall.

After giving rain on the windward side, when these winds reach the other slope, they descend and their temperature rises and their capacity to take in moisture increases. Hence, the leeward slopes remain rainless and dry. The area situated on the leeward side which gets less rainfall is known as rain shadow area. Orographic rain is also known as the relief rain.

The rainfall which occurs after temperate and tropical cyclone is called cyclonic rainfall.

12. "In last years, the intensity of occurrence of drought has increased. Uncertainty has also increased in the rainfall". What are the causes behind these? Suggest some ways/measures for the conservation of water.

Ans. The intensity of drought has increased in India, due to global changing trend in the pattern of rainfall.

Causes for changing rainfall trend

- The global average temperature is increasing which causes drastic climatic change in the various parts of the world.
- The cutting of trees is also a significant cause behind shifting of monsoon.
- The use of concrete reduces the evaporation.
- The use of fossil fuel and other greenhouse gases have caused global warming which is responsible for the deviation of rainfall.

Ways/measures for the conservation of water are

- Rain water harvesting should be promoted in all possible regions.
- Check dams and ponds should be developed for the efficient use of water.
- Water treatment plants should be installed to refine the waste water and to reuse it.
- The value of 'saving' and 'protection' should be developed in the society and specially among the children.

• Long Answer (LA) Type Questions

1. Define the term humidity. Also elaborate the various types of humidity.

Ans. The amount of water vapour in the air is called humidity. Humidity is a significant term in the atmospheric contents. There are three types of humidity:

(i) **Absolute Humidity** It is the actual amount of water vapour present in a volume of air at a given temperature. It is the density of water vapour present in a mixture of air which is the ratio of the mass of water vapour to the volume occupied by the mixture. It is usually measured in grams per cubic metre. Cold air cannot contain as much water vapour as warm air, so cold air has a low absolute humidity than warm air.

(ii) **Specific Humidity** It is the mass of water vapour (in grams) per unit mass of air (in kilograms) at any specific temperature. Specific humidity has no relation with pressure or temperature as it is measured in units of weight.

(iii) **Relative Humidity** It is a widely used measure of water vapour in the atmosphere. The calculation of relative humidity depends on the maximum amount of moisture that air can hold i.e. saturation level. Relative humidity is expressed in percentage. When relative humidity is 100 per cent, the atmosphere is said to be saturated.

2. Explain in brief the different forms of condensation.

Ans. Different forms of condensation on the basis of temperature and location are

Dew When the moisture is deposited in the form of water droplets on cooler surfaces of solid objects (rather than nuclei in air above the surface) such as stone, grass blades and plant leaves, it is known as dew.

Frost It forms on cold surface when condensation takes place below freezing point ($0°$ C) i.e. dew point is at or below the freezing point. The excess moisture is deposited in the form of minute ice crystals instead of water droplets. Air temperature must be at or below the freezing point for the formation of white frost.

Fog and Mist When the temperature of an air mass containing a large quantity of water vapour falls all of a sudden, condensation takes place within itself on fine dust particles. So, the fog is a cloud with its base near the ground. When fog is mixed with smoke it is called as **smog**.

Mists are frequent over mountains as the rising warm air up the slopes meets a cold surface. Each nuclei of mist contains thicker layer of moisture.

Cloud It is a mass of minute water droplets or tiny crystals of ice formed by the condensation of the water vapour in free air at considerable elevations. As the clouds are formed at some height over the surface of the earth, they take various shapes.

3. Briefly describe the world distribution of rainfall.

Ans. Different places on the earth's surface receive different amount of rainfall in a year and that too in different seasons. Rainfall decreases steadily when moves upward i.e. from the equator to poles. The coastal areas of the world receive greater amount of rainfall than the interior of the continents. The rainfall is more over the oceans than on the landmasses as being the great source of water.

Between the latitude $35°$ and $40°$N and S of the equator, the rain is heavier on the Eastern coast and goes on decreasing towards the West. But between $45°$ and $65°$ N and S of the equator, due to westerlies, the rainfall is first received on the Western margins of the continents and then it goes on decreasing towards the East. Wherever mountins run parallel to the coast, the rain is greater on the coastal plain, on the windward side and it decreases towards the leeward side.

4. "In India all three types of rainfall are responsible for the precipitation." Give your argument in support of the statement.

Ans. It is correct that all three types of rain fall are responsible for the precipitation in India as it has monsoon climate and more than 50 per cent rainfall occurs in the four months of monsoon. There is a significant role of convectional and cyclonic rainfall in the climatic conditions of India. The three types of rainfall are

(i) **Convectional Rainfall** This rain is caused by the convection process in the atmosphere. Mostly pre-monsoonous rainfall are of convectional type. It largely occurs in the month of April and May.

(ii) **Orographic Rainfall** This is also known as relief rainfall. It occurs where the saturated air mass comes across a mountain. In India, due to the Himalayas, monsoon winds cause sufficient amount of rainfall in the whole part of India.

(iii) **Cyclonic Rainfall** Rain associated with the passage of cyclone is known as cyclonic rainfall. It is also known as frontal rainfall. Winter rainfall in the Northern part of India is also the result of cyclonic rainfall. It not only causes rainfall but also a sufficient amount of snowfall.

5. Discuss the major precipitation regimes of the world.

Ans. On the basis of the total amount of annual precipitation, major precipitation regimes of the world are identified as

- **Receive more than 200 cm per annum of Rainfall** The equatorial belt, the windward slope of mountains along the Western coasts in the cool temperate zone and the coastal area of monsoon land receive heavy rainfall.
- **Receive 100-200 cm per annum of Rainfall** Interior continental areas and coastal areas of continents receive moderate rainfall.
- **Receive 50-100 cm per annum of Rainfall** Central parts of the tropical land and the Eastern and interior parts of the temperate land.
- **Receive less than 50 cm per annum of Rainfall** Areas lying in the rain shadow zone of the interior continents and areas of high latitudes receive very low rainfall. Seasonal distribution of rainfall provides an important aspect to judge its effectiveness. In some of the regions, rainfall distributed evenly throughout the year i.e. in equatorial and in Western parts of cool temperate regions.

• Case Based Questions

1. Read the case/source given and answer the following questions.

Clouds

Cloud is a mass of minute water droplets or tiny crystals of ice formed by the condensation of the water vapour in free air at considerable elevations. As the clouds are formed at some height over the surface of the earth, they take various shapes. According to their height, expanse, density and transparency or opaqueness clouds are grouped under four types : (i) cirrus; (ii) cumulus; (iii) stratus; (iv) nimbus.

Cirrus

Cirrus clouds are formed at high altitudes (8,000 - 12,000 m). They are thin and detatched clouds having a feathery appearance. They are always white in colour.

Cumulus

Cumulus clouds look like cotton wool. They are generally formed at a height of 4,000 - 7,000 m. They exist in patches and can be seen scattered here and there. They have a flat base.

Stratus

As their name implies, these are layered clouds covering large portions of the sky. These clouds are generally formed either due to loss of heat or the mixing of air masses with different temperatures.

(i) Explain the process of cloud formation

Ans. Clouds are mass of minute water droplet or tiny ice crystals which are formed by the condensation of the water vapour in free air. They are formed at considerable elevations in the atmosphere.

(ii) Identify the four types of cloud formation and briefly describe what determines the type of cloud formation?

Ans. The four types of cloud formations are cirrus, cumulus, stratus and nimbus.

The type of cloud formation is determined by the height, expanse, density, and transparency and opaqueness of the clouds.

(iii) Differentiate between cirrus and cumulus clouds?

Ans. Cirrus clouds are formed at high altitudes between 8000-12000 m, whereas, cumulus is formed at elevations between 4000-7000 m. Cirrus are thin and detached with a feathery appearance. Cumulus exists in patches, have a flat base, and can be seen scattered.

2. Read the passage given below and answer the following questions.

The process of continuous condensation in free air helps the condensed particles to grow in size. When the resistance of the air fails to hold them against the force of gravity, they fall on to the earth's surface. So after the condensation of water vapour, the release of moisture is known as precipitation. This may take place in liquid or solid form. The precipitation in the form of water is called rainfall, when the temperature is lower than the 0°C, precipitation takes place in the form of fine flakes of snow and is called snowfall.

Moisture is released in the form of hexagonal crystals. These crystals form flakes of snow. Besides rain and snow, other forms of precipitation are sleet and hail, though the latter are limited in occurrence and are sporadic in both time and space.

Sleet is frozen raindrops and refrozen melted snow-water. When a layer of air with the temperature above freezing point overlies a subfreezing layer near the ground, precipitation takes place in the form of sleet.

Raindrops, which leave the warmer air, encounter the colder air below. As a result, they solidify and reach the ground as small pellets of ice not bigger than the raindrops from which they are formed.

Sometimes, drops of rain after being released by the clouds become solidified into small rounded solid pieces of ice and which reach the surface of the earth are called hailstones. These are formed by the rainwater passing through the colder layers. Hailstones have several concentric layers of ice one over the other.

(i) Briefly describe the process of precipitation .

Ans. Precipitation is release of moisture from air. Continuous condensation results in increase in size of condensed particles which falls to earth's surface due to lack of sufficient resistance of the air. Precipitation may take place in liquid or solid form.

(ii) Identify the different types of precipitation as well as the key difference in their formation.

Ans. The precipitation can be of four types, i.e., rainfall, snowfall, sleet and hailstone. The key difference in their formation is the temperature at which precipitation is taking takes place. For example, precipitation takes place above freezing temperature is in liquid form as rainfall, whereas, precipitation at temperature lower than 0°C (freezing temperature) is in solid form as snowfall.

(iii) Differentiate between hailstone and sleet.

Ans. Hailstones are formed by solidification of raindrops passing through colder layers in the atmosphere and have several concentric layers one over the other. On the other hand, sleet is frozen raindrops and refrozen melted snow water. It is formed when raindrops from an upper warmer layer passes through underlying subfreezing layer and solidifies to form small pallets of ice with same size as the rain drops.

Chapter Test

Objective Questions

1. Relative humidity is greater over.
   (a) Continents
   (b) Oceans
   (c) Atmosphere
   (d) Both (a) and (b)

2. The temperature at which saturation occurs in a given sample of air is known as ....
   (a) Saturation
   (b) Relative humidity
   (c) Absolute humidity
   (d) Dew Point

3. If the excess water vapour directly condenses into solid form, it is known as
   (a) Condensation
   (b) Evaporation
   (c) Dew point
   (d) Sublimation

4. In free air, condensation which results from cooling around very small particles is termed as ....
   (a) Condensation
   (b) Hygroscopic condensation nuclei
   (c) Evaporation
   (d) None of these

5. Consider the following statements and choose the correct option.
   I. Nimbus clouds are opaque to the rays of the sun.
   II. Nimbus clouds are extremely dense and are black and dark grey in colour.
   (a) Only I is correct
   (b) Only II is correct
   (c) Both statements are incorrect
   (d) Both statements are correct and statement II correctly explains statement I

Short Answer Type Questions

6. How does atmosphere loose moisture?
7. Differentiate between specific humidity and absolute humidity.
8. Define relative humidity.
9. Explain the process of condensation.
10. Distinguish between fog and mist.
11. How does rainfall occur in cyclone?

Long Answer Type Questions

12. Explain in brief the various types of clouds.
13. Give an account of distribution of rainfall.
14. Describe the region where precipitation is received throughout the year.

Answers

1. (b) Oceans
2. (d) Dew Point
3. (d) Sublimation
4. (b) Hygroscopic condensation nuclei
5. (d) Both statements are correct and statement II correctly explains statement I

CHAPTER 05

Movements of Ocean Water

In this Chapter...

- Movement of Ocean Water
- Ocean Resources and Pollution
- Submarine Relief

The water of the ocean is highly dynamic. The movement of ocean water is influenced by its physical features, e.g. temperature, salinity and density. The external forces like gravitational forces of the moon and the sun, the winds, etc also influence the movement of ocean water.

Movement of Ocean Water

The horizontal and vertical movements are common in ocean water bodies. The horizontal motion refers to the ocean currents and waves. The vertical motion refers to tides.

Ocean currents are continuous flow of huge amount of water in a definite direction over long distances. Water moves ahead from one place to another through ocean currents, whereas in the waves the water does not move but it is the wave that moves ahead.

The vertical motion of the oceans and sea water occurs in the form of rise and fall of water. The attraction force caused by the Sun and the Moon forces ocean water to move up-down twice a day. The other forms of vertical movement of ocean water are **upwelling**[1] of cold water from sub surfaces and sinking of surface water.

Types of Movement

The movement of ocean water are primarily studied through following three forms

  (i) Waves   (ii) Tides

 (iii) Ocean Currents

Waves

Waves are energy and not the water as such, that moves across the ocean surface and wind provides energy to the waves. Water particles only travel in a small circle as a wave passes. Wind causes waves to travel in the ocean and the energy is released on **shorelines**[2]. The motion of the surface water seldom affects the motionless deep bottom water of the oceans.

Some of the important features of the waves are

- When a waves approaches to the beach, it slows down due to the **friction**[3] occurring between the dynamic water and sea floor.
- When the depth of water is less than half the wavelength of wave, the wave breaks.

---

1 **Upwelling** When the cold water comes up at the surface of the oceans from the deep bottom, it is known as upwelling.

2 **Shoreline** Line of contact between land surface and ocean surface.

3 **Friction** The force that opposes relative motion of two bodies which are in direct contact of each other.

- The largest waves are found in the open oceans.
- Waves continue to grow larger as they move and absorb energy from the wind.
- Most of the waves are caused by the wind driving against water.
- When a breeze of two knots or less blows over calm water, small ripples form and grow as the wind speed increases until white caps appear in the breaking waves.
- Waves may travel thousands of km before rolling ashore, breaking and dissolving as surf.

Origin of Waves

The origin of waves are traced by the size and shape of the waves. **Steep waves**[4] are fairly young ones and are probably formed by local wind, whereas, slow and steady waves originate from far away places, possibly from another hemisphere.

The maximum wave height is determined by the strength of the wind, i.e. how long it blows and the area over which it blows in a single direction.

Motion of Wave

As wind pushes the water body in its course the wave travels forwards. However, the crests of waves move downwards as gravity pulls it down. The falling water pushes the former troughs upward and the wave moves to new position. The actual motion of the water beneath the waves is circular. This shows that there is a continuous upward-forward and downward-backward motion in a wave.

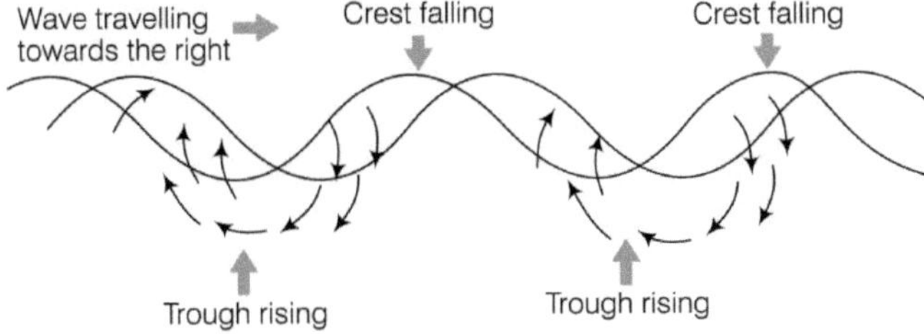

Motion of Waves and Water Molecules

Characteristics of Waves

Some of the important characteristics of waves are given as under

- **Wave Crest and Trough** The highest and lowest points of a wave are called the crest and trough, respectively.
- **Wave Height** It is the vertical distance from the bottom of a trough to the top of a crest of a wave.

- **Wave Amplitude** It is one-half of the wave height.
- **Wave Period** It is the time interval between two successive wave crests or trough, as they pass a fixed point.
- **Wavelength** It is horizontal distance between two successive crests.
- **Wave Speed** It is the rate at which the wave moves through the water, and is measured in knots.
- **Wave Frequency** It is the number of waves passing a given point during time interval of one second.

Tides

The Periodical rise and fall of the sea level, once or twice in a day due to the attraction of the sun and the moon is called a tide. The movement of ocean water brought about by meteorological phenomena like winds and atmospheric pressure gradient are known as **surges**. The tides are more regular than surges.

Causes of Tides

The tides have great variation in terms of frequency, magnitude and height, therefore, the study of tides is highly complex, spatially as well as temporally. Several factors responsible for the origin of tides are

- The tides occur due to great extent of gravitational pull of the Moon and to a smaller extent to gravitational pull of the Sun.
- The **centrifugal force**[5] which acts to counter balance the gravity is another important causal factor of tides.
- The 'tides generating' force is the difference between the two forces i.e. Moon's gravitational pull and the centrifugal force. Together these forces are responsible for creating the two major tidal bulges on the earth.
- On the side of the earth facing the moon, a tidal bulge is caused by a net force i.e. force equal to moon's gravitational force which is greater than centrifugal force. However, on the opposite side, the second tidal bulge is caused by the force which is equal to centrifugal force which is greater than moon's gravitational force.
- On the earth's surface, the horizontal tide generating forces are more important than vertical forces in generating tidal bulges.
- On wide continental shelves, the tidal bulges are of greater height. However, the tidal bulges lose their height as they hit the **mid-oceanic islands**[6].

4　**Steep waves** Steep waves is a characteristic of plunging waves. Plunging waves break when the ocean floor is steep or has sudden depth changes. They can be powerful barrels or enormous close-outs.

5　**Centrifugal Force** It is the apparent force that is felt by an object moving in a curved path that acts outwardly away from the centre of rotation.

6　**Mid Oceanic Islands** Large scale linear islands found along mid oceanic ridge. They are found on the divergent plate boundary.

- The intensity of tides is also magnified depending upon shape of bays and estuaries along a coastline. For example, the tidal magnitude is greatly changed by Funnel-shaped bays.
- When the tide is channelled between islands or into bays and estuaries, they are called **tidal currents**.

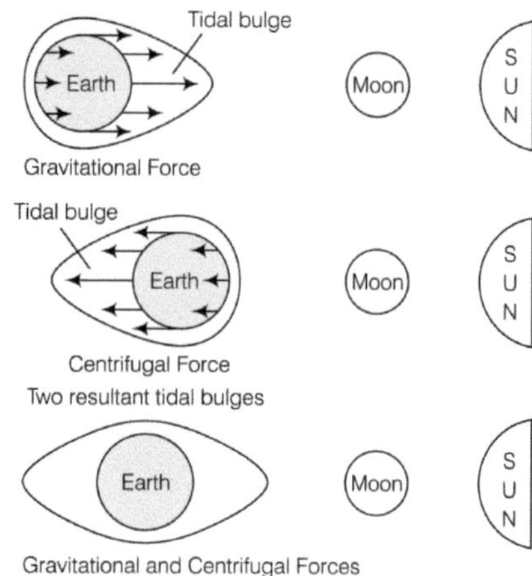

Relation between Gravitational Forces and Tides

Tides of Bay of Fundy, Canada

The highest tidal waves occur in the Bay of Fundy in Nova Scotia in Canada. The tidal bulge may reach upto 15-16 metre because there are two high and two low tides everyday, then a tide must come in within about a six hour period. In the Bay of Fundy, the tide rises about 240 cm per hour.

Types of Tides

Tides vary in their frequency, direction and movement from place to place and also from time to time. Tides are generally classified on the basis of their frequency of occurrence (in a day or 24 hours), their height, etc. The major groups of tides are given as under:

Tides Based on Frequency

On the basis of frequency of their occurrence, the tides are classified as

- **Semi-diurnal Tide** It is the most common form of tides. In this, two high tides and two low tides occur everyday. Here, the height of successive high or low tides is generally same.
- **Diurnal Tide** In this type of tides, there is only one high tide and one low tide occur everyday. Here also the height of successive high tide and low tide remains same.
- **Mixed Tide** The tides having variations in their height are called mixed tides. These type of tides occur along the West coast of North America and Islands of the Pacific Ocean.

Tides based on the Sun, Moon and the Earth Positions

The position of the sun and moon in respect of the earth plays an important role by bringing in variations in the height of rising water (high tide). On the basis of these positions, tides are classified as

- **Spring Tides** The position of both the sun and the moon in relation to the earth has direct bearing on tide height. When the sun, the moon and the earth are in straight line, the height of the tide will be higher. These are known as spring tides. Spring tides occur on full moon and on new moon i.e. twice a month.
- **Neap Tides** When the sun and the moon are at right angles to each other and forces of the sun and moon tend to counteract one another neap tides occur. In other words, the attraction force of sun and moon counter balance each other. Though moon's attraction force is twice than that of the sun, but sun's attraction (gravitational force) force diminishes it considerably. The neap tides occur at a seven days interval time from spring tides.

Perigee and Apogee Once in a month, when the moon's orbit is closest to the earth (Perigee), unsually high and low tides occur. During this time the tidal range is greater than normal. Two weeks later, when the moon is farthest from earth (apogee), the moon's gravitational force is limited and the tidal ranges are less than their average heights.

When the earth is closest to the sun (perihelion), around 3rd January, each year, tidal ranges are also much greater, with unusually high and unusually low tides. When the earth is farthest from the sun (aphelion), around 4th July each year, tidal ranges are much less than average. The time between the high tide and low tide, when the water level is falling, is called the ebb. The time between the low tide and high tide, when the tide is rising, is called the flow or flood.

Importance of Tides

The tides can be predicted well in advance as the position of the sun, the moon with respect to the earth known accurately. The main importance of tides are

- The prediction of tides helps navigators and fishermen to plan their activities in the open oceans, as tides help in navigation.
- Tidal heights or harbours located near the mouth of rivers and estuaries having shallow bars at entrance prevent the ships and boats from entering into the harbour.
- The tides also help in **desilting**[7] of sediments and removal of pollutants from estuaries.
- The tides are also used for generating electricity. It is being developed in countries like France, Canada, Russia and China. A 3 MW tidal power project is under way which is located at Durgaduani in Sunderbans of West Bengal.

---

7   Desilting   The removal of silt from a body of water.

Ocean Currents

A regular volume of water which flows like a river in oceans in a definite path and direction is known as ocean current. Forces influencing the ocean currents are

Primary Forces The forces which initiate the movement of water are primary forces. Some of the important primary forces are

- **Heating by Solar Energy** It causes water to expand because of thermal expansion. Because of this, the water level is 8 cm higher at the equator than middle latitudes. This very small gradient causes water to flow from the equator towards middle latitudes.
- **Wind** It pushes the surface ocean water to move in the direction of their blowing. However, this wind generated water movement is affected by friction between wind and ocean surface.
- **Gravity** It creates gradient variation as water is pulled down the pile.
- **Coriolis force** This force intervenes and causes the water to move towards right in the Northern hemisphere and towards left in the Southern hemisphere. Thus, water accumulates in large volume and a flow around them is started. It is known as Gyres. The Gyre produces large circular ocean currents in all ocean basins.

Secondary Forces The forces which influence the currents to flow are secondary forces.

Movement of Ocean Currents

Existence of density differences in the different layers of ocean water causes vertical mobility of ocean currents. High salinity water is denser than low salinity water and in the same way cold water is denser than the warm water.

Therefore, the denser water sinks and lighter water rise up. At the poles, the cold water sinks down and moves towards the equator. It is termed as cold water currents. To replace this cold water, warm water from the equator moves towards poles along the surface, it is termed as warm water currents.

Characteristics of Ocean Currents

Important characteristics of ocean currents are

- Currents are referred by their drift or speed. We refer to the speed of a current as its 'drift'. The drift is measured in terms of knots.
- The strength of a current refers to the speed of the current. A fast moving current is generally taken as strong current.
- The currents are strongest at surface and their speed (strength) decreases with depth. Generally, the ocean currents move at a speed less than or equal to 5 knots. At surface, the speed of current is over 5 knots. However, at depths, the speed of current is less around 0.5 knots.

Types of Ocean Currents

Broadly, the ocean currents are classified according to their depth and temperature.

On the Basis of Depth

On the basis of depth, the ocean currents are classified as

- **Surface Currents** They move on the surface of ocean water upto 400 metres of depth. They constitute about 10% of all the waters in the oceans.
- **Deep Water Currents** At the higher latitudes, due to low temperature, the density of water increases that makes cold water to sink into the ocean basins. Due to density and gravity differences, ocean water moves at greater depth i.e. around the ocean basins. These make upto 90% of the total ocean water. These are known as deep water currents.

On the Basis of Temperature

On the basis of temperature, the ocean currents are classified as

- **Cold Currents** Currents which bring cold waters into warm water areas are known as cold currents. These currents are found on the West coast of continents in the low and middle latitudes (in both hemispheres) and on the East coast in the higher latitudes (only in the Northern hemisphere).
- **Warm Currents** Currents which bring warm water into cold water areas are known as warm currents. They are generally found on the East coasts of continents in the low and middle latitudes (in both hemispheres). In the Northern hemispheres these are found on the West Coasts of continents in high latitudes.

Major Oceans Currents

Major oceanic currents are greatly influenced by two forces i.e. coriolis force and stresses exerted by the prevailing winds. The oceanic circulation pattern corresponds to the atmospheric circulation pattern such as

- In mid latitudes, the air circulation over the oceans is mainly anti-cyclonic i.e. anti-clockwise (more effective in the Southern Hemisphere than in the Northern Hemisphere), the oceanic circulation pattern follows the same pattern.
- At higher latitudes, winds flow in cyclonic way, ocean circulation also follows same clockwise pattern (in the Southern hemisphere).
- In regions of pronounced monsoonal flow, the monsoon winds influence the current movements. Due to coriolis force, the warm currents from low latitudes tend to move to the right in the Northern Hemisphere and to their left in the Southern Hemisphere.
- Ocean circulation transports heat from one latitude belt to another as heat transported by general circulation of atmosphere.
- The cold water of the Arctic and Antarctic circles moves towards warmer water in the tropical and equatorial regions, while the warmer water at lower latitudes moves polewards.

Effects of Ocean Currents

The ocean currents bring a large number of direct and indirect influence on the areas through which they pass and on human activities in those areas. The major effects of ocean currents are

- On the Western coasts of continents in tropical and sub-tropical latitudes (except close to the equator) the cold currents are found which bring fog and make these areas arid. These currents have low average temperatures as well as narrow diurnal and annual ranges.
- On the Western coasts of the continents in the middle and higher latitudes, warm ocean currents are found which bring a distinct marine climate to the surrounding regions. They bring cool summers and mild winters and keep annual range of temperature low.
- In tropical and sub-tropical latitudes, the warm currents flow parallel to the Eastern coasts of the continents. They bring warm and rainy climates to the surrounding regions. Such areas are located on the Western margins of sub-tropical anti-cyclones.
- In the regions, where warm and cold currents meet, the high growth of **planktons**[8] is found, as currents help to replenish the oxygen. Since, the planktons are basic food of fish, world's best fishing grounds are found in these mixing regions.

Ocean Resources and Pollution

Ocean Resources

The ocean is one of the Earth's most valuable natural resources. It provides important living and non-living resources. Food resources, mineral resources and energy resources are the main types of ocean resources.

Some living resources include algae which is used in detergents, shampoo, cosmetics, ice cream, etc and diatoms which are used in paints and abrasives.

Non-living resources include water, fuels and minerals(magnesium, salt, gold, manganese, iron, cobalt, sand and gravel).

Importance of ocean is

- The ocean plays a critical role in removing carbon from the atmosphere and providing oxygen. It regulates earth's climate.
- The ocean is an increasingly important source of biomedical organisms with enormous potential for fighting disease.
- Oceans are important source of fishes. The oceans have been fished for thousands of years and are an integral part of human society.
- Oceans are used for navigation purposes, especially, for trade and tourism.

- Oceans are rich sources of many minerals and metals. Humans began to mine the oceans floor for diamonds, gold, silver, metal ores like manganese, nodules and gravel mines. Diamonds are found in greater number and quality in the ocean than on land but are much harder to mine.
- The ocean is an integral component of the world's climate due to its capacity to collect, drive and mix water, heat and carbon dioxide. The ocean and the atmosphere work together to form complex weather phenomena like the North Atlantic Oscillation and EL Nino.

Ocean Pollution

Although some ocean pollution is the result of natural occurrences, most pollution is the result of human activities. Natural occurrences include weather like heavy rains add freshwater lowering salinity. Human activities include sewage, chemicals, and trash dumped into waters, runoff from fields, oil pollution from tankers or damaged oil drilling platforms ocean mining and soon.

Submarine Relief

There are mountains, basins, plateaus, ridges, canyons and trenches beneath the ocean water too. These relief features found on the ocean floor are called submarine relief. Some of the main relief features are

- **Mid-Oceanic Ridges** It is composed of two chains of mountains separated by large depression. The mountain ranges can have peaks as high as 2,500 m and some even reach above the ocean's surface, e.g. Iceland is the part of mid-Atlantic ridge.
- **Seamount** It is a mountain with pointed summits, rising from the seafloor that does not reach the surface of the ocean. Seamount is volcanic in origin and can be 3,000-4,500 m tall. For example, Emperor seamount in the Pacific Ocean is an extension of the Hawaiian Islands.
- **Submarine Canyons** These are deep valleys some comparable to the Grand Canyon of the Colorado river. They are sometimes found cutting across the continental shelves and slopes, often extending from the mouth of large rivers. For example, the **Hudson Canyon** is the best known submarine canyon in the world.
- **Guyot** It is a flat topped seamount. They show evidences of gradual subsidence through stages to become flat topped submerged mountains. It is estimated that more than 10,000 seamounts and guyots exist in the Pacific Ocean alone.
- **Atoll** They are low islands found in the Tropical Oceans consisting of coral reefs surrounding a central depression. It may be a part of sea (lagoon) or form enclosing a body of fresh, brackish, or highly saline water.

---

8 **Planktons** These are micro-organisms which are favoured by fishes.

Chapter Practice

Objective Questions

• Multiple Choice Questions

1. Which of the following is the vertical movement of ocean water?
   (a) Tides   (b) Ocean currents
   (c) Waves   (d) All of these

Ans. (a) Tides is the vertical movement of ocean water.

2. The attraction force caused by the sun and the moon forces ocean water to move up down
   (a) once in a day   (b) twice a day
   (c) thrice a day   (d) None of these

Ans. (b) The attraction force caused by the sun and the moon forces ocean water to move up down twice a day

3. The other forms of vertical movement of ocean water are
   (a) upwelling of cold water from sub-surfaces
   (b) sinking of surface water
   (c) tides
   (d) Both (a) and (b)

Ans. (d) The other forms of vertical movement of ocean water are upwelling of cold water from sub-surfaces and sinking of surface water.

4. The movements of ocean water are primarily studied through
   (a) waves   (b) tides
   (c) ocean currents   (d) All of these

Ans. (d) The movements of ocean water are primarily studied through waves, tides and ocean currents.

5. Which of the following causes waves to travel in the ocean?
   (a) Temperature   (b) Precipitation
   (c) Winds   (d) None of these

Ans. (c) Winds causes waves to travel in the ocean.

6. The maximum wave height is determined by the strength of the
   (a) evaporation   (b) wind
   (c) temperature conditions   (d) precipitation

Ans. (b) The maximum wave height is determined by the strength of the wind.

7. The crests of waves move in which direction due to gravity?
   (a) Forward   (b) Downward
   (c) Upward   (d) None of these

Ans. (b) The crests of waves move downward due to gravity.

8. Which among the following pairs is correctly matched?
   (a) Semi-diurnal Tide – Two high tides and one low tide
   (b) Diurnal Tide – Only one high tide and two low tides occur everyday
   (c) Mixed Tide – Tides having variations in their height
   (d) None of the above

Ans. (c) Mixed tides have variations in their height.

9. Find the incorrect pair.
   (a) Wave Crest and Trough- The highest and lowest points of a wave
   (b) Wavelength- Vertical distance between two successive crests
   (c) Wave Amplitude- one half of the wave height
   (d) Wave Height- Vertical distance from the bottom of a trough to the top of a crest of a wave

Ans (b) Wavelength is the horizontal (not vertical) distance between two successive crests.

10. Match the following.

	List - I		List - II
A.	Spring Tides	1.	Seven days interval time from spring tides
B.	Neap Tides	2.	Full moon and on new moon.
C.	Perigee	3.	Farthest from earth
D.	Apogee	4.	Closest to the earth

Codes

	A	B	C	D
(a)	1	2	3	4
(c)	2	1	4	3

	A	B	C	D
(b)	2	1	3	4
(d)	1	4	3	2

Ans. (c)

11. Match the following.

	List - I		List - II
A.	Friction	1.	The highest points of a wave
B.	Shoreline	2.	The force that opposes relative motion of two bodies which are in direct contact of each other
C.	Plunging waves	3.	Line of contact between land surface and ocean surface
D.	Wave Crest	4.	It breaks when the ocean floor is steep or has sudden depth
E.	Mid Oceanic Islands	5.	Favoured by fishes
F.	Planktons	6.	Found on the divergent plate boundary

Codes

	A	B	C	D	E	F
(a)	4	3	1	2	5	6
(c)	1	2	3	4	5	6

	A	B	C	D	E	F
(b)	2	3	4	1	6	5
(d)	6	2	3	4	1	5

Ans. (b)

12. Which of the following statements are correct regarding the causes of tides?

I. The tides occur due to great extent of gravitational pull of the Sun.

II. On the side of the earth facing the moon, a tidal bulge is caused by a net force.

III. On wide continental shelves, the tidal bulges are of lower height.

IV. The tidal magnitude is greatly changed by funnel-shaped bays.

Codes

(a) I, II and III
(b) II, III and IV
(c) Both II and IV
(d) Both I and III

Ans. (c) Statements II and IV are correct. Statements I and III are incorrect because the tides occur due to great extent of gravitational pull of the Moon and to a smaller extent to gravitational pull of the Sun. On wide continental shelves, the tidal bulges are of greater height.

13. Which the following statements is/are incorrect regarding the importance of tides?

I. Tides help in navigation.

II. Tidal heights or harbours located near the mouth of rivers and estuaries having shallow bars at entrance.

III. The tides help in desilting of sediments and removal of pollutants from estuaries.

IV. The tides are not used for generating electricity.

Codes

(a) Both I and II
(b) Both II and IV
(c) Only III
(d) Only IV

Ans. (d) Statements IV is incorrect as the tides are used for generating electricity. It is being developed in countries like France, Canada, Russia and China.

14. Which the following statements is incorrect regarding the movement of Ocean currents?

I. High salinity water is less dense than low salinity water.

II. Cold water is denser than the warm water.

III. At the poles, the cold water sinks down and moves towards the equator.

IV. Warm water from the equator moves towards poles along the surface.

Codes

(a) Only I
(b) Only II
(c) Only III
(d) Only IV

Ans (a) Statement I is incorrect as high salinity water is less dense than low salinity water.

15. Which the following statements are correct regarding the Ocean resources?

I. Algae is used in detergents, shampoo, cosmetics and ice cream.

II. Diatoms are used in paints and abrasives.

III. The ocean plays a critical role in removing carbon from the atmosphere and providing oxygen.

IV. The ocean and the atmosphere work together to form complex weather phenomena.

V. The ocean is an increasingly important source of biomedical organisms with enormous potential for fighting disease.

Codes

(a) I, II and III
(b) II, III and IV
(c) I, III and IV
(d) All of these

Ans. (d) All the given statements are correct.

• Case Base MCQs

16. Read the case/source given and answer the questions that follow by choosing the correct option.

Ocean currents are like river flow in oceans. They represent a regular volume of water in a definite path and direction. Ocean currents are influenced by two types of forces namely, (i) primary forces that initiate the movement of water. (ii) secondary forces that influence the currents to flow. The primary forces that influence the currents are: (i) heating by solar energy; (ii) wind; (iii) gravity; (iv) Coriolis force. Heating by solar energy causes the water to expand. That is why, near the equator the ocean water is about 8 cm higher in level than in the middle latitudes. This causes a very slight gradient and water tends to flow down the slope. Wind blowing on the surface of the ocean pushes the water to move. Friction between the wind and the water surface affects the movement of the water body in its course. Gravity tends to pull the water down the pile and create gradient variation. The Coriolis force intervenes and causes the water to move to the right in the Northern Hemisphere and to the left in the Southern Hemisphere. These large accumulations of water and the flow around them are called Gyres. These produce large circular currents in all the ocean basins.

The oceanic circulation transports heat from one latitude belt to another in a manner similar to the heat transported by the general circulation of the atmosphere. The cold waters of the Arctic and Antarctic circles move towards warmer water in tropical and equatorial regions, while the warm waters of the lower latitudes move pole wards. Ocean currents have a number of direct and indirect influences on human activities. West coasts of the continents in tropical and sub-tropical latitudes (except close to the equator) are bordered by cool waters. Their average temperatures are relatively low with a narrow diurnal and annual ranges. There is fog, but generally the areas are arid. West coasts of the continents in the middle and higher latitudes are bordered by warm waters which cause a distinct marine climate. They are characterised by cool summers and relatively mild winters with a narrow annual range of temperatures. Warm currents flow parallel to the East coasts of the continents in tropical and sub-tropical latitudes. This results in warm and rainy climates.

(i) Ocean currents are important for which of the following functions?
(a) Redistribute nutrients in oceans
(b) Redistribute heat on Earth
(c) Provide oxygen to organisms
(d) All of the above

Ans. (b) Ocean current are important for redistributing heat on Earth.

(ii) Which of the following forces provides a primary push to the oceanic waters?
(a) Friction   (b) Solar insolation
(c) Wind   (d) Both (b) and (c)

Ans. (d) Solar insolation and wind provides a primary push to the oceanic waters.

(iii) Which of the following forces is responsible for the drift of oceanic water to the right-hand side in the Northern Hemisphere?
(a) Gravity   (b) Tidal repulsion
(c) Coriolis force   (d) Radioactivity

Ans. (c) Coriolis force is responsible for the drift of oceanic water to the right-hand side in the Northern hemisphere and to the left in the Southern hemisphere.

(iv) Oceanic currents are responsible for occurrence of which of the following phenomena on the Western coast of continents?
(a) Rainfall   (b) Fog   (c) Tide   (d) Gyre

Ans. (b) Oceanic currents are responsible for occurrence of fog on the Western coasts of continents.

PART 2
Subjective Questions

• Short Answer (SA) Type Questions

1. What are the horizontal and vertical movements of ocean water? Explain.

Ans. The ocean water is highly dynamic. It keeps moving all the time both vertically as well as horizontally.

The horizontal motion of the ocean surface occurs across the latitudes. It occurs mainly in the form of ocean currents and waves. The ocean currents are definite flow of huge volume of water along a definite path and direction. Whereas, the waves are movement of energy through the ocean water.

The vertical movement of ocean water occurs in the form of tides. The tides are periodical rise and fall of seawater under the gravitational force of the sun and the moon.

2. Define waves. What are the major characteristics of waves?

Ans. Waves are energy which move across the surfaces of the oceans.

Major characteristics of waves are
• Waves are flow of energy through water.
• The energy for waves is given by winds.
• The shape and size of waves reveal their origin.

- The waves break when depth of water is less than half the wavelength of the wave.
- Circular water movements are found beneath the waves.

3. Why tides have great variation with respect to frequency, magnitude and height? Explain.

Ans. Tides have great variation with respect to frequency, magnitude and height due to a combination of all primary and marginal factors. The primary factors are gravitational force of the sun and the moon alongwith centrifugal force. There are other marginal factors which play their roles in the occurrence of tides. The atmospheric factors like cyclones further accentuate the tides. The shape of bay and estuary also magnifies the intensity of tides.

The variations in tide with respect to frequency, magnitude and height are

- The coastal areas having narrow outlets have larger tidal range.
- On wide continental shelves, the tidal bulges are of greater heights.

4. Define tide-generating force. Also explain how tides are generated.

Ans. The tide generating force is the net difference between gravitational force of the moon and centrifugal force. On the earth's side facing moon, gravitational force is dominant, whereas on the opposite side, the centrifugal force dominates over gravitational force.

Tides are generated in the following ways

- The tides generate in the form of bulge, on the earth's side facing the moon.
- Similar bulge occurs on the opposite side because of centrifugal force.
- The tides occur primarily because of gravitational force of the moon, as it is stronger than gravitational force of the sun.

5. What is the importance of tides?

Ans. The importance of tides is

- The prediction of tides helps navigators and fishermen to plan their activities in the open oceans, as tides help in navigation.
- Tidal heights or harbours located near the mouth of rivers and estuaries having shallow bars at entrance prevent the ships and boats from entering into the harbour.
- The tides also help in desilting of sediments and removal of pollutants from estuaries.
- The tides are also used for generating electricity. It is being developed in countries like France, Canada, Russia and China.

6. The moon's gravitational force has more influence over tides in comparison with the sun's gravitational force. Discuss.

Ans. The effect of gravitational force depends upon the distance between the objects. Although, the sun has more gravitational energy as compared to the moon, yet moon's gravitational force has more influence over tides in comparison with the sun's gravitational force.

The distance between the earth and the moon is 3.6 lakhs km, whereas the distance between the earth and the sun is 14.5 crore kms. Therefore, the moon exerts more gravitational attraction over the earth than the sun.

7. 'Inspite of vast potential, tidal power is not so popular'. Give reason.

Ans. Tidal energy is one of the significant resources of renewable energy. But its use is not so popular because of the following reasons

- Tidal power plants are based on location. It can't be established everywhere.
- It is technology intensive as complete technology to harness tidal energy has not been developed till the date.
- There are also some ecological concerns about development of tidal power plant.

8. How are ocean currents affected by the prevailing winds and the coriolis force?

Ans. Ocean currents are affected by the prevailing winds and the coriolis force in the following ways

- The oceanic circulation pattern roughly corresponds with atmospheric circulation pattern. Over middle latitude, the atmospheric circulation is anti-cyclonic, the oceanic pattern also becomes anti-cyclonic. Similarly in higher latitudes, the oceanic circulation is cyclonic and atmospheric circulation is anti-cyclonic.
- In the North Indian Ocean, the ocean currents reverse their direction seasonally with winds.
- According to coriolis force, the ocean currents move towards their right in the Northern Hemisphere and towards their left in the Southern Hemisphere.

9. The ocean waves are very important for weather forecasting and climate studies. Discuss its role for the welfare of human beings.

Ans. The role of ocean waves for the welfare of human beings is

- Ocean waves are very important for weather forecasting and climate modelling.
- These are also important for coastal communities, shipping route and offshore industry.

- Ocean waves are thought to play a role in weather forecasting such as improving hurricane intensity forecasts by regulating surface friction.
- Extreme ocean waves continued to be a threat for coastal community and the offshore industry. Hence, its study and proper analysis will help to protect the welfare of human beings.

10. Coastal regions have great advantage in the form of connectivity with rest of the world through oceans. But it is compensated with the loss of coastal ecology. Discuss the measures which are necessary to protect coastal ecology.

Ans. The coastal regions and countries are rich in trade and transport and have more strong economy because of swift connectivity with rest of the world. But due to shipping and other human activities, coastal ecology is harmed very much. Coastal regions posses good amount of biodiversity in the form of flora and fauna which is harmed with pollution and human encroachment in ecosensitive areas.

Measures to protect coastal ecology are

- There is need to make balance between development and environment.
- Ecological loss should be added in production cost.
- Proper rules and regulations should be adopted for activites in ecologically active areas.
- Ecologically sensitive zone should be identified and human activities should be completely restricted in core areas.

11. How do currents affect the temperature? How does it affect the temperature of coastal areas in the North-Western Europe?

Ans. The ocean currents affect the temperature in the following ways

- The cold currents bring down the temperature of the region through which they pass. As winds blow over cold currents and move towards land these further bring the temperature down.
- The warm currents act in an opposite manner. The warm currents increase the temperature of the surrounding regions. As winds blow over warm currents, they bring warm and rainy climates to the surrounding region.

The effect of currents of coastal areas on the temperature of North-Western Europe is that the Gulf stream moves in the coastal areas of North-West Europe as North Atlantic Drift. It is a warm current which has higher temperature than surrounding areas. It keeps the coastal areas and parts frost-free during winter months.

12. Discuss the measures to come out of the problem of marine pollution.

Ans "With the increasing pressure of population and international trade, the excess use of oceans have caused marine pollution".

Some suggestive measures for marine pollution are

- Foremostly, dumping of wastes should be strictly restricted in the ocean.
- There should be proper mechanism for the disposal of radioactive waste.
- The offshore drilling and oil refineries should be made capable to clean the surrounding ocean from their waste.
- Oil spill should be prevented for which the leakage proof tanker and ship should be made.
- Navigation agency should take responsibility of any harm caused by their navigation.

• Long Answer (LA) Type Questions

1. Explain the various types of tides based on the sun, moon and the earth positions.

Ans The various types of tides on the basis of the sun, moon and the earth positions are

- **Spring Tides** The position of both the sun and the moon in relation to the earth has direct bearing on tide height. When the sun, the moon and the earth are in straight line, the height of the tide will be higher. These are known as spring tides. Spring tides occur on full moon and on new moon i.e. twice a month.
- **Neap Tides** When the sun and the moon are at right angles to each other and forces of the sun and moon tend to counteract one another neap tides occur. In other words, the attraction force of sun and moon counter balance each other. Though moon's attraction force is twice than that of the sun, but sun's attraction (gravitational force) force diminishes it considerably. The neap tides occur at a seven days interval time from spring tides.
- **Perigee and Apogee** Once in a month, when the moon's orbit is closest to the earth (Perigee), unsually high and low tides occur. During this time the tidal range is greater than normal.Two weeks later, when the moon is farthest from earth (apogee), the moon's gravitational force is limited and the tidal ranges are less than their average heights.

When the earth is closest to the sun (perihelion), around 3rd January, each year, tidal ranges are also much greater, with unusually high and unusually low tides. When the earth is farthest from the sun (aphelion), around 4th July each year, tidal ranges are much less than average. The time between the high tide and low tide, when the water level is falling, is called the ebb. The time between the low tide and high tide, when the tide is rising, is called the flow or flood.

2. "Along with multiple merits, tides are also supportive to economy of the nation". Give your argument in support of this statement.

Ans. Tides generally help in navigation, desilting of sediments and wash out pollutants from estuaries. Apart from all these significances, there are various economic importance of tides, some of them are

- **Shipping** Harbours located near the mouth of rivers and estuaries having shallow bars at entrance prevent the ship and boats from entering into the harbours. Tides help ships to move in and come out smoothly.
- **Electricity** Tidal force is also used as a source for generating electricity. The generation of tidal energy was started by France. India also produces tidal energy in the Gulf of Khambat and Kuchchh.
- **Minerals** Tides bring jems and minerals near the coast which are used by the industries to produce the products.
- **Fishery** Due to tides, fish comes nearer to coast and help the fishermen to catch them easily. Tides can be predicted in advance and hence fishermen can plan their activities.
- **Salt Industries** Tide also provides support to salt industries as sea water accumulates in the depressions near the coasts which is further converted into salt.

3. What are the causes of currents?

Ans. The major causes of ocean currents are classified into two broad groups, primary forces and secondary forces.

(i) **Primary Forces** These are those forces which initiate the movement of ocean currents. The primary forces are further classified as

Heating by the Solar Energy It creates slope gradient between equatorial and middle latitudes. This causes currents to move towards higher latitudes from lower latitudes.

Wind It pushes the ocean water to move. Under the influence of easterlies, the ocean water moves westwards.

Gravity It pulls the water down and creates gradient variation.

Coriolis Force This force makes ocean currents to move towards right in the Northern hemisphere and towards left in the Southern hemisphere. This deflected motion creates a circular motion known as Gyre.

(ii) **Secondary Forces** The other forces which are small but do affect the ocean current to flow are known as secondary forces. Factors like temperature, pressure, density difference, local topography, ocean basin relief, etc. are some of the important secondary forces which cause ocean currents.

4. Describe the types of ocean currents according to their depth and temperature.

Ans On the basis of depth, the ocean currents are classified as

- **Surface Currents** They move on the surface of ocean water upto 400 metres of depth. They constitute about 10% of all the waters in the oceans.
- **Deep Water Currents** At the higher latitudes, due to low temperature, the density of water increases that makes cold water to sink into the ocean basins. Due to density and gravity differences, ocean water moves at greater depth i.e. around the ocean basins. These make upto 90% of the total ocean water. These are known as deep water currents.

On the basis of temperature, the ocean currents are classified as

- **Cold Currents** Currents which bring cold waters into warm water areas are known as cold currents. These currents are found on the West coast of continents in the low and middle latitudes (in both hemispheres) and on the East coast in the higher latitudes (only in the Northern hemisphere).
- **Warm Currents** Currents which bring warm water into cold water areas are known as warm currents. They are generally found on the East coasts of continents in the low and middle latitudes (in both hemispheres). In the Northern hemispheres these are found on the West Coasts of continents in high latitudes.

5. What are the major effects of ocean currents?

Ans The ocean currents bring a large number of direct and indirect influence on the areas through which they pass and on human activities in those areas. The major effects of ocean currents are

- On the Western coasts of continents in tropical and sub-tropical latitudes (except close to the equator) the cold currents are found which bring fog and make these areas arid. These currents have low average temperatures as well as narrow diurnal and annual ranges.
- On the Western coasts of the continents in the middle and higher latitudes, warm ocean currents are found which bring a distinct marine climate to the surrounding regions. They bring cool summers and mild winters and keep annual range of temperature low.
- In tropical and sub-tropical latitudes, the warm currents flow parallel to the Eastern coasts of the continents. They bring warm and rainy climates to the surrounding regions. Such areas are located on the Western margins of sub-tropical anti-cyclones.
- In the regions, where warm and cold currents meet, the high growth of planktons is found, as currents help to replenish the oxygen. Since, the planktons are basic food of fish, world's best fishing grounds are found in these mixing regions.

• Case Based Questions

1. Read the case/source given and answer the following questions.

The ocean water is dynamic. Its physical characteristics like temperature, salinity, density and the external forces like of the sun, moon and the winds influence the movement of ocean water. The horizontal and vertical motions are common in ocean water bodies. The horizontal motion refers to the ocean currents and waves. The vertical motion refers to tides. Ocean currents are the continuous flow of huge amount of water in a definite direction while the waves are the horizontal motion of water. Water moves ahead from one place to another through ocean currents while the water in the waves does not move, but the wave trains move ahead. The vertical motion refers to the rise and fall of water in the oceans and seas. Due to attraction of the sun and the moon, the ocean water is raised up and falls down twice a day. The upwelling of cold water from subsurface and the sinking of surface water are also forms of vertical motion of ocean water.

Waves are actually the energy, not the water as such, which moves across the ocean surface.

Water particles only travel in a small circle as a wave passes. Wind provides energy to the waves. Wind causes waves to travel in the ocean and the energy is released on shorelines. The motion of the surface water seldom affects the stagnant deep bottom water of the oceans. As a wave approaches the beach, it slows down. This is due to the friction occurring between the dynamic water and the sea floor. And, when the depth of water is less than half the wavelength of the wave, the wave breaks. The largest waves are found in the open oceans.

Waves continue to grow larger as they move and absorb energy from the wind. Most of the waves are caused by the wind driving against water. When a breeze of two knots or less blows over calm water, small ripples form and grow as the wind speed increases until white caps appear in the breaking waves. Waves may travel thousands of km before rolling ashore, breaking and dissolving as surf.

(i) What is wave frequency and wave period?

Ans. Wave frequency is the number of waves passing a given point during a time interval of one second. Wave period is merely the time interval between two successive wave crests or troughs as they pass a fixed point.

(ii) Explain how size and shape of a wave reveal its origin?

Ans. A wave's size and shape reveal its origin as steep waves are fairly young ones and are probably formed by local wind. Slow and steady waves originate from faraway places, possibly from another hemisphere.

(iii) Define wave crest and trough.

Ans. The highest and lowest points of a wave are called the crest and trough respectively in other words, in a wave, the maximum value of upward displacement is called its crest. On the other hand, trough is just opposite to the crest. In a wave, the minimum value of downward displacement is called its trough.

2. Read the case/source given and answer the following questions.

Tides vary in their frequency, direction and movement from place to place and also from time to time. Tides may be grouped into various types based on their frequency of occurrence in one day or 24 hours or based on their height. Tides based on Frequency Semi-diurnal tide : The most common tidal pattern, featuring two high tides and two low tides each day. The successive high or low tides are approximately of the same height. Diurnal tide : There is only one high tide and one low tide during each day. The successive high and low tides are approximately of the same height. Mixed tide : Tides having variations in height are known as mixed tides. These tides generally occur along the west coast of North America and on many islands of the Pacific Ocean.

(i) What is ebb and flow in tide?

Ans. The time between the high tide and low tide, when the water level is falling, is called the ebb. The time between the low tide and high tide, when the tide is rising, is called the flow or flood.

(ii) What are the tide generating forces?

Ans. The tide-generating force is the difference between the two forces, i.e. the gravitational attraction of the moon and the centrifugal force.

(iii) What are the different tides based on frequency?

Ans. Different tides based on frequency are

Semi-diurnal tide It is the most common tidal pattern, featuring two high tides and two low tides each day. The successive high or low tides are approximately of the same height.

Diurnal tide In this pattern, there is only one high tide and one low tide during each day. The successive high and low tides are approximately of the same height.

3. Read the case/source given and answer the following questions.

Ocean currents are like river flow in oceans. They represent a regular volume of water in a definite path and direction. Ocean currents are influenced by two types of forces namely : (i) primary forces that initiate the movement of water; (ii) secondary forces that influence the currents to flow.

Ocean currents are like river flow in oceans. They represent a regular volume of water in a definite path and direction. Ocean currents are influenced by two types of forces namely : (i) primary forces that initiate the movement of water; (ii) secondary forces that influence the currents to flow. The primary forces that influence the currents are: (i) heating by solar energy; (ii) wind; (iii) gravity; (iv) coriolis force. Heating by solar energy causes the water to expand. That is why, near the equator the ocean water is about 8 cm higher in level than in the middle latitudes. This causes a very slight gradient and water tends to flow down the slope. Wind blowing on the surface of the ocean pushes the water to move. Friction between the wind and the water surface affects the movement of the water body in its course.

Gravity tends to pull the water down the pile and create gradient variation. The Coriolis force intervenes and causes the water to move to the right in the northern hemisphere and to the left in the southern hemisphere. These large accumulations of water and the flow around them are called Gyres. These produce large circular currents in all the ocean basins.

(i) Define Gyres.

Ans. The large accumulations of water and the flow around them are called Gyres. These produce large circular currents in all the ocean basins.

(ii) What are the different types of ocean currents based on their depth?

Ans. The ocean currents may be classified based on their depth as surface currents and deep water currents. Surface currents constitute about 10 per cent of all the water in the ocean. Deep water currents make up the other 90 per cent of the ocean water.

(iii) Name the different primary forces that influence the currents.

Ans. The primary forces that influence the currents are Heating by solar energy, wind, gravity and coriolis force.

• Map Based Question

1. Identify the following currents marked on the map of the world given below.

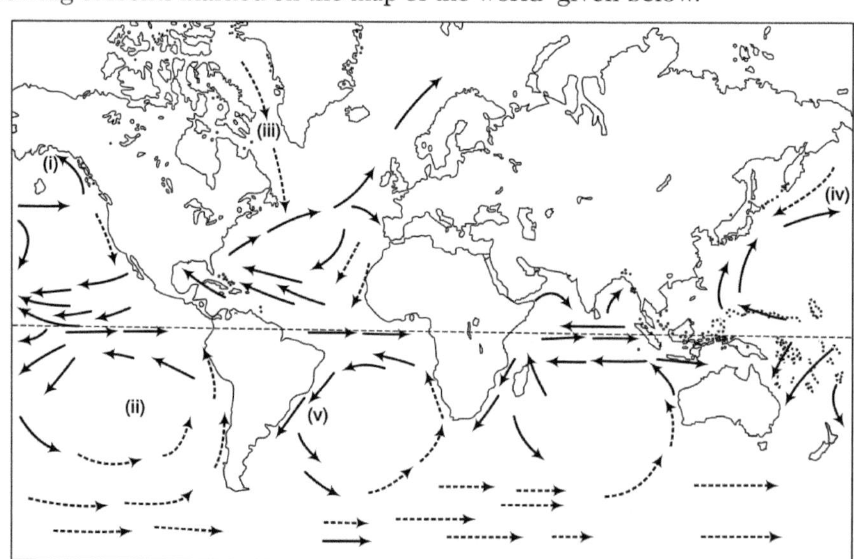

Ans

(iii) Labrador Current
(i) Alaska Current
(iv) Oyashio Current
(ii) South Equatorial Current
(v) Brazilian Current

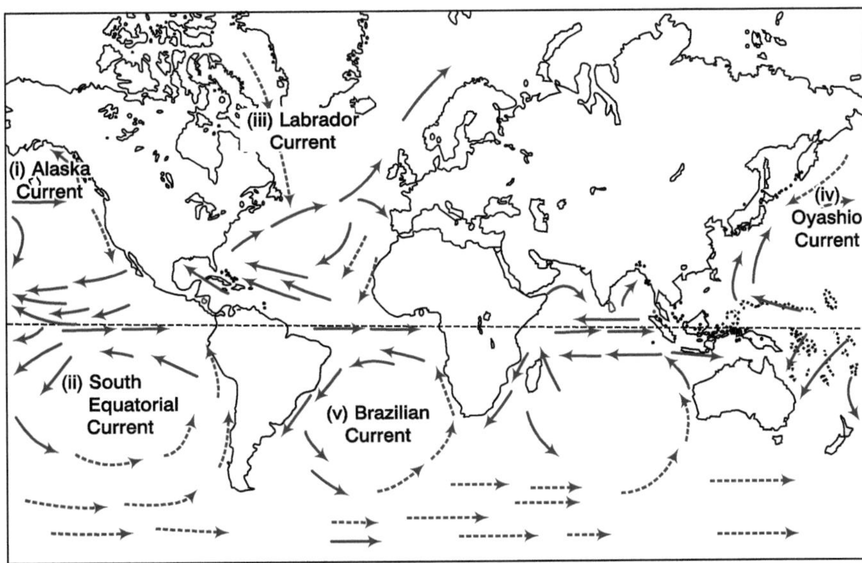

Chapter Test

Objective Questions

1. Which of the following is the horizontal movement of ocean water?
   (a) Tides
   (b) Ocean currents
   (c) Waves
   (d) Both (b) and (c)
2. Which of the following is the important feature of the waves?
   (a) When wave approaches to the beach, it slows down due to the friction occurring between the dynamic water and sea floor.
   (b) When the depth of water is less than half the wavelength of wave, the wave breaks.
   (c) The largest waves are found in the open oceans.
   (d) All of the above
3. The actual motion of the water beneath the waves is
   (a) horizontal
   (b) vertical
   (c) circular
   (d) diagonal
4. Which of the following motions is found in a wave?
   (a) Upward
   (b) Forward
   (c) Downward
   (d) All of these
5. Consider the following statements and choose the correct option.
   I. At the higher latitudes the density of water increases.
   II. Temperature is very low at higher latitudes.
   Codes
   (a) Only I is correct
   (b) Only II is correct
   (c) Both statements are incorrect
   (d) Both statements are correct

Short Answer Type Questions

6. What are the major causes of tides?
7. What do you mean by upwelling of ocean water? How does it help in the movement of ocean water?
8. How waves break upon reaching the shoreline? Explain.
9. List down the factors on which a wave depends.
10. List down major characteristics of ocean currents.

Long Answer Type Questions

11. Why spring tide occurs only on new moon or full moon day? Explain in detail.
12. Describe the major ocean currents of the Pacific, Atlantic and Indian Oceans taking one cold current and one warm current from every ocean.
13. The ocean currents bring a large number of direct and indirect influence on areas through which they pass and on human activities. Explain in brief.

Answers

1. (d) Both (b) and (c)
2. (d) All of the above
3. (c) circular
4. (d) All of these
5. (d) Both statements are correct

Life on the Earth

Life on the earth is found almost everywhere. Living organisms are found from the poles to the equator, from the bottom of the sea to several km in the air, from freezing waters to dry valleys, from under the sea to underground water lying below the earth's surface.

Biosphere

The biosphere comprises all the living components of the earth which interacts with other environmental realms like, lithosphere, atmosphere and hydrosphere. It includes plants, animals and all micro-organisms and also includes the interactions of these living organisms with their environment. Most of the organisms exist on the lithosphere, hydrosphere as well as in the atmosphere. There are also many organisms that move freely from one realm to the other.

The biosphere and its components are very significant elements of the environment. These elements are in direct interaction with other components found in natural landscape like land, water and soil. Atmospheric elements like temperature, rainfall, moisture and sunlight also influence these components. The interactions of biosphere with land, air and water are important to the growth, development and evolution of the organism.

Ecology

The term ecology is made up of two Greek words i.e. *oikos* meaning 'house' and *logy* meaning 'the science of or the study of'. Therefore, ecology is the study of the earth as a household. It study the different aspects of the plants, human beings, animals and micro-organisms. They all live together as a interdependent component.

The term 'ecology' was first used by a German zoologist named as **Ernst Haeckel**. He used the word *oekologie* in 1869. The science of ecology is the study of interactions between **life forms** (biotic) and the **physical environment** (abiotic). Hence, ecology is defined as a scientific study of the interactions of organisms with their physical environment and with each other.

Abiotic and biotic components together make our **environment**. In order to maintain a balance in the environment, a certain degree of diversity of life-forms is required. To sustain a healthy interaction between biotic and abiotic components of the environment, the balance is maintained in a particular proportion. Ecological systems are interactions of certain organisms within a particular habitat. It results in well-defined energy flows and cycles of material on land, water and air. In the ecological sense, a habitat is assemblage and totality of physical and chemical factors constituting the general environment.

Ecosystem

An ecosystem is nothing but a system which consists of biotic and abiotic components. In an ecosystem, all these components are not only inter-related, but also interact with each other. Different ecosystems have evolved due to the process of ecological adaptation. It is the adaptation of various plants and animals with varying ranges of environmental conditions that are found in various types of ecosystems.

Types of Ecosystems

Generally, the ecosystem is broadly classified into two types i.e. **terrestrial** and **aquatic**. The terrestrial ecosystem is then classified into **biomes**. The aquatic ecosystems are further classified as marine ecosystems and freshwater ecosystems. The marine ecosystem comprises of oceans, estuaries and coral reefs; whereas the freshwater ecosystems are consisted of lakes, ponds, streams, marshes and bogs.

Structure of Ecosystem

The description of available plants and animals species are known as structure of ecosystem. It is consisted of all the **biotic** and **abiotic** factors. Some of the important abiotic factors are rainfall, temperature, sunlight, atmospheric humidity, soil conditions and inorganic substances like carbon dioxide, water, nitrogen, calcium, phosphorus, potassium, etc.

However, the biotic factors of an ecosystem are the producers, the consumers (primary, secondary, tertiary) and the decomposers

- **Producers** All the green plants which manufacture their own food through **photosynthesis**[1] are known as the producers.

- **Consumers** Those organisms that receive all their energy by consuming other types of organisms or organic matters are called consumers.

  They are of three types

  (i) **Primary Consumers** These include herbivorous animals like deer, goat, mice and all plant eating animals.

  (ii) **Secondary Consumers** Carnivores include all flesh eating animals like snakes, tigers and lions.

  (iii) **Tertiary Consumers** Carnivores which feed on other carnivores are known as top carnivores like hawks and mongooses.

- **Decomposers** Those organisms which feed on the remains of dead organisms are called decomposers. For example, scavengers like vultures and crows. The decomposers further breakdown matter through bacteria and other micro-organisms which act as decomposing agents.

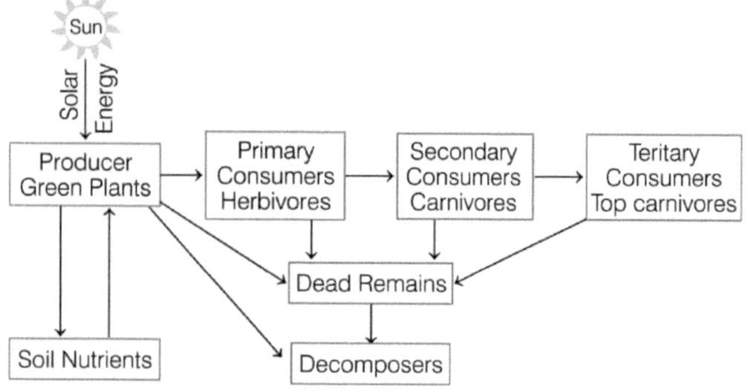

Structure and Functions of Ecosystems

Functions of Ecosystem

The primary consumers eat producers, whereas secondary consumers eat primary consumers. Tertiary consumers eat secondary consumers. At each and every level, the dead remains are eaten by the decomposers. The decomposers convert these dead remains into nutrients, organic and inorganic salt, etc. All these are essential for soil fertility.

Food Chain

Organisms of an ecosystem are linked together through a foodchain. For example, a plant eating beetle eats paddy stalk, this beetle is eaten by a frog, and frog is eaten by snake, and finally snake is consumed by a hawk. This sequence of eating and being eaten and the resultant transfer of energy from one level to another is known as the food chain.

This transfer of energy from one level of food chain to another one is known as **flow of energy**. Food chains are not isolated from each other which means that they are inter-linked with each other. In fact, all food chains are interlocked. This interconnecting network of species is known as **food web**. For example, a mouse which eats grain may be consumed by any of secondary consumers (carnivores) and these secondary consumers may be eaten up by any of tertiary consumers (top carnivores). In such situations, each of the carnivones may consume more than one type of prey. Broadly two types of food chains are classified in the ecosystem. These are

  (i) **Grazing Food Chain** The first level starts with primary producers i.e. plants. The plants are eaten up by herbivores like goat, deer, etc. which are at intermediate level. This food chain ends at the level of carnivores which eat up herbivores. These make last level. In this types of food chain, energy is lost at each level by means of respiration, excretion or decomposition. In a grazing food chain the number of levels vary from three to five. The energy is lost at each of these levels.

  (ii) **Detritus Food Chain** It is based on autotrophs energy capture initiated by grazing animals and involves the decomposition or breaking down of organic wastes and dead matter derived from the grazing food-chain.

Biomes

A biome is a plant and animal community that covers a large geographical area. Climate determines the boundaries of different biomes on land. Biomes can be defined as the total assemblage of plant and animal species interacting within specific conditions. These include rainfall, temperature, humidity and soil conditions.

Types of biomes

There are five major biomes, that include:

  (i) Forest　　　　(ii) Aquatic　　　　(iii) Desert

  (iv) Altitudinal biomes　　　　　　(v) Grassland

1　Photosynthesis A complex process occurring within the cells of green plants where sunlight is utilised in combination with carbon dioxide and water to produce oxygen and carbohydrates.

Characteristics of World Biomes

Biomes	Sub-types	Regions	Climatic Characteristics	Soil	Flora and fauna
Forest	A. Tropical 1. Equatorial 2. Deciduous	A1.10° N-S A2.10°-25° N-S	A1.Temperature 20-25°C evenly distributed. A2.Temperature 25-30° C, Rainfall average annually 1,000 mm, seasonal.	A1. Acidic, poor in nutrients. A2. Rich in nutrients.	A1. Multi- layered canopy, tall and large trees. A2. Less dense, trees of medium height, many varieties co-exist. Insects, bats, birds and mammals are common species in both.
	B. Temperate	B. Eastern North America, N.E Asia, Western and Central Europe.	B. Temperature 20-30° C, Rainfall evenly distributed 750-1,500 mm, well-defined seasons and distinct winters.	B. Fertile, enriched with decaying litter.	B. Moderately dense broad leaved trees. With less diversity of plant species. Oak, Beach, Maple, etc are some common species, squirrels, rabbits, skunks, birds, black bears, mountain lions, etc.
	C. Boreal	C. Broad belt of Eurasia and North America (Parts of Siberia, Alaska, Canada and Scandinavia).	C. Short moist moderately warm summers and long cold dry winter, very low temperatures. Precipitation mostly snowfall 400-1,000 mm.	C. Acidic and poor in nutrients, thin soil cover.	C. Evergreen conifers like pine, fur and spruce, etc. Wood peckers, hawks, bears, wolves, deer, hares and bats are common animals.
Desert	A. Hot and Dry desert	A. Sahara, Kalahari, Marusthali, Rub-el-Khali.	A. Temperature 20-45° C	Rich in nutrients with little or no organic matter.	A-C, Scanty vegetation, few large mammals, insects, reptiles and birds.
	B. Semi-arid desert	B. Marginal areas of hot deserts.	B. 21-38° C		
	C. Coastal desert	C. Atacama.	C. 15-35° C		
	D. Cold desert	D. Tundra climatic regions.	D. 2-25° C A-D Rainfall is less than 50 mm.		D. Rabbits, rats, antelopes and ground squirrels.
Grassland	A. Tropical Savannah	A. Large areas of Africa, Australia, South America and India.	A. Warm hot climates, Rainfall 500-1,250 mm.	A. Porous with thin layer of humus.	A. Grasses, trees and large shrubs absent; giraffes, zebras, buffaloes, leopards, hyenas, elephants, mice, moles, snakes and worms, etc are common animals.
	B. Temperate Steppe	B. Parts of Eurasia and North America.	B. Hot summers and cold winters, rainfall 500- 900 mm.	B. Thin flocculated soil, rich in bases.	B. Grasses, occasional trees such as cotton, wood, oaks and willows; gazelles, zebras, rhinoceros, wild horses, lions, varieties of birds, worms, snakes, etc are common animals.
Aquatic	A. Freshwater	A. Lakes, streams, rivers, and wetlands.	A-B Temperatures vary widely with cooler air temperatures and high humidity.	A. Water swamps and marshes.	Algal and other aquatic and marine plant communities with varieties of water dwelling animals.
	B. Marine	B. Oceans, coral reefs, lagoons and estuaries.		B. Water, tidal swamps and marshes.	
Altitudinal		Slopes of high mountain ranges like the Himalayas, the Andes and the Rockies.	Temperature and precipitation vary depending upon latitudinal zone.	**Regolith**[2] over slopes.	Deciduous to tundra vegetation varying according to altitude.

---

2 **Regolith** It is the layer of unconsolidated solid material covering the bedrock of a planet.

Biogeochemical Cycles

The sun is the basic source of energy on which all life depends. The sun's energy initiates life processes through photosynthesis in the biosphere and this photosynthesis is the main source of food and energy for the green plants. During the processes of photosynthesis, carbon dioxide is converted into organic compounds and oxygen. However, in the photosynthesis only a small fraction i.e. 0.1 per cent of solar energy that reaches on the earth's surface is fixed.

Out of this energy, more than half is used for plant respiration and the rest is temporarily stored. This remaining part may also be shifted to the other portions of the plant. A great variety of living organisms are found on the earth. These living organisms exist and survive in a diversity of associations which involves the presence of systemic flows such as, flows of energy, water or nutrients. These flows show variations in different parts of the world, in different seasons of the year and under varying local circumstances.

Studies show that for the last one billion years, atmosphere and hydrosphere have been composed of the same balance of chemical components. This balance has been maintained by a cyclic passage through the tissues of plants and animals. This cyclic process starts when organisms absorb the chemical elements and are returned to air, water and soil through decomposition. Solar energy provides necessary energy to these cycles.

Collectively, these cyclic movements of chemical elements of biosphere between organisms and their environment is known as **biogeochemical cycles**, whereas bio refers to living organisms and geo to rocks, soil, air and water of the earth.

Types of Biogeochemical Cycles

Broadly, there are two main types of biogeochemical cycles:

(i) Gaseous cycle

(ii) Sedimentary cycle

The main reservoirs of nutrients in a gaseous cycle are the atmosphere and the oceans. However, the main reservoirs of nutrients in sedimentary cycle are soils, sedimentary and other rocks of the earth's crust.

Some of the important biogeochemical cycles are:

- The water cycle
- The oxygen cycle
- Other mineral cycles
- The carbon cycle
- The nitrogen cycle

The Water Cycle

Circulation of water in its all three forms i.e solid, liquid or gaseous is found among living organisms, the atmosphere and the lithosphere. It is known as **hydrological cycle.**

The Carbon Cycle

Carbon is one of the important basic elements of all living organisms which forms the basic constituent of all the organic compounds. The biosphere contains more than half a million carbon compounds in them. Some of the important features of carbon cycle are

- In a carbon cycle, mainly the conversion of carbon dioxide takes place.
- It starts through the process of photosynthesis, which fixes the carbon dioxide from the atmosphere.
- This conversion results into production of carbohydrates, glucose, etc. These products are further converted into organic compounds like sucrose, starch or cellulose. Some of the carbohydrates are directly consumed by the plants.
- During the process of photosynthesis in the day time more carbon dioxide is generated and released through its leaves and roots. However, remaining carbohydrates which are not used by the plants become part of plant tissue.

These plant tissues are either being eaten by herbivorous or get decomposed by micro-organisms. Some of the consumed carbohydrates are converted into carbon dioxide by herbivorous. It is released in the atmosphere through respiration. The remaining carbohydrates are decomposed by micro-organisms after the animal dies. It then gets oxidised into carbon dioxide to return back into atmosphere.

The Oxygen Cycle

Oxygen is the principle by-product of photosynthesis. It is involved in the **oxidation**[3] of carbohydrates with the release of energy, carbon dioxide and water. Some of the important features of the oxygen cycle are

- It is a highly complex process.
- Oxygen occurs in a number of chemical forms and combinations. It combines with nitrogen to form nitrates and with many other minerals and elements to form various oxides such as the iron oxide, aluminium oxide and others.
- The decomposition of water molecules by sunlight during the process of photosynthesis produces oxygen. This oxygen is then released into atmosphere through the transpiration and respiration processes of plants.

The Nitrogen Cycle

Out of all atmospheric gases, nitrogen is the major constituents which constitutes about 78% of the atmosphere. Nitrogen is an essential constituent of many types of organic compounds like amino acids, nucleic acids, proteins, vitamins and pigments. The nitrogen is utilisable in direct form (gaseous form) only by a few types of organisms like certain species of soil bacteria and blue- green algae.

---

3 Oxidation A chemical reaction involving oxygen dissolved in water.

Main features of nitrogen cycle are

- Nitrogen can be used only when it is fixed. In the environment, out of the total nitrogen found, 90% of fixed nitrogen is biological.
- The principal source of free nitrogen is the action of soil micro-organism and associated plant roots on atmospheric nitrogen found in pore spaces of the soil.
- It can also be fixed by lightening and **cosmic radiation**[4] in the atmosphere. It is also fixed by marine organisms in the oceans.
- Once free nitrogen has been fixed into an available form it is assimilated by green plants. Herbivorous consume this nitrogen by eating plants.
- Soil bacteria converts nitrogenous wastes of excreta and of dead plants and animals remain into nitrites. This nitrite is then converted into nitrates by some bacteria.
  These nitrates are then again used by green plants. Some bacteria then convert these nitrates into free nitrogen. This process is known as **denitrification**.

Other Mineral Cycles

Apart from the principal geochemical components of the biosphere like carbon, oxygen, nitrogen and hydrogen, some minerals are also found as critical nutrients for plants and animal life. All these mineral elements are required by living organisms.

They are obtained from inorganic sources like phosphorus, sulphur, calcium and potassium. These minerals are found as dissolved salts in soil water, lakes, streams and seas. The earth crust directly provides the mineral salts through weathering, whereas soluble salts directly reaches the sea, as they enter into water cycle.

Through the process of sedimentation, some salts return back to the earth's surface and again move into the mineral cycle through weathering. Mineral solutions of the environment provide necessary minerals to living organisms. Some organisms receive these salts through plants and animals they consume. Finally, after the death of living organisms, the minerals are returned to the soil and water through decomposition and flow.

Ecological Balance

A state of dynamic equilibrium within a community of organisms in an ecosystem or habitat is known as ecological balance. The main characteristics of ecological balance are

- The ecological balance can be achieved only when the diversity within living organisms remains relatively stable. Gradual changes take place but that happens only through natural succession.
- These changes can also be explained as a stable balance in the number of each species in an ecosystem. This balance is

achieved through cooperation and competition among different organisms. However, their population stability is maintained in this.

- To achieve the ecological balance different species compete with each other in a given environment. This balance is also attained by the fact that some species are always dependent on other species for food and sustenance.
- There are many types of mechanisms to maintain ecological balance. In large grasslands, herbivorous like deer, zebra, buffaloes, etc are found in abundance, whereas the carnivores (like tigers, lions, etc) which feed on herbivorous are not found in large numbers. Thus, the population stability of both herbivorous and carnivores is maintained.

Succession

In plant communities, any disturbance in the native forests such as clearing the forest for shifting cultivation usually brings about a change in the species distribution. This change is due to competition where the secondary forest species such as grasses, bamboos or pines overtake the native species changing the original forest structure. This is called **Succession**.

Disturbance of Ecological Balance

The factors responsible for disturbance of ecological balance are

- Ecological balance may be disturbed due to the introduction of new species, natural hazards or human causes.
- The balance of plant communities has been greatly affected by human interference which has led to disturbances in the ecosystems. These disturbances have brought about numerous secondary successions.
- The earth's resources are under immense pressure from rising human demands. It is threatening for the ecosystem. Due to this, the originality of the ecosystem has been lost forever and this adversely affects the general environment.
- Many natural calamities like floods, landslides, diseases, erratic climatic occurrences are happening because of ecological imbalances only.
- There is a very close relationship between the plant and animal communities within particular habitats.
- The diversity of life is a good indicator of habitat factor of any area. To have a solid base for protection and conservation of ecosystems, a proper understanding and knowledge of all these factors is essential.

---

4 Cosmic radiation Cosmic radiation or rays are high-energy protons and atomic nuclei which move though space at nearly the speed of light. They originate from the sun, from outside of the solar system and from distant galaxies.

Chapter Practice

Objective Questions

• Multiple Choice Questions

1. Biosphere comprises which of the following?
(a) Plants   (b) Animals
(c) Micro-organisms   (d) All of these

Ans. (d) The biosphere comprises all the living components of the earth use plants, animals and all micro-organisms.

2. In which year Ernst Haeckel, a German Zoologist, used the word 'Oekologie'?
(a) 1804   (b) 1850
(c) 1869   (d) 1899

Ans. (c) In 1869, Ernst Haeckel, a German Zoologist, used the word 'Oekologie'.

3. Which of the following components together makes our environment?
(a) Abiotic only   (b) Biotic only
(c) Both Abiotic and Biotic   (d) None of these

Ans. (c) Abiotic and biotic components together makes our environment. Abiotic component includes, soil, air, water etc and biotic component includes plants, animals and micro-organism.

4. In the ecological sense, which of the following is the assemblage and totality of physical and chemical factors constituting the general environment?
(a) Abiotic component   (b) Biotic component
(c) Habitat   (d) None of these

Ans. (c) In the ecological sense, a habitat is assemblage and totality of physical and chemical factors constituting the general environment.

5. Which of the following is a type of Biome?
(a) Forest biomes   (b) Aquatic biomes
(c) Desert biomes   (d) All of these

Ans. (d) There are five major biomes, that include Forest, Aquatic, Desert, Altitudinal and Grassland biomes.

6. Which of the following is not an important biogeochemical cycle?
(a) Water cycle
(b) Carbon cycle
(c) Nutrient cycle
(d) Nitrogen cycle

Ans. (c) Nutrient cycle is not an important biogeochemical cycle.

7. Which among the following pair is correctly matched?
(a) Biosphere - The part of the earth where life exists.
(b) Ecology - The study of relationship of organisms with their environment.
(c) Ecosystem - It includes all the living things in a given area interacting with each other and also with their non - living environment
(d) All of the above

Ans. (d) All the given pairs are correctly matched.

8. Find the incorrect pair.
(a) Life forms-Biotic
(b) Physical environment-Abiotic
(c) Ecology-Ernst Haeckel
(d) None of the above

Ans. (d) All the given pairs are correctly matched.

9. Match List I with List II and select the correct answer using the codes given below.

	List I (Biotic factors of an ecosystem)		List II (Examples)
A.	Producers	1.	Tertiary
B.	Primary consumers	2.	Snakes
C.	Secondary consumers	3.	Deer
D.	Tertiary consumers	4.	Plants

Codes

	A	B	C	D
(a)	1	2	3	4
(b)	4	3	2	1
(c)	3	2	1	4
(d)	2	4	3	1

Ans. (b)

10. Match List I with List II and select the correct answer using the codes given below.

	List I		List II
A.	Biosphere	1.	It is the part of the earth where life exists.
B.	Ecology	2.	The study of relationship of organisms with their environment.
C.	Ecosystem	3.	It includes all the living things in a given area interacting with each other and also with their non-living environment.
D.	Photosynthesis	4.	A complex process occurring within the cells of green plants
E.	Oxidation	5.	Chemical reaction involving oxygen dissolved in water.
F.	Regolith	6.	It is the layer of unconsolidated solid material covering the bedrock of a planet.

Codes

	A	B	C	D	E	F
(a)	2	3	4	5	1	6
(b)	1	2	3	4	5	6
(c)	6	2	4	5	1	3
(d)	5	1	2	4	3	6

Ans. (b)

11. Which of the following statements is/ are correct about the Ecology?

  I. Ecological systems are interactions of certain organisms within a particular habitat.

  II. It results in well-defined energy flows and cycles of material on land, water and air.

  III. In the ecological sense, a habitat is totality of physical and chemical factors constituting the general environment.

Codes
(a) Only I and II   (b) Only II and III
(c) Only III   (d) All of these

Ans. (d) All the given statements are correct about ecology.

12. Which of the following statements is/ are correct about the biomes?

  I. Multi- layered canopy, tall and large trees can be seen on Tropical Equatorial biomes.

  II. Evergreen conifers like pine, fur and spruce, etc. Wood peckers, hawks, bears, wolves, deer, hares and bats are common animals are found in Boreal Biomes.

  III. Scanty vegetation, few large mammals, insects, reptiles and birds are found in Desert Biomes.

Codes
(a) Only I and II   (b) Only I and III
(c) Only II and III   (d) All of these

Ans. (d) All the statements are correct about the biomes.

13. Which of the following statements is /are incorrect about the disturbance of ecological balance?

  I. Ecological balance can not be disturbed due to the introduction of new species.

  II. The balance of plant communities has been greatly affected by human interference.

  III. There is a very close relationship between the plant and animal communities within particular habitats.

Codes
(a) Only I   (b) Only II
(c) Only III   (d) None of these

Ans. (a) Statement I is incorrect as ecological balance can be disturbed due to the introduction of new species.

14. Living organisms are found in which of the following areas?

  I. From the poles to the Equator.

  II. From the bottom of the sea to several km in the air.

  III. From freezing waters to dry valleys.

Codes
(a) Only I   (b) Only II
(c) I and II   (d) All of these

Ans. (d) Living organisms are found in all the given regions.

15. Arrange the biotic factors (Producers and Consumers) in sequence.

  1. Green Plants

  2. Goats

  3. Lions

  4. Hawks

Codes
(a) 1, 2, 3, 4   (b) 4, 3, 2, 1
(c) 4, 2, 1, 3   (d) 1, 4, 2, 3

Ans. (a) 1, 2, 3, 4

• Case Based MCQs

16. Read the case/source given and answer the questions that follow by choosing the correct option.

The structure of an ecosystem involves a description of the available plant and animal species. From a structural point of view, all ecosystems consist of abiotic and biotic factors. Abiotic factors include rainfall, temperature, sunlight, atmospheric humidity, soil conditions, inorganic substances (carbon dioxide, water, nitrogen, calcium, phosphorus, potassium, etc.). Biotic factors include the producers, the consumers (primary, secondary, tertiary) and the decomposers. The producers include all the green plants, which manufacture their own food through photosynthesis. The primary consumers include herbivorous animals like deer, goats, mice and all plant-eating animals. The carnivores include all the flesh-eating animals like snakes, tigers and lions. Certain carnivores that feed also on carnivores are known as top carnivores like hawks and mongooses. Decomposers are those that feed on dead organisms (for example, scavengers like vultures and crows), and further breaking down of the dead matter by other decomposing agents like bacteria and various microorganisms.

The producers are consumed by the primary consumers whereas the primary consumers are, in turn, being eaten by the secondary consumers. Further, the secondary consumers are consumed by the tertiary consumers. The decomposers feed on the dead at each and every level. They change them into various substances such as nutrients, organic and inorganic salts essential for soil fertility.

(i) Which of these is an abiotic factor in the ecosystem?
(a) Primary producer   (b) Decomposer
(c) Secondary consumer   (d) Carbon dioxide

Ans. (d) Carbon dioxide is an abiotic factor in the ecosystem.

(ii) Which of the following process will result in a loss of energy in a food web?
(a) Respiration   (b) Decomposition
(c) Excretion   (d) All of these

Ans. (d) All the given options are correct because, respiration, decomposition, excretion are the process through which energy is being loss in a food web.

(iii) The detritus food chain involves which one of the following organism at the top?
(a) Bio-decomposers   (b) Producer
(c) Carnivore   (d) Herbivore

Ans. (a) The detritus food chain involves bio-decomposers at the top.

Detritus food chain is based on autotrophs energy capture initiated by grazing animals and involves the decomposition or breaking down of organic wastes and dead matter derived from the grazing food-chain.

(iv) Which of the following organism cannot be categorised as Top carnivore?
(a) Lion   (b) Tiger
(c) Deer   (d) Hawk

Ans. (c) Deer cannot be categorised as a top carnivore.

17. Study the following diagram and answer the questions that follow by choosing the correct option.

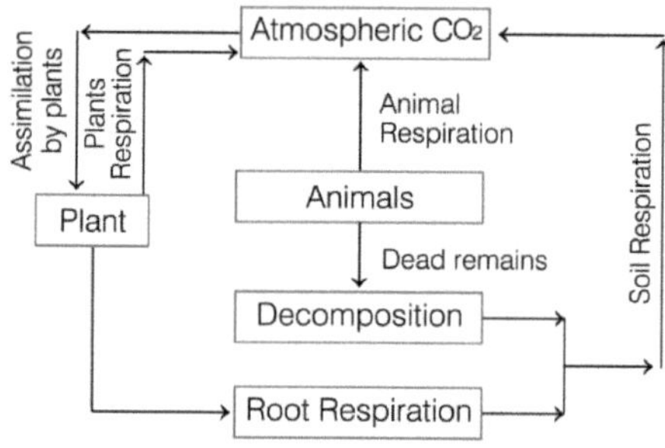

(i) Which of these process releases carbon dioxide in the atmosphere?
(a) Respiration   (b) Photosynthesis
(c) Decomposition   (d) Both (a) and (c)

Ans. (d) Respiration along with photosynthesis are the process by which   can be released in the atmosphere.

(ii) Carbon dioxide is released through which of the following parts of plants?
(a) Roots   (b) Trunk
(c) Fruits   (d) All of these

Ans. (a) During the process of photosynthesis in the day time more carbon dioxide is generated and released through its leaves and roots.

(iii) The role of bacteria in the carbon cycle is
(a) Breakdown of organic compounds
(b) Chemosynthesis
(c) Photosynthesis
(d) Assimilation of nitrogen compound

Ans. (a) The role of bacteria (micro-organism) in the carbon cycle is to breakdown the organic compounds after the animal dies.

(iv) Which of the following is a storehouse of carbon?
(a) Soil
(b) Oceans
(c) Forests
(d) All of the above

Ans. (d) Soil, oceans and forests are a storehouse of carbon.

Subjective Questions

• Short Answer (SA) Type Questions

1. The biosphere and its components are very significant elements of the environment. Discuss.

Ans. The biosphere includes all the living components of the earth and their interaction with surrounding environment as they are very significant elements of the environment as these component are responsible for the smooth functioning of the environment.

The components of biosphere i.e. plants and animals interact with other components of natural landscape such as land, water and soil. These components are also influenced by the atmospheric elements such as temperature, rainfall, moisture and sunlight. The interaction of biosphere with land, air and water are important for the growth, development and evolution of the organism.

2. Establish the relationship among producers, consumers and decomposers.

Ans. The producers, consumers and decomposers are interlinked with each other. In an ecosystem, the producers produce food by using solar energy and nutrients through the process of photosynthesis. The food produced by producers is consumed by consumers. The consumers may have different level i.e. herbivorous, carnivores, etc. The herbivorous eat carnivores and some carnivores eat other carnivores. As the consumers die, their dead remains are decomposed by bacterial activities. The decomposition involves breaking down of wastes and dead remains by which the chemical elements are released in the biosphere. This is the relationship among producers, consumers and decomposers.

3. What do you mean by photosynthesis? Why is it important in ecosystem?

Ans. Photosynthesis is a complex process occurring within the cells of green plants where sunlight is utilised in combination with carbon dioxide and water to produce oxygen and simple sugar.

The importance of photosynthesis is

- The life in the biosphere is initiated through the process of photosynthesis using sunlight.
- Through the process of photosynthesis, chemical compounds are turned into food. Carbon dioxide is fixed by plants by photosynthesis.
- The transfer of energy starts at the level of primary producers, which produce food by photosynthesis. Thus, it is the first step of food chain.
- It helps in maintaining flow of energy, nutrients and water.

4. Differentiate between habitat and ecosystem.

Ans. The differences between habitat and ecosystem are

Habitat	Ecosystem
Totality of physical and chemical factors that constitute the general environment is known as habitat.	A broad system comprising biotic and abiotic components is known as ecosystem.
It is easy to understand and recognise different component of habitat.	It is complex in nature.
It is a part of ecosystem which offers favourable conditions for life to survive.	Ecosystem is a wider concept than habitat.

5. Explain tropical biome in detail.

Ans. The tropical biome is sub type of forest biome. The main features of forest tropical biomes are

- The tropical forest biome are of two types i.e. equatorial and deciduous forests.
- The equatorial forests are found between $10°$ N and $10°$ S latitudes, whereas the deciduous forests are found between $10°$ - $25°$ N and S latitudes.
- The temperature and rainfall are high throughout the year.
- The rainfall is evenly distributed in equatorial forests, whereas in deciduous forests rainfall is confined to rainy season only.
- The soil of tropical forests are biome is acidic in nature. Whereas, the soils of deciduous forests are rich in nutrients.

6. Write down the difference between hot desert and cold deserts

Ans. The differences between hot deserts and cold deserts are

Hot Deserts	Cold Deserts
In hot deserts the temperature ranges between $20°$ C and $45°$ C.	In cold deserts the temperature ranges between $2°$ C and $25°$ C.
Temperature extremes are highest in hot deserts.	The temperature extremes are high in cold deserts but less than hot deserts.
Main regions of hot deserts are Sahara, Kalahari, etc.	Main regions of cold deserts are Greenland, Antarctica, etc.

7. Give differences between tropical and temperate grasslands.

Ans. The major differences between tropical and temperate grasslands are

Tropical Grasslands	Temperate Grasslands
These are found in warm, hot climates. They have rainfall between 50 and 125 cms.	They are found in warm temperate climate with warm summers and cool winters. The rainfall ranges between 50 to 90 cm.
The tropical grasslands are found in large areas of Africa, Australia, South America and India.	The temperate grasslands are found in Eurasia and parts of North America.
Trees are absent and tall grasses are found. Big animals are found here.	Short grasses are found. Big animals are generally absent in temperate grasslands.

8. What are the factors which disturb the ecological balance? Explain.

Ans. The factors which distrubs the ecological balance are

- Ecological balance may be disturbed due to the introduction of new species, natural hazards or human causes.
- The balance of plant communities has been greatly affected by human interference which has led to disturbances in the ecosystems.
- The earth's resources are under immense pressure from rising human demands. It is threatening for the ecosystem.
- Many natural calamities like floods, landslides, diseases, erratic climatic occurrences are happening because of ecological imbalances only.

9. What are the consequences of ecological imbalance?

Ans. The ecological imbalance is very harmful for survival of living beings in the long run. The main consequences of ecological imbalance are

- The ecological imbalance may increase or reduce diversity of life and associations to such an extent that it is not possible to maintain balance within biotic factors and between biotic and abiotic factors.
- As the flow of energy, nutrients and water is disturbed, it may result into either excess or scarcity of these elements. Their excess turns toxic, whereas their scarcity results in poor growth of plants and animals.
- The ecological balance may result into species selection as only better adopted species survive in ecological imbalances. It results into loss of genetic and species diversity in the ecosystem. It has resulted into secondary successions.
- Intensity and frequency of natural calamities like floods, landslides, etc have increased.

10. How other minerals besides carbon, oxygen, nitrogen and hydrogen, move in the ecosystem? Explain.

Ans. Other minerals are obtained from inorganic sources like phosphorus, sulphur, calcium and potassium.

These minerals move into ecosystem by either of the following ways

- By dissolving in the water through water cycle.
- By weathering of rocks i.e. sedimentation.

They usually occur as salts dissolved in soil water or lakes, streams and seas. The salts dissolved in water are reached directly to plants and animals, whereas the salts sedimented in rocks are taken up by plants. These minerals return back by decomposition of wastes or dead remains.

11. Plants are the most valuable items for the human being on this planet as they give oxygen for the respiration and breathing. Elucidate the statement.

Ans. Plants are the most valuable item on this planet for human beings and without plants, it is difficult to imagine life on the planet earth. Oxygen is the main by-product of photosysthesis and it is released in the atmosphere through transpiration and respiration processes of plants. Therefore, oxygen released by plants is the main component which is used by the human beings. Besides oxygen, there are many other life giving things which are provided by plants to human beings such as food, energy and wood for shelter.

• Long Answer (LA) Type Questions

1. "Organisms of an ecosystem are linked together through a food chain." Give your arguments to justify this statement.

Ans. Food chain is the sequence of eating and being eaten and the resultant transfer of energy from one level to another. In the food chain, all the organisms are interlinked together through nutrient cycle and energy flow.

The organisms includes producers, consumers and the decomposers.

Producers develop their own food through photosynthesis. Producers are consumed by the primary consumers. Primary consumers are then in turn being eaten by the secondary consumers. Secondary consumers are consumed by tertiary consumers. Finally, decomposers feed on the dead at each and every level. They change them into various substances such as nutrients, organic and inorganic salts essential for soil fertility.

All organisms are mutually linked together such as a plant eating beetle feeding on a paddy stalk is eaten by frog which is in turn, eaten by snake, which is then consumed by a hawk. Therefore, organisms of an ecosystem are linked together through a food chain.

2. Give a detailed account of world distribution of biomes.

Ans. A large community of plant and animals covering a large geographical area is known as biome.

The account of world distribution of biomes is

- **Forest Biomes** The forest biomes are broadly classified as tropical, temperate and boreal. The tropical forests are found in tropical areas having high temperature and heavy rainfall in the form of equatorial and deciduous forests. Temperate forests are found in temperate zones whereas the boreal forests are found in taiga vegetation belts.

- **Desert Biomes** These are broadly divided into hot deserts and cold deserts. The hot deserts are further divided into arid and semi-arid zones. The range of temperature is always high, whereas the precipitation is less. Mainly xerophyte vegetation is found in desert biomes.

- **Grassland Biomes** These are divided into tropical grasslands and temperate grasslands. These grasslands are practically treeless. The tropical grasslands are famous for its diverse animal population, whereas the temperate grasslands have been cleared for intensive wheat cultivation.

- **Aquatic Biomes** These biomes are divided into fresh water and marine biomes.

- **Altitudinal Biomes** These are found on the slopes of high mountains like Himalayas, Alps, Andes, etc.

3. What do you understand by altitudinal biomes? How is it different from tundra biomes?

Ans. The biomes found on slope of high mountain ranges like the Himalayas, the Andes and the Rockies are known as altitudinal biomes. Here the altitude is the main determining factor, therefore, these are known as altitudinal biomes.

In the altitudinal biomes, the temperature and precipitation vary according to latitude of the region. The precipitation occurs in the form of both rainfall and snowfall. The soil is not perfectly built here. The soil is found in the form of regolith over slopes. The vegetation varies from deciduous forests to Tundra vegetation according to altitude.

Differences between altitudinal biomes and tundra biomes are

Altitudinal Biomes	Tundra Biomes
In altitudinal vegetation, the frozen conditions are found only in winter months or above snowline. The climate depends upon altitude as well as latitude.	The tundra biomes are essentially found in frozen climates. Even in the warmest month, the temperature remains below 0° C.

Altitudinal Biomes	Tundra Biomes
In altitudinal vegetations, the precipitation may be as high as 200cm. The precipitation includes both snowfall and rainfall.	In tundra biomes, the precipitation is below 50 cm and occurs in the form of snowfall.
In altitudinal biomes, vegetation varies from deciduous to alpine vegetation.	In tundra, the vegetation consists of lichens, mosses, etc.

4. Describe in brief the carbon cycle and its characteristics.

Ans. Carbon is one of the important basic elements of all living organisms which forms the basic constituent of all the organic compounds. The biosphere contains more than half a million carbon compounds in them.

Some of the important features of carbon cycle are

- In a carbon cycle, mainly the conversion of carbon dioxide takes place.

- It starts through the process of photosynthesis, which fixes the carbon dioxide from the atmosphere.

- This conversion results into production of carbohydrates, glucose, etc. These products are further converted into organic compounds like sucrose, starch or cellulose. Some of the carbohydrates are directly consumed by the plants.

- During the process of photosynthesis in the day time more carbon dioxide is generated and released through its leaves and roots. However, remaining carbohydrates which are not used by the plants become part of plant tissue.

These plant tissues are either being eaten by herbivorous or get decomposed by micro-organisms. Some of the consumed carbohydrates are converted into carbon dioxide by herbivorous. It is released in the atmosphere through respiration. The remaining carbohydrates are decomposed by micro-organisms after the animal dies. It then gets oxidised into carbon dioxide to return back into atmosphere.

5. Discuss the main features of Nitrogen cycle.

Ans. Main features of nitrogen cycle are

- Nitrogen can be used only when it is fixed. In the environment, out of the total nitrogen found, 90% of fixed nitrogen is biological.

- The principal source of free nitrogen is the action of soil micro-organism and associated plant roots on atmospheric nitrogen found in pore spaces of the soil.

- It can also be fixed by lightening and cosmic radiation in the atmosphere. It is also fixed by marine organisms in the oceans.

- Once free nitrogen has been fixed into an available form it is assimilated by green plants. Herbivorous consume this nitrogen by eating plants.

- Soil bacteria converts nitrogenous wastes of excreta and of dead plants and animals remain into nitrites. This nitrite is then converted into nitrates by some bacteria. These nitrates are then again used by green plants. Some bacteria then convert these nitrates into free nitrogen. This process is known as denitrification.

6. What is an ecological balance? Discuss the important measures needed to prevent ecological imbalances.

Ans. A state of dynamic equilibrium within a community or organisms in a habitat or ecosystem is known as ecological balance. It is also referred to as a stable balance in the numbers of each species in an ecosystem.

Some of the important measures needed to prevent the ecological imbalances are

- The human interference in the ecologically sensitive areas should be minimised.
- Construction, mining and other activities should not be allowed in the ecologically sensitive areas.
- Proper measures should be adopted to minimise the impact of natural calamities on ecology and forest.
- Measures like afforestation, rain water harvesting, protection of flora and fauna, in-situ should be encouraged.
- Introduction of new species in native forest should be avoided as maximum as possible. If introduced already then native species should be given due care and protection.
- More areas should be brought under the umbrella of biosphere reserves. Ecologically sensitive areas must be protected with the help of people.

7. "There are the human activities which are maximum responsible for ecological disturbance." Highlight such human activities and also suggest some measures to prevent the ecological disturbance.

Ans. Some of the major human activities which are harmful for ecological balance are

- **Clearing of Forest** Deforestation for jhoom cultivation, urbanisation, agriculture, industrialisation, etc have reduced the ecological sustainable forest cover. It has disturbed the natural cycle of nutrient water and energy.
- **Construction of Big Dams** The construction of big dams for the purpose of building multi-purpose river valley projects have submerged thousands of acres of forest under river water. This have disturbed the ecology of surrounding areas.
- **Mining Activities** This results into large scale deforestation of ecological disturbance mostly in the hilly and plateau areas. The loss of shelter for large number of species of animal has brought about serious danger for ecological balance.

- **Suggestions to prevent Ecological Disturbance** There is need for strict regulation of mining and construction activities to protect the ecology and environment. Cutting of forest for materialistic pleasure should be demotivated. There should be proper conservation or preservation for native and endangered species to make the ecology sustainable.

• Case Based Questions

1. Read the case/source given and answer the following questions.

The living organisms of the earth, constituting the biosphere, interact with other environmental realms. The biosphere includes all the living components of the earth. It consists of all plants and animals, including all the micro-organisms that live on the planet earth and their interactions with the surrounding environment. Most of the organisms exist on the lithosphere and/or the hydrosphere as well as in the atmosphere. There are also many organisms that move freely from one realm to the other. The biosphere and its components are very significant elements of the environment. These elements interact with other components of the natural landscape such as land, water and soil. They are also influenced by the atmospheric elements such as the temperature, rainfall, moisture and sunlight. The interactions of biosphere with land, air and water are important to the growth, development and evolution of the organism.

Life on the earth is found almost everywhere. Living organisms are found from the poles to the equator, from them bottom of the sea to several km in the air, from freezing waters to dry valleys, from under the sea to underground water lying below the earth's surface.

(i) Define Biosphere.

Ans. The biosphere is the narrow zone where we find land, water and air together, which contains all forms of life.

(ii) Define ecological systems.

Ans. The interactions of a particular group of organisms with abiotic factors within a particular habitat resulting in clearly defined energy flows and material cycles on land, water and air are called ecological systems.

(iii) What do you mean by ecology?

Ans. The term ecology is derived from the Greek word 'oikos' meaning 'house', combined with the word 'logy' meaning the 'science of' or 'the study of'. Literally, ecology is the study of the earth as a 'household', of plants, human beings, animals and micro-organisms. They all live together as interdependent components.

2. Read the case/source given and answer the following questions.

The sun is the basic source of energy on which all life depends. This energy initiates life processes in the biosphere through photosynthesis, the main source of food and energy for green plants.

During photosynthesis, carbon dioxide is converted into organic compounds and oxygen. Out of the total solar insolation that reaches the earth's surface, only a very small fraction (0.1 per cent) is fixed in photosynthesis. More than half is used for plant respiration and the remaining part is temporarily stored or is shifted to other portions of the plant.

Life on earth consists of a great variety of living organisms. These living organisms exist and survive in a diversity of associations. Such survival involves the presence of systemic flows such as flows of energy, water and nutrients.

(i) What is biome? What are the five major biomes?

Ans. Biome refers to the community of plants and animals that occur naturally in an area, often sharing common characteristics specific to that area. The five major biomes are forest, desert, grassland, aquatic and altitudinal biomes.

(ii) What do you mean by biogeochemical cycle?

Ans. The cyclic movements of chemical elements of biosphere between living organisms and their environment are known as biogeochemical cycles. 'Bio' refers to living organisms and 'geo' to rocks, soil, air and water of the earth.

(iii) What are the two different types of biogeochemical cycles?

Ans. Two types of biogeochemical cycles are the gaseous and the sedimentary cycle. In the gaseous cycle, the main reservoir of nutrients is the atmosphere and the ocean. In the sedimentary cycle, the main reservoir is the soil and sedimentary and other rocks of earth's crust.

Chapter Test

Objective Questions

1. Which of the following elements of atmosphere influences the components of biosphere?
  (a) Temperature   (b) Rainfall
  (c) Moisture   (d) All of these

2. The ecosystem is broadly classified into which types?
  (a) Terrestrial ecosystem   (b) Aquatic ecosystem
  (c) Coral reefs   (d) Both (a) and (b)

3. The transfer of energy from one level of foodchain to another is known as
  (a) Food web   (b) Food net
  (c) Flow of energy   (d) None of these

4. The inter connecting network of species is known as ....
  (a) Food web   (b) Food network
  (c) Food chain   (d) Flow of energy

5. Marine ecosystem comprises of which of the following?
  I. Oceans   II. Estuaries   III. Coral reefs
  Codes
  (a) Only I   (b) I and II
  (c) I and III   (d) All of these

Short Answer Type Questions

6. How are life processes initiated on the earth?

7. How is balance of chemical elements maintained? Explain.

8. How do climatic factors determine boundaries of biome? Explain with the help of examples.

9. List down the factors influencing the terrestrial ecosystems.

10. Give a scientific definition of ecology. Also explain first order and second order consumers.

Long Answer Type Questions

11. How is ecological balance maintained? Explain with the help of examples.

12. Give a detailed account of vegetation found in each of these biomes.

Answers

1. (d) All of these   **2.** (d) Both (a) and (b)   **3.** (c) Flow of energy
4. (c) Food chain   **5.** (d) All of these

CHAPTER 07

Biodiversity and Conservation

In this Chapter...

- Biodiversity
- Loss of Biodiversity
- Conservation of Biodiversity

The term biodiversity refers to biological diversity. The biodiversity is our living wealth, as it is a result of hundreds of millions of years of evolutionary history of life on our planet.

Weathering mantle is the basis for the diversity of vegetation and hence, the biodiversity. The basic cause for such weathering variations and resultant biodiversity is the input of solar energy and water. It is common that the areas that are rich in these inputs are the areas of wide spectrum of biodiversity.

Biodiversity

The word biodiversity is comprised of two words i.e., *Bio* (life) and *diversity* (variety). In simple terms, biodiversity refers to number and variety of organisms found in a given geographical region. The varieties of plants, animals, micro-organisms, their **genes**[1] and their ecosystem are all parts of biodiversity. Therefore, biodiversity relates to the variability among living organisms on the earth, including the variability within and between the species and the ecosystems.

Characteristics of Biodiversity

- Today's biodiversity is the result of continuous process of evolution over 2.5 to 3.5 billions of years.
- The earth had more biodiversity before the existence of human beings. However, later biodiversity began to decline with one species after another due to overuse by human beings.
- The number of species globally varies from 2 to 100 millions, with 10 million being the best estimate. However, tropical forests are very rich in biodiversity.

- The average half life of a species is between one and four million years and 99% of the species that have ever lived on the earth, are now **extinct**[2].
- Studies have shown that more than 40% of freshwater fishes from South America are not classified yet. Besides, new species are regularly discovered.
- The biodiversity is not evenly distributed on the earth. Biodiversity is richer in the tropics. It decreases from the equator towards the poles. In the Polar regions, larger populations of fewer species are found.

Levels of Biodiversity

Broadly, the biodiversity can be discussed at three levels

(i) Genetic Diversity

It refers to the variation of genes within species, as genes are the basic building blocks of various life forms. A species is a group of individual organisms which have certain similarities in their physical features. The human beings belong, genetically to the *Homo sapiens* group. Within this group, the differences are found in respect of height, colour, physical appearance etc. It happens due to genetic diversity. It is essential for healthy breeding of population of a species.

(ii) Species Diversity

It refers to variety as well as number of species in a given area. The species diversity is measured through its richness, abundance and types. There are some regions which have more species diversity than others.

---

1 **Gene** Basic physical and functional unit of heredity is known as gene. It is made up of DNA.
2 **Extinct** The species is declared as extinct when there is no chance of its appearance again.

These areas which are rich in species biodiversity are known as **hotspots of diversity** in the world.

(iii) Ecosystem Diversity

The ecosystem diversity is constituted within the broad differences between ecosystem types and the diversity of habitats and also ecological processes. The boundaries of communities (associations of species) and ecosystems are not clearly defined. Therefore, the demarcation of ecosystem boundaries is difficult and complex.

Importance of Biodiversity

Biodiversity involves in many ways to develop human culture, in return humans play significant role in shaping the diversity of nature at the genetic, species and ecological levels. Therefore, biodiversity and human influence each other. Biodiversity plays three important roles within its defined boundaries, these include ecological, economic and scientific.

Ecological Role of Biodiversity

In an ecosystem, species of many kinds perform some functions or the other. Nothing in an ecosystem evolves and sustains without any reason. It means every organism, besides extracting its needs, also contributes something of useful to other organisms.

The functions of species within an ecosystem plays a significant role for ecosystem function and human survival. The functions of species are

- They capture and store energy.
- They produce and decompose organic materials.
- They help to cycle water and nutrients throughout the ecosystem.
- They fix atmospheric gases.
- They help in regulation of climates.

The diverse ecosystem is a more productive ecosystem because it makes chances for the species to survive through adversities and attacks higher. Any loss of species decreases the ability of the system to maintain itself. Just like an ecosystem with high biodiversity, always has greater chances to adapt to environmental changes as in the case of a species having high genetic diversity. More the variety of species an ecosystem has, more stable it is likely to be.

Economic Role of Biodiversity

Biodiversity plays a significant role in the promotion of economic benefits. Biodiversity itself is an important resource for human beings in their day to day life. **Crop-diversity** also known as **agro-biodiversity**[3] is an important part of biodiversity.

Biodiversity as a reservoir of resources used for manufacturing of food, medicines and cosmetic products.

The above concept of biological resources is responsible for the deterioration of biodiversity. At the same time, it is also the origin of new conflicts dealing with rules of division and appropriation of natural resources. Some of the important economic commodities that biodiversity supplies to human beings are, foodcrops, livestock, forestry, fish, medicinal resources, etc.

Scientific Role of Biodiversity

Biodiversity is important as every species provides a clue as to how life has evolved in the past and will evolve in the future, therefore biodiversity is important. The biodiversity also helps us in understanding how life functions.

It is our ethical responsibility to consider that each and every species has the right to exist. Hence, it is morally wrong to voluntarily cause the extinction of any species. The level of biodiversity is a good indicator of the state of our relationship with other living species. In fact, the concept of biodiversity is an integral part of many human cultures.

Loss of Biodiversity

The rate of consumption of natural resources has been increased in last few decades because of growth in human population. The population increase has resulted in accelerated rate of loss of species and their habitats across the world. About three-fourth of human population lives in tropical areas which is just one-fourth area of the world. It has led to exploitation of resources and **deforestation**[4] in these areas in order to fulfill the demands and needs of human beings.

Apart from this, biodiversity loss is heavily caused by

- About 50% of total species are found in **tropical rainforests**[5] alone, the destruction of their natural **habitat**[6] is harmful for entire biosphere.
- The biodiversity of a given area changes considerably because of natural calamities like earthquakes, floods, volcanic eruptions, forest fires, droughts, etc. These are the causes which damage **flora and fauna**[7] of the earth.
- The weak and senstive species are further get destroyed by excessive use of pesticides and pollutants like hydrocarbons and heavy toxic metals.

---

3 **Agro-biodiversity** It is the diversity of crops and their wild relatives, trees, animals, microbes and other species that contribute to agricultural production.

4 **Deforestation** Clearing of forest for land or for the purpose of timber is known as deforestation.

5 **Tropical Rainforest** Forest found in the tropical areas having high temperature and more than 200 cm rainfall.

6 **Habitat** Location where a plant or animal lives.

7 **Flora and Fauna** The plant and animal species found in any regions is known as flora and fauna of that region, respectively.

- Exotic species are those species which are introduced in an ecosystem from outside and are not native to that ecosystem. The introduction of exotic species brings extensive damage to a natural biotic community.
- Some animals have been rendered into endangered category in last few years because of their merciless hunting by poachers for their horn, tusks, hides, etc. These animals are tigers, elephants, rhinoceros, crocodiles, minks, birds etc.

Classification of Threatened Species

The classification of threatened species of plants and animals is done by the International Union of Conservation of Nature and Natural Resources (IUCN). These animals are categorised into following three categories for the purpose of their conservation

(i) **Endangered Species** Those species which are in danger of extinction are included in this list. Information about these species is published world wide by IUCN in Red List of threatened species. For example, Red Panda.

(ii) **Vulnerable Species** Those species which are likely to be in danger of extinction in near future are included in this list, if the threatening factors continue. The population of these species have reduced considerably and therefore, their survival is not assured.

(iii) **Rare Species** These species have very small population in the world which is either confined to a limited area or thinly scattered over a large area. For example, humbodtia decurrens Bedd, a highly-rare endemic tree of Southern Western Ghats.

Conservation of Biodiversity

Life-forms are so closely related to each other that disturbance in one creates disturbance in other. Therefore, biodiversity is essential for human existence. It happens because if any species existence is in danger, it degrades the environment which ultimately threatens existence of human beings. To conserve the biodiversity following steps need to be taken

- Educate people about environment friendly activities is a need of hour.
- There is a need to reorient our activities in such a way that development process is sustainable and is harmonious with other life-forms.
- It is increasingly being realised that conservation and sustainable use of resources can be carried out only with the help of local communities and individuals. To make this happen, institutional structures should be developed at local level.
- The continuation of process of conservation is more important along with conservation of species and their habitat.

Earth Summit

The convention of Biodiversity was signed at the Earth Summit held at **Rio de Janeiro, Brazil** in June 1992. It was signed by 155 countries including India.

Following steps have been suggested by world conservation strategy for biodiversity conservation.

- Efforts should be made to preserve the species that are endangered.
- Prevention of extinction requires proper planning and management.
- Varities of food crops, forage plants, timber trees, livestock, animals and their wild relatives should be preserved.
- Each country should identify habitats of wild relatives and ensure their protection.
- Habitats where species, breed, rest and nurse their young ones should be safeguarded and protected.
- International trade in wild plants and animals be regulated.

Wildlife Protection Act, 1972

Government of India passed the Wildlife Protection Act, 1972 to protect, preserve and propagate the variety of species within natural boundaries. To achieve these objectives, national parks and wildlife sanctuaries were established. Certain areas were declared as **biosphere reserves**.

Mega Diversity Centres

Countries located in tropical areas possess a large number of world's species diversity. These regions are referred to as Mega Diversity Centres.

There are 12 such countries in number where these centres are located. They are Mexico, China, Columbia, India, Ecuador, Malaysia, Peru, Indonesia, Brazil, Australia, Democratic and Republic of Congo and Madagascar.

Hotspots

The International Union for the Conservation of Nature and Natural Resources (IUCN) has identified **biodiversity hotspots**[8] in order to concentrate resources on most vulnerable areas. Hotspots have been identified on the basis of dominant vegetation. The vegetation is important in these hotspots because it determines the primary productivity of an ecosystem.

However, most of these hotspots, rely on species rich ecosystems for forests produces like food, firewood, cropland, timber etc. 85% of plants and animal species found in the Madagascar are native to that region. These species are not found anywhere else in the world.

The hotspots of rich and wealthy countries are facing other threats. For example, Hawaii islands which have unique plants and animals are threatened by introduction of new species and land development.

---

8 Biodiversity Hotspots These are areas that support natural ecosystems that are largely intact and where native species and communities associated with these communities are well represented. They are also areas with a high diversity of locally endemic species.

Chapter Practice

Objective Questions

• Multiple Choice Questions

1. Which of the following regions is very rich in biodiversity?
(a) Temperate region   (b) Polar region
(c) Tropical region   (d) Steppe region

Ans. (c) Tropical region is very rich in biodiversity. About 50% of total species are found in tropical rainforests alone.

2. Biodiversity relates to the variability among?
(a) Non-Living Organisms   (b) Living Organisms
(c) Both (a) and (b)   (d) None of these

Ans. (b) Biodiversity relates to the variability among living organisms on the earth, including the variability within and between the species and the ecosystem.

3. Around 40% of freshwater fishes of which region have not been classified yet?
(a) North America   (b) South America
(c) Europe   (d) Asia

Ans. (b) Studies have shown that more than 40% of freshwater fishes from South America have not been classified yet. Besides, new species are regularly discovered.

4. The biodiversity is divided into how many levels?
(a) 2   (b) 3
(c) 4   (d) 5

Ans. (b) Biodiversity is divided into three levels, which are Genetic Diversity, Species Diversity and Ecosystem Diversity.

5. The ecological hotspot found in the South America is
(a) Queensland
(b) Central American lowland forest
(c) Western Ecuador and Colombian Congo
(d) Northern Borneo.

Ans. (c) Western Ecuador and Colombian Congo are the as ecological hotspots of the South America.

6. Which of the following diversities refers to variety as well as number of species in a given area?
(a) Genetic diversity
(b) Species diversity
(c) Ecosystem diversity
(d) None of the above

Ans. (b) Species diversity refers to variety as well as number of species in a given area. The species diversity is measured through its richness, abundance and types.

7. In which year, the convention of Biodiversity was signed at the Earth summit held at Rio de Janeiro, Brazil?
(a) 1940   (b) 1948
(c) 1960   (d) 1992

Ans. (d) The convention of Biodiversity was signed in the year 1992 at the Earth summit held at Rio de Janeiro, Brazil.

8. Which of the following pairs are correctly matched?
(a) Habitat - Location where a plant or animal lives.
(b) Biodiversity Hotspots- Areas that support natural ecosystems that are largely intact.
(c) IUCN- The International Union for the Conservation of Nature and Natural Resources
(d) All of the above

Ans. (d) All the given pairs correctly matched.

9. Match the following.

List I (Classification of Threatened Species)		List II (Meaning)
A.	Endangered species	1.	Species which are in danger of extinction
B.	Vulnerable species	2.	Species which are likely to be in danger of extinction in near future.
C.	Rare species	3.	Species which have very low population.

Codes

	A	B	C			A	B	C
(a)	1	2	3	(b)		2	3	1
(c)	3	1	2	(d)		1	3	3

Ans. (a)

10. Match the following

	List I		List II
A.	Biodiversity	1.	Basic physical and functional unit of heredity.
B.	Gene	2.	The number and variety of organisms found within a specified geographic region.
C.	Species	3.	Groups of individuals organisms having certain similarities in their physical characteristics.
D.	Extinct	4.	The diversity of crops and their wild relatives, trees, animals, microbes and other species that contribute to agricultural production.
E.	Agro-biodivers ity	5.	The species is declared as extinct when there is no chance of its appearance again.
F.	Deforestation	6.	Clearing of forest for land or for the purpose of timber.

Codes

	A	B	C	D	E	F
(a)	1	2	3	4	5	6
(b)	2	1	3	5	4	6
(c)	3	4	5	6	2	1
(d)	5	4	6	3	2	1

Ans. (b)

11. Which of the following statements is/ are incorrect about Wildlife Protection Act?

I. Government of India passed the Wildlife Protection Act in 1972

II. To achieve these objectives, national parks and wildlife sanctuaries were established

III. Certain areas were declared as biosphere reserves.

Codes

(a) Only I   (b) Only III

(c) Only I and III   (d) None of these

Ans. (b) Statement III is incorrect as Biosphere Reserves are established by the provisions of the Wildlife Protection Act, 1972. All the other statements are correct.

12. Which of the following statements is/ are incorrect about the importance of Biodiversity?

I. Biodiversity involves in many ways to develop human culture.

II. Biodiversity and human influence each other.

III. Biodiversity plays four important roles within its defined boundaries.

Codes

(a) Only I   (b) Only III

(c) Only I and III   (d) Only II and III

Ans. (b) Statement III is incorrect as biodiversity plays three important roles within its defined boundaries, these include ecological, economic and scientific.

• Case Based MCQs

13. Read the case/source given and answer the questions that follow by choosing the correct option.

Biodiversity is important because each species can give us some clue as to how life evolved and will continue to evolve. Biodiversity also helps in understanding how life functions and the role of each species in sustaining ecosystems of which we are also a species. This fact must be drawn upon every one of us so that we live and let other species also live their lives. It is our ethical responsibility to consider that each and every species along with us have an intrinsic right to exist. Hence, it is morally wrong to voluntarily cause the extinction of any species. The level of biodiversity is a good indicator of the state of our relationships with other living species. In fact, the concept of biodiversity is an integral part of many human cultures.

Since the last few decades, growth in human population has increased the rate of consumption of natural resources. It has accelerated the loss of species and habitation in different parts of the world. Tropical regions which occupy only about one-fourth of the total area of the world, contain about three-fourth of the world human population. Overexploitation of resources and deforestation have become rampant to fulfil the needs of large population. As these tropical rainforests contain 50 per cent of the species on the earth, destruction of natural habitats have proved disastrous for the entire biosphere. Natural calamities such as earthquakes, floods, volcanic eruptions, forest fires, droughts, etc. cause damage to the flora and fauna of the earth, bringing change the biodiversity of respective affected regions. Pesticides and other pollutants such as hydrocarbons and toxic heavy metals destroy the weak and sensitive species.

Species which are not the natural inhabitants of the local habitat but are introduced into the system, are called exotic species. There are many examples when a natural biotic community of the ecosystem suffered extensive damage because of the introduction of exotic species. During the last few decades, some animals like tigers, elephants, rhinoceros, crocodiles, minks and birds were hunted mercilessly by poachers for their horn, tusks, hides, etc. It has resulted in the rendering of certain types of organisms as endangered category.

(i) Which of the following is the most important factor that has led to decline in biodiversity?
(a) Earthquakes   (b) Rising population
(c) Agriculture
(d) Mining and quarrying

Ans. (b) Rising population is the most important factor that has led to the decline in biodiversity. The population increase has resulted in accelerated rate of loss of species and their habitats across the world.

(ii) Which of the following species is originally not a part of an ecosystem and are introduced from the outside?

(a) Vulnerable species
(b) Endangered species
(c) Exotic species
(d) Near threatened species

Ans. (c) Exotic species are originally not a part of an ecosystem and are introduced from the outside.

(iii) Which of the following biome has the highest biodiversity?
(a) Deserts   (b) Coastal region
(c) Rain forests   (d) Oceans

Ans. (c) Rain forests has the highest biodiversity.

(iv) Which of the following are the natural causes of declining biodiversity?
(a) Chlorofluoro carbons   (b) Pesticides
(c) Droughts
(d) Deforestation

Ans. (c) Among the given options, droughts are the only natural cause of declining biodiversity.

14. Study the map and answer the questions that follow by choosing the correct option.

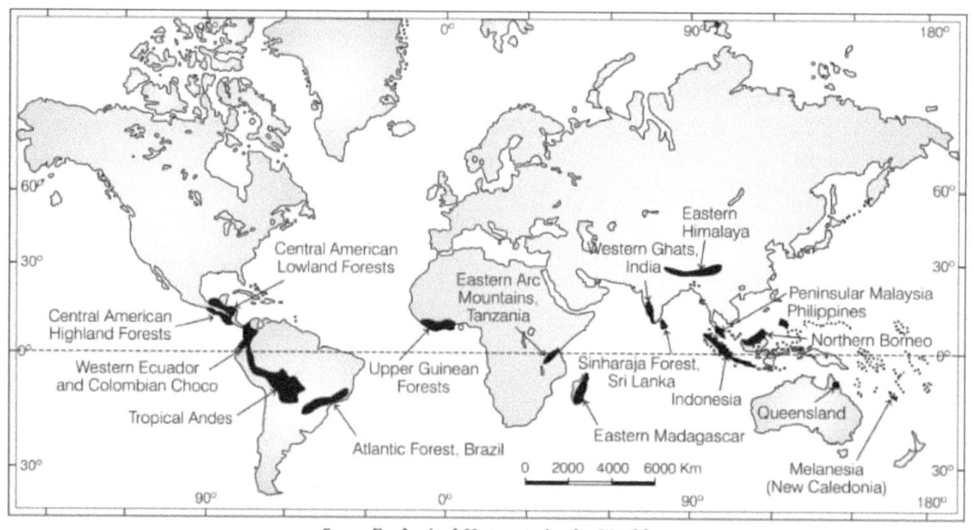

Some Ecological Hotspots in the World

(i) Ecological hotspot from Southern hemisphere is
(a) Eastern Himalayas   (b) Peninsular Malayasia
(c) Lowland forest   (d) Queensland

Ans. (d) Ecological hotspot from Southern hemisphere is Queensland.

(ii) Equator cut the hotspot of
(a) Northern Borneo
(b) Sinharaja Forest
(c) Eastern Ghat
(d) Peninsular Malaysia

Ans. (a) The equator cut the hotspot of Northern Borneo.

(iii) World's most diverse hotspot is
(a) Tropical Andes
(b) Sinharaja Forest
(c) Eastern Ghat
(d) Peninsular Malaysia

Ans. (a) The most diverse Hotspot of world is Tropical Andes.

(iv) How many Hotspots are there in India?
(a) 2   (b) 4
(c) 8   (d) 10

Ans. (b) There are 4 hotspots in India.

Subjective Questions

• Short Answer (SA) Type Questions

1. What do you mean by diversity? What are its types? Why diversity is important?

Ans. The physical or biological complexity of a system is known as diversity.

There are three main types of diversity.

(i) **Genetic Diversity** Diversity of genes within a species.

(ii) **Species Diversity** Diversity of species within an ecosystem.

(iii) **Ecosystem Diversity** Diversity of ecosystem within the biosphere.

The importance of diversity is

- The diversity of life forms is essential to maintain balance in the ecosystem.
- The diversity of species is essential for survival of life forms.
- Diversity of associations smoothens flow of energy, water and nutrients.

2. What does ecosystem diversity and species diversity refer to?

Ans. Ecosystem diversity refers to broad differences between ecosystem types and variety of habitats and Ecological processes occurring within each ecosystem type.

The demarcation of ecosystem boundaries is a very difficult and complex process, as the boundaries of communities and the ecosystem are not clearly defined.

Species diversity refers to variety as well as number of species in a given area. The species diversity is measured through its richness, abundance and types. There are some regions which have more species diversity than others. These areas which are rich in species biodiversity are known as hotspots of diversity in the world.

3. Why is biodiversity so important for an ecosystem? Explain.

Ans. Biodiversity is very important for an ecosystem. Following features establish importance of an ecosystem

- Various functions performed by various species are essential for functioning of ecosystem. These functions include capture of energy, cycling of nutrients, fixing up gases etc.
- If the amount of diversity in an ecosystem is greater there will be more the productive ecosystem.
- With more biodiversity, species ability to survive through adversities and attacks also increase.
- With greater diversity, ecosystem has greater chances of adaptation with environment.
- Biodiversity provides stability to the ecosystem.

4. Explain ecological role of biodiversity.

Ans. Biodiversity plays a very significant role in the ecosystem.

Some of the important ecological roles played by the biodiversity are

- Species capture and store energy which is a part of flow of energy in the ecosystem.
- In an ecosystem, the organic materials are produced and decomposed by various species.
- Various species help in cycling of nutrients and water in the ecosystem.
- Species fix up atmospheric gases which are used in the food chain.
- Species also help in regulation of climate.

5. "Concept of biodiversity is the integral part of many human cultures." Justify the statement.

Ans. The concept of biodiversity is the integral part of many human cultures as biodiversity has contributed in many ways to the development of human culture and biodiversity of any region determines the cultural activities prevailing in the region. For example, the culture of Meghalaya is totally different from the culture of Rajasthan mainly because of the variations in biodiversity.

Human being is highly associated with the nature and the biological diversity for their surrounding. The level of biodiversity is a good indicator of the state of human relationships with other living species. Custom, tradition, way of worship, clothing and living patterns are also determined by biodiversity of the region.

6. "Economic importance of biodiversity is responsible for its deterioration". Discuss.

Ans. Biodiversity is seen as a reservoir of resources to be drawn upon for the manufacture of food, pharmaceutical and cosmetic products.

Biodiversity supplies various commodities for the day to day life use for all humans such as food crops, livestock, forest, fish, medicinal resources etc.

To obtain these resources as much as it is available, human beings are exploiting nature more than its ecological footprint.

Mass level of deforestation, mining, illegal trafficking of plants and animals results into the deterioration of biodiversity.

7. What is the scientific role of biodiversity? Explain.

Ans. The importance or scientific role of biodiversity is

- In biodiversity, each species provides insight about how life has evolved in the history and how life will evolve in the future.
- It also gives us an understanding about how life functions.
- It explains about the role of each species in sustaining ecosystem.
- It gives us an idea about what is the place and the role of human beings in the ecosystem.
- It gives us a responsibility to ensure existence of other species also and to live in harmony with other species.

8. Why are tropical forests so important with the point of view of biodiversity? Explain.

Ans. Tropical rainforests are very important with the point of view of biodiversity due to their following features

- Tropical rainforests are found in tropical regions of the globe. These areas are 1/4 area of earth and 3/4 of the world population lives there.
- These tropical rain forests contain 50% species of the earth.
- The biodiversity is highest in these forests. They are called lungs of the earth.
- All the 12 hotspots and mega diversity centres are located in the tropical rainforests areas.
- New species are being discovered in the tropical areas regularly.

9. List down the measures to conserve biodiversity.

Ans. The measures which can be adopted for the conservation of biodiversity are

- To educate people about environment friendly activities is a need of hour.
- There is a need to reorient our activities in such a way that development process is sustainable and is harmonious with other life-forms.
- It is increasingly being realised that conservation and sustainable use of resources can be carried out only with the help of local communities and individuals. To make this happen, institutional structures should be developed at local level.
- The continuation of process of conservation is more important along with conservation of species and their habitat.

10. Discuss the human activities which are responsible for deteriorating the biodiversity. Also suggest some measures to come out from this problem.

Ans. Some major human activities responsible for loss of biodiversity are

- Changes in land usage i.e. conversion of forest land to agriculture or residential land.
- Increasing pollution which includes air pollution, water pollution and soil pollution.

- Emission of carbon and change in   concentration in the atmosphere. These have increased the global temperature and give rise to global warming which is responsible for loss of biodiversity.
- Change in nitrogen cycle and acid rain. This change is also responsible for biodiversity destruction. The change in nitrogen cycle will decrease the amount of nitrogen content into soils which is much needed for plant growth. Acid rain is equally harmful for biodiversity.

Some measures to reduce deterioration of biodiversity are

- Sustainable mode of development is needed to be adopted.
- We should use resources judiciously.
- We should also consume our nature and ecology.

• Long Answer (LA) Type Questions

1. Discuss about the three categories of endangered species of plants and animals, as released by IUCN.

Ans. The classification of threatened species of plants and animals is done by the International Union of Conservation of Nature and Natural Resources (IUCN). The three categories of endangered species of plants and animals as released by IUCN are

(i) **Endangered Species** Those species which are in danger of extinction are included in this list. Information about these species is published world wide by IUCN in Red List of threatened species. For example, Red Panda.

(ii) **Vulnerable Species** Those species which are likely to be in danger of extinction in near future are included in this list, if the threatening factors continue. The population of these species have reduced considerably and therefore, their survival is not assured.

(iii) **Rare Species** These species have very small population in the world which is either confined to a limited area or thinly scattered over a large area. For example, humbodtia decurrens Bedd a highly-rare endemic tree of Southern Western Ghats.

2. Discuss some important steps taken on national and international level for conservation of biodiversity.

Ans. Various significant steps or initiatives that have been taken on national and international level for the conservation of biodiversity are

- **At International Level Earth Summit** United Nation Conference on Environment and Development (UNCED) also called Earth Summit held in 1992 at Rio de Janeiro. It was the first instrument to address all the aspects of biodiversity. Every year, Summit held in the form of Conference of Parties (COP) meeting to discuss the issues for conservation of biodiversity.
- **International Union of Conservation of Nature and Natural Resources** It is an international organisation which has classified the threatened species of plants and animals into three categories for the purpose of their conservation.

- **Hotspots** In order to concentrate resources on those areas that are most vulnerable, the IUCN has identified certain areas as biodiversity hotspots. These hotspots are defined according to their vegetation.
- **On National Level** Government of India alongwith 155 other nations have signed the Convention of Biodiversity at the Earth Summit. Government of India passed the Wildlife Protection Act 1972 to protect, preserve and propagate the variety of species within the national boundaries.

3. What do you understand by mega diversity centres? Why are they so important? Provide a list of these centres.

Ans. Ecological centres, situated in the tropical areas of the earth, which have very high amount of biodiversity, are known as mega diversity centres.

Mega diversity centres are important as

- They are located in tropical areas where around 3/4 of world population lives.
- These areas have around 50% of the world species.
- They have world's highest biodiversity.
- Many researches are being done in these areas to classify newly discovered species.
- They are playing critical role in the conservation of biodiversity.
- These mega-centres are important to maintain the ecological balance in the earth. They provide lot of ecological services.

The Mega diversity centres are located in following countries

- Mexico
- Columbia
- Ecuador
- Peru
- Brazil
- Democratic Republic of Congo
- Austrialia
- Madagascar
- China
- India
- Malaysia
- Indonesia

4. "The critical problem is not merely the conservation of species nor the habitat but the continuation of process of conservation." Give your argument in support of this statement.

Ans. The critical problem in the context of conservation of species is the continuation of the process of conservation.

Large number of species are facing threat of extinction, therefore, Governments and authorities around the world have also many initiative and programmes for their conservation. They have launched the initiative and programmes with great encouragement but their implementation was not continued.

Launching the initiative will not help in conserving bio diversity, it implementation in true sense is also important. Many countries are not able to continue the

process of conservation due to high monetary budget. Many countries do not acknowledge the seriousness of the problem hence, they show negative attitude towards the conservation process. Many have still not realised the importance of conserving biodiversity.

• Case Based Questions

1. Read the case/source given and answer the following questions.

Biodiversity as we have today is the result of 2.5-3.5 billion years of evolution. Before the advent of humans, our earth supported more biodiversity than in any other period. Since, the emergence of humans, however, biodiversity has begun a rapid decline, with one species after another bearing the brunt of extinction due to overuse. The numbers of species globally vary from 2 million to 100 million, with 10 million being the best estimate. New species are regularly discovered most of which are yet to be classified (an estimate states that about 40 per cent of fresh water fishes from South America are not classified yet). Tropical forests are very rich in bio-diversity.

(i) Define species.

Ans. Groups of individual organisms having certain similarities in their physical characteristics are called species.

(ii) What do you mean by term biodiversity?

Ans. Biodiversity itself is a combination of two words, bio (life) and diversity (variety). In simple terms, biodiversity is the number and variety of organisms found within a specified geographic region.

(iii) What are the different levels of biodiversity? What are the constituents of biodiversity?

Ans. Biodiversity can be discussed at three levels i.e. Genetic diversity, species diversity and ecosystem diversity. The varieties of plants, animals, micro-organisms, their genes and their ecosystem are all constituents of biodiversity.

2. Read the case/source given and answer the following questions.

Biodiversity is important because each species can give us some clue as to how life evolved and will continue to evolve. Biodiversity also helps in understanding how life functions and the role of each species in sustaining ecosystems of which we are also a species. This fact must be drawn upon every one of us so that we live and let other species also live their lives.

It is our ethical responsibility to consider that each and every species along with us have an intrinsic right to exist. Hence, it is morally wrong to voluntarily cause the extinction of any species.

The level of biodiversity is a good indicator of the state of our relationships with other living species. In fact, the concept of biodiversity is an integral part of many human cultures.

Since the last few decades, growth in human population has increased the rate of consumption of natural resources. It has accelerated the loss of species and habitation in different parts of the world. Tropical regions which occupy only about one-fourth of the total area of the world, contain about three fourth of the world human population. Overexploitation of resources and deforestation have become rampant to fulfil the needs of large population.

(i) How IUCN help in conservation of biodiversity?

Ans. IUCN stands for International Union for Conservation of Nature and Natural Resources. It is a democratic union that brings together the world's most influential organisations and top experts in a combined effort to conserve nature and promote sustainable development.

(ii) What due you mean by exotic species?

Ans. Species which are not the natural inhabitants of the local habitat but are introduced into the system, are called exotic species.

(iii) Examine any two causes of biodiversity loss.

Ans. Two causes of loss of biodiversity are

  (i) **Habitat Loss and Degradation** This reduced the food resources and living space for many species which resulted in their death and decline.

  (ii) **Overexploitation**: It means the harvesting or use of any animal or any other organism beyond a limit. It results in rapid declination in the number of species.

3. Read the case/source given and answer the following questions.

Biodiversity is important for human existence. All forms of life are so closely interlinked that disturbance in one gives rise to imbalance in the others. If species of plants and animals become endangered, they cause degradation in the environment, which may threaten human being's own existence.

There is an urgent need to educate people to adopt environment-friendly practices and reorient their activities in such a way that our development is harmonious with other life forms and is sustainable. There is an increasing consciousness of the fact that such conservation with sustainable use is possible only with the involvement and cooperation of local communities and individuals. For this, the development of institutional structures at local levels is necessary. The critical problem is not merely the conservation of species nor the habitat but the continuation of process of conservation.

(i) What is the significance of Earth Summit?

Ans. The Government of India along with 155 other nations have signed the Convention of Biodiversity at the Earth Summit held at Rio de Janeiro, Brazil in June 1992.

(ii) Which countries have mega diversity centres?

Ans. There are some countries which are situated in the tropical region; they possess a large number of the world's species diversity. They are called mega diversity centres. There are 12 such countries, namely Mexico, Columbia, Ecuador, Peru, Brazil, Democratic Republic of Congo, Madagascar, China, India, Malaysia, Indonesia and Australia in which these centres are located.

(iii) How the hotspots are defined? Why plants are important?

Ans. Hotspots are defined according to their vegetation. Most of the hotspots rely on species-rich ecosystems for food, firewood, cropland and income from timber. Plants are important because these determine the primary productivity of an ecosystem.

• Map Based Question

1. Mark the following on the map of the world.
   (i) Central American Lowland Forests
   (ii) Upper Guinean Forests
   (iii) Atlantic Forest, Brazil
   (iv) Sinharaja Forest, Sri Lanka
   (v) Eastern Madagascar

Ans.

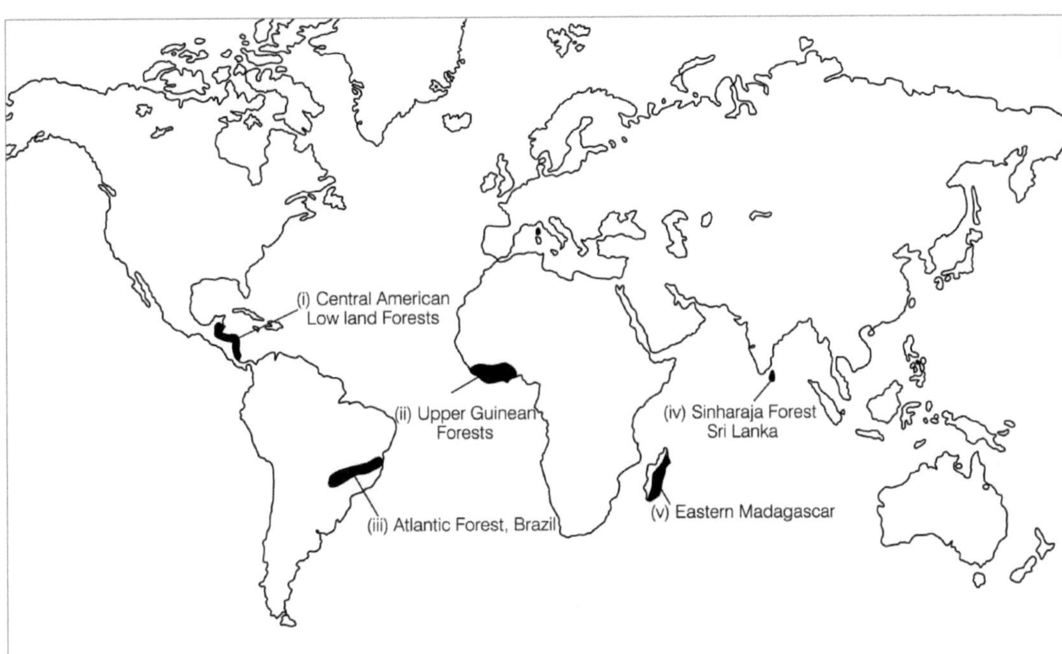

Chapter Test

Objective Questions

1. After the appearance of human beings the biodiversity rapidly
(a) declined
(b) increased
(c) remain constant
(d) no change is observed

2. How much percentage of freshwater fishes from South America are not classified yet?
(a) 10%
(b) 30%
(c) 40%
(d) 60%

3. Within Homo sapiens group, the differences are found in respect of which of the following?
(a) Height
(b) Colour
(c) Physical appearance
(d) All of these

4. Which of the following statements are correct in the context of the biodiversity?

I. species diversity refers to the variation in genes with in a species.

II. Crop diversity is also known as agro-diversity.

III. Biodiversity has many scientific roles.

Codes
(a) Only I
(b) Both II and III
(c) Only III
(d) All of these

Short Answer Type Questions

5. Establish the relationship among genes, species and ecosystems.

6. How has human beings affected the biodiversity?

7. Suggest measures to conserve biodiversity.

8. How all life forms are interlinked with each other? Explain.

9. List down the steps suggested by world conservation strategy.

10. Explain in detail the role played by IUCN for conservation of species.

Long Answer Type Questions

11. What do you understand by hotspots? What are their main characteristics?

12. Explain the main provisions of Wildlife Protection Act, 1972.

13. What is the responsibility of human beings towards other species? Write in detail.

Answers

1. (a) declined
2. (c) 40%
3. (d) All of these
4. (b) Both II and III

CHAPTER 01

Climate

In this Chapter...

- Unity and Diversity in Monsoon Climate of India
- Factors Determining the Climate of India
- The Nature of Indian Monsoon
- The Rhythm of Seasons
- Traditional Indian Seasons

The momentary state of the atmosphere is defined as **weather**. There are variations in weather conditions during different seasons due to changes in the elements of weather like temperature, pressure, wind direction and velocity, precipitation, etc.

The average of weather conditions over a longer period of time is called **climate**. The weather changes quickly, for example, in a day or in a week but climate changes very slowly and may be noted after 50 years or more.

Unity and Diversity in Monsoon Climate of India

The climate of India is **monsoonal** in rhythm and character. Monsoon denotes the climate associated with seasonal reversal in the direction of winds. India with the rest of South-East Asia has the **Tropical Monsoon Climate** because a large area of it lies in the tropical zone and largely affected by the monsoon winds which emphasises the unity of the region. But regional variations in such a vast area cannot be ignored which differentiate the weather and climate of different regions of India.

For example, the climate of Kerala and Tamil Nadu in the South are so different from that of Uttar Pradesh and Bihar in the North. The climate of India has many regional variations in the patterns of winds, temperature and rainfall, rhythm of seasons and degree of wetness or dryness. These regional variations may also be described as sub-types of monsoon climate.

It can be justified by the following examples

Regional Variations in Temperature of India

There are seasonal variations in temperature from place to place and from region to region in India. In Western Rajasthan, the temperature rises to 55°C in summer and drops down to minus 45°C in winters in Leh region of Ladakh.

Churu in Rajasthan may record a temperature of 50°C or more on a day in June, while the mercury hardly touches 19° C in Tawang in Arunachal Pradesh on the same day. On a December night, the temperature in Drass (Ladakh) may drop to minus 45°C while Chennai or Thiruvananthapuram records 20°C or 22°C.

The difference between day and night temperature in Kerala and Andaman islands is quite low, may be 7°C or 8°C, whereas in the Thar desert, if the day temperature is around 50°C, night temperature may drop to 15°C-20°C. Thus, the difference becomes 30– 35°C.

Regional Variations in Precipitation of India

The types of precipitation varies according to the topography. High mountains of the Himalayas receive snowfall while rest of the country gets rainfall. Variations are also noticeable in amount of precipitation. Cherrapunji and Mawsynram in the Khasi hills of Meghalaya receive more than 1,080 cm of rainfall in a year and Jaisalmer in Rajasthan hardly gets 9 cm of rainfall during the same period.

Tura situated in the Garo hills of Meghalaya may receive an amount of rainfall equal to 10 years of rainfall at Jaisalmer in one day. Annual rainfall in Meghalaya exceeds 400 cm, while it is less than 10 cm in the North-West Himalayas and the Western deserts. During the months of July and August, the total amount of rainfall received in the Ganga delta and the coastal plains of Odisha is much more (above 200 cm) than the Coromandal coast, which is dry.

Most parts of the country gets rainfall during June to September, while the coastal plains of Tamil Nadu receives rainfall in the beginning of the winter season.

Factors Determining the Climate of India

India's climate is controlled by a number of factors which can be broadly divided into two groups:

Factors Related to Location and Relief

Latitude

The angular distance of a location from the equator in the North-South direction is called latitude. The Tropic of Cancer passes through the central part of India in East-West direction. Thus, Northern part of the India lies in sub-tropical and temperate zone and the part lying South of the Tropic of Cancer falls in the tropical zone.

The tropical zone being nearer to the equator, experiences high temperatures throughout the year with small daily and annual range. Area North of the Tropic of Cancer being away from the equator experiences extreme climate with high daily and annual range of temperature.

The Himalayan Mountains

The entire stretch of the mountains acts as climatic divide. It saves India from being a cold desert as it stops the cold Northern winds which originate near the Arctic circle and blow across Central and Eastern Asia. The Himalayas trap the monsoon winds and force them to shed moisture which saves the subcontinent from being a dry region.

Distribution of Land and Water

India is girdled (belt) by high continuous mountain wall in the North and flanked (surrounded) by the Indian Ocean (Arabian sea and Bay of Bengal) on three sides in the South. Landmass and water heat up and cool down at different rate because water heats up or cools down slowly than the landmasses. This differential heating and cooling of land and sea creates difference in air pressure in different seasons which further causes reversal in the direction of monsoon winds.

Distance from the Sea

The areas near the coast have an equable climate (neither very hot nor very cold) due to the moderating effect of the sea. Therefore, the people of Mumbai, and the Konkan coast hardly experience the change of season. The areas far away from the sea experience extremes of temperature or seasonal contrast as they are not affected by moderating influence of sea.

Altitude

Temperature decreases with height due to lapse rate. Air is thick near the sea level and the density of air decreases with height. Therefore, due to thin air, places in the mountains are cooler than plains. For example, Agra and Darjiling are located at the same latitude, but temperature on a day in winters (January) in Agra is 16° C, whereas it is only 4° C in Darjiling.

Relief

The relief of India also affects the temperature, air pressure, direction and speed of wind and the amount and distribution of rainfall. The slopes which face the moisture laden winds (windward sides) receive heavy rainfall whereas on the other side of mountain slopes (leeward side) wind becomes dry and rainfall received is less.

As a result, the windward sides of the Western Ghats and Assam receive high rainfall during rainy season (June-September), whereas the Central part of the Southern plateau situated on leeward side receive less amount of rainfall.

Factors Related to Air Pressure and Wind

To understand the differences in local climates of India, one needs to understand the mechanism of monsoon during winter and summer season under the following three factors

(i) Distribution of air pressure and winds on the surface of the earth.

(ii) Upper air circulation caused by factors controlling global weather and the inflow of different air masses and **jet streams**[1].

(iii) Inflow of Western cyclones known as Western disturbances during winter season and tropical cyclones/ depressions during South-West monsoon period into India, creating weather conditions favourable to rainfall.

---

1 Jet Stream A very strong and steady westerly wind blowing just below the tropopause is called jet stream.

The mechanism of these three factors can be understood with reference to winter and summer seasons of the year separately.

Mechanism of Weather in the Winter Season

Surface Pressure and Winds

In winter months, the weather conditions over India are generally influenced by the distribution of pressure in Central and Western Asia. A high pressure centre in the region lying to the North of the Himalayas develops during winter. This centre of high pressure gives rise to the flow of air at the low level from the North towards the Indian subcontinent, South of the mountain range.

The surface winds blowing from the high pressure centre over central Asia reach India in form of a dry continental air mass. These continental winds come in contact with trade winds over North-Western India and this contact zone may shift upto the middle Ganga valley. Thus, whole of North-Western and Northern India upto middle Ganga valley comes under influence of dry North-Western winds.

Jet Stream and Upper Air Circulation

About 3 km above the surface of the earth, a different pattern of air circulation is observed. The winds blowing across Asian continent at latitudes North of Himalayas roughly parallel to the Tibetan highlands at the height of 9-13 km from West to East under the influence of Westerly winds are known as Jet Streams.

Tibetan highlands act as a barrier in the path of these jet streams. As a result, jet streams get divided into two branches. One of its branches blows to the North of the Tibetan highlands, while the Southern branch blows in an Eastward direction, South of the Himalayas. It has its mean position at 25°N in February at 200-300 mb level. It is believed that this Southern branch of the jet stream exercises an important influence on the winter weather in India.

Western Cyclonic Disturbance and Tropical Cyclones

The Western cyclonic disturbances or temperate cyclones that originate over the Mediterranean Sea are dragged by the Westerly jet streams towards the Indian sub-continent and cause rainfall in the North-Western part of India. An increase in the night temperature generally indicates the arrival of cyclonic disturbances.

Tropical cyclones originate over the Bay of Bengal and the Indian Ocean. They move towards the East coast of India causing destruction due to high wind velocity and torrential rain on the coast of Tamil Nadu, Andhra Pradesh and Odisha.

Mechanism of Weather in the Summer Season

Surface Pressure and Winds

As the summer sets in and the sun shifts Northwards, weather condition, reversed, get temperature rises and low pressure conditions prevail in the Northern part of India.

The **Inter Tropical Convergence Zone** (ITCZ) Shifts Northwards and Westerly jet streams withdraws from India by the middle of July. Meteorologists have found a cause and effect relationship between these two. The ITCZ, a zone of low pressure, attracts inflow of winds from different directions.

The Maritime Tropical Airmass (mT) from the Southern Hemisphere rushes to the low pressure zone. After crossing the equator, their direction is changed due to **coriolis force**[2] and they start blowing from South-West to North-East direction, known as **South-West monsoon winds**. These winds are moist winds.

> ## Inter Tropical Convergence Zone (ITCZ)
>
> The Inter Tropical Convergence Zone (ITCZ) is a low pressure zone located at the equator where trade winds converge, and so, it is a zone where air tends to ascend. In July, the ITCZ is located around 20° N-25° N latitudes (over the Gangetic plain), sometimes called the **monsoon** or **equatorial** trough. This monsoon trough encourages the development of thermal low over North and North-West India.
>
> Due to shift of ITCZ, trade winds of Southern hemisphere cross the equator and start blowing from South-West to North-East due to coriolis force. It is known as South-West monsoon.
>
> In winter, ITCZ moves Southward. This results in reversal of winds from North-East to South and South-West. The are called **North-East monsoon**.

Jet Stream and Upper Air Circulation

An Easterly jet stream flows over Southern part of Peninsula in June and has a maximum speed of 90 km/hr. It is confined to 15° N latitude in August and upto 22° N latitude in September. The easterlies normally do not extents to North of 30° N latitude in upper atmosphere.

Easterly Jet Streams and Tropical Cyclones

The Easterly jet stream steers (guide) the tropical depressions into India. These depressions play a significant role in the distribution of monsoon rainfall over the Indian subcontinent. The tracks of these depressions are the areas of highest rainfall in India. The frequency at which these depressions visit India, their direction and intensity, all go a long way in determining the rainfall pattern during the South-West monsoon period.

---

2 Coriolis Force Once air has been set in motion by the pressure gradient force, it undergoes an apparent deflection from its path, as seen by an observer on the earth. This apparent deflection is called the ''coriolis force'' and is a result of the earth's rotation.

The Nature of Indian Monsoon

Systematic studies of the causes of rainfall in the South Asian region have helped in understanding the causes and salient features of the monsoon such as

- Onset of the Monsoon
- Rain Bearing Systems (e.g. tropical cyclones) and relationship between their frequency and distribution of monsoon rainfall.
- **Break in the Monsoon**[3]

Onset of the Monsoon

When the sun shines vertically over the Tropic of Cancer during summer months of April and May, the large landmass in the North of the Indian Ocean gets intensely heated. This causes the formation of an intense low pressure in the North-Western part of the subcontinent. The pressure in the Indian Ocean is high due to slow heating of water.

The ITCZ shifts Northwards and the South-East trade winds cross the equator due to the intense low pressure cell formed over the Northern part. The South-East trade winds are deflected towards the sub-continent between 40° E to 60° E longitudes.

The monsoon sets in over the Kerala coast by 1st June, Mumbai by 10th, Kolkata by 13th June and by mid-July it engulfs (cover) the entire sub-continent.

The shift of ITCZ is also related to the phenomenon of the withdrawal of the Westerly jet streams from the Northern plain and South of the Himalayas. Then, the Easterly jet streams sets in along 15° N latitude from the Eastern coast and is responsible for the **burst of monsoon** which means continuous heavy rainfall for few days.

Rain-bearing System and Rainfall Distribution

There are two rain bearing systems in India due to the peninsular shape of the country. First originates in the Bay of Bengal causing rainfall over the plains of the North. Second in the Arabian Sea branch of South-West monsoon which brings heavy rain to the West coast of India.

As the Western Ghats obstruct the rain bearing winds and force them to rise along the Ghats, it is known as the **orographic** or **relief type of rainfall**. The amount of rainfall decreases from West to East on the West coast and from South-East to North-West over North Indian plain and Northern part of Peninsula.

The intensity of rainfall over the West coast of India is related to two factors

  (i) The offshore meteorological conditions.

  (ii) The position of Equatorial jet stream along the Eastern coast of Africa.

The frequency of the tropical cyclones originating from the Bay of Bengal varies from year to year. Their paths over India are mainly determined by the position of ITCZ which is termed as **monsoon trough**. As the position of ITCZ or monsoon trough oscillates, there are fluctuations in the track and direction of depressions. The intensity and the amount of rainfall also vary from year to year.

Break in the Monsoon

After having rains for a few days during the monsoon period, the rain fails to occur for one week or more, this **dry spell** is known as break in the monsoon. These are quite common during rainy season. This break can be seen on the West coast when winds blow parallel to the coast. In the Northern part of India, the break in the monsoon occurs when rain bearing storms are not very frequent along the monsoon trough or low pressure zone or ITCZ over this region.

> ### Effects of El-Nino on Indian Monsoon
>
> El-Nino is a complex weather system that appears once every three to seven years around December which brings droughts, floods and other weather extremes to different parts of the world.
>
> This system involves oceanic and atmospheric phenomena which replaces the **cold Peruvian current** or **Humbolt current** temporarily by warm currents off the coast of Peru in the Eastern Pacific and affects weather in many places including India. This current increases the temperature of water on the Peruvian coast by 10°C.

The Rhythm of Seasons

The meteorologists recognise the following four seasons to describe the climate conditions of India

1. Cold Weather Season

Temperature

In the Northern hemisphere, the cold weather season begins in mid-November upto the month of February. In the North parts of India, mean daily temperature remains below 21° C. December and January are the coldest months in Northern plain.

The night temperature may be quite low, sometimes going below freezing point in Punjab and Rajasthan. There are three main reasons for the excessive cold in North India during this season

---

3 **Break in the Monsoon** During the South-West monsoon period after having rains for a few days, if rain fails to occur for one or more weeks, it is known as break in the monsoon.

(i) States like Punjab, Haryana and Rajasthan being far away from the moderating influence of sea experience continental climate.

(ii) The snowfall on the high mountain ranges of the Himalayas creates **cold wave** situation.

(iii) Cold waves caused by the winds coming from the **Caspian sea** and **Turkmenistan** bring cold wave along with frost and fog over the North-Western parts of India.

In the Peninsular region, there is no well-defined cold season as it has sea on three sides and a close proximity to equator. For example, the mean maximum temperature of Thiruvananthapuram in January is about 31° C and 29.5° C in June. The temperature at the hills of Western Ghats remains comparatively low.

Pressure And Winds

Due to the Sun's position over the Tropic of Capricorn on 22nd December and low temperature conditions in Northern plains and the Central Asia, a feeble high pressure is formed over North and slightly low pressure in South. As a result, wind start blowing from North-Western high pressure zone to low pressure zone over the Indian Ocean in South. The **isobars** of 1019 mb and 1013 mb pass through North-West India and far South, respectively.

The light winds having a low velocity of about 3-5 km/hr begin to blow outwards due to low pressure gradient. Wind direction is influenced by the topography. They are North-Westerly down the Ganga valley, become northerly in the Ganga-Brahmaputra delta and North-Easterly over the Bay of Bengal.

The weather conditions are pleasant in India during winters and get disturbed by shallow cyclonic depressions originating over the East **Mediterranean Sea**. These depressions (temperate cyclones) travel Eastwards across West Asia, Iran, Afghanistan and Pakistan and then reach the North-Western parts of India. On their way, the moisture content gets augmented from the **Caspian Sea** in the North and the **Persian Gulf** in the South.

Rainfall

Winter monsoons do not cause rainfall because they have little humidity and also due to anti-cyclonic circulation on land. So, most parts of India do not receive rainfall in winter season. However, some exceptions to it are

- The temperate cyclones from the Mediterranean sea cause rainfall in Punjab, Harayana, Delhi and Western Uttar Pradesh. Though the amount is not enough but highly beneficial for **rabi** crops.

- The precipitation is in the form of snowfall in the lower Himalayas. It goes on decreasing from West to East in the plains and from North to South in the mountains. The average rainfall in Delhi is around 53 mm. In Punjab and Bihar, rainfall remains between 25 mm and 18 mm respectively.

- Central parts of India and Northern parts of Southern Peninsula also gets winter rainfall occasionally.

- Arunachal Pradesh and Assam in the North-Eastern parts of India also gets winter rainfall between 25 mm and 50 mm during winter season.

- The coast of Tamil Nadu, Southern Andhra Pradesh, South-East Karnataka and South-East Kerala gets torrential rainfall during October and November from the North-East monsoon, as they pick up moisture while crossing over the Bay of Bengal.

2. The Hot Weather Season

Temperature

April, May and June are the months of summer in North India when temperature starts rising due to the apparent movement of the Sun towards the Tropic of Cancer in March.

In most parts of India, temperatures recorded are between 30°- 32°C. The highest day temperature of about ° occurs in the Deccan Plateau in March while in April, temperature ranging between 38°C and 43°C are found in Gujarat and Madhya Pradesh. In May, the heat belt moves further North, and in the North-Western part of India, temperatures around 48°C are recorded.

The hot weather season in South India is mild and not so intense as in North India. The Peninsular of South India which is surrounded by ocean from three sides has moderating effect and keeps the temperatures lower than in North India. The temperatures remain between 26°C and 32°C.

Due to altitude, the temperatures in the hills of Western Ghats remain below 25°C. In the Coastal regions, the North-South extent of **isotherms** parallel to the coast is the proof that temperature does not decrease from North to South but it increases from the coast to the interior. The mean daily minimum temperature during the summer months also remains quite high and doesn't go below 26°C.

Pressure and Winds

High temperature in North India leads to low pressure condition and the ITCZ moves Northwards at 25° N in July. This elongated low pressure trough, extends from Thar desert in North-West to Patna and Chotanagpur plateau in East-South-East.

The location of ITCZ attracts surface circulation of winds which are Easterly or South-Easterly over North Bengal and Bihar and South-Westerly on West coast as well as along the coast of West Bengal and Bangladesh.

Local Storm

The hot, dry and oppressing winds known as **Loo**[4] blow in afternoon in Northern plains from Punjab to Bihar with higher intensity between Delhi and Patna.

In the evening, dust storms are very common during May in Punjab, Haryana, Eastern Rajasthan and Uttar Pradesh. Some famous local storms of hot weather season apart from loo are

(i) There are pre-monsoon showers towards the end of summer which are a common phenomena in Kerala and coastal areas of Karnataka. They are known as **mango showers**[5] because they help in early ripening of mangoes.

(ii) **Blossom Shower**[6] It helps coffee flowers to blossom in Kerala and nearby areas.

(iii) **Nor Westers** These are dreaded (causing fear) evening thunderstorms in Bengal and Assam. They are known as **Kalbaisakhi** i.e. calamity of the month of Baisakh. It is useful for tea, jute and rice cultivation. In Assam, these storms are known as **Bardoli chheerha**.

3. The South-West Monsoon Season/Rainy Season

Rainy season begins in June and ends in September. The low pressure conditions over the North-Western plains get further intensified and are powerful enough to attract the trade winds of the Southern Hemisphere coming from Indian Ocean. The South-East trade winds cross the equator and are deflected towards the right which flows over Bay of Bengal and the Arabian Sea. Passing over the equatorial warm currents, they bring with them moisture in abundance. After crossing the equator, they follow a southwesterly direction.

The sudden onset of moisture laden winds associated with violent thunder and lightening is known as **break** or **burst** of the monsoons. The monsoon may burst in coastal areas of Kerala, Karnataka, Goa and Maharashtra in the first week of June and in the interior parts of the country, it may be delayed to first week of July.

Due to the tapering shape of Peninsular India, and thermal low pressure over North-West India, the South-Westerly direction of the approaching winds get modified. The South-West monsoon winds divided into two branches

(i) Monsoon Winds of the Arabian Sea

The Arabian Sea branch blows on the Western coast of the Peninsular India in South-West direction. These winds further spilt into three branches

(a) One branch is obstructed by Western Ghats. As the winds climb the slopes of Western Ghats from 900-1200 m, the winds become cool. This results in heavy rainfall ranging between 250 cm and 400cm on the windward side of Sahyadris and Western Coastal Plain. After crossing the Western Ghats, these winds descend and get heated up which reduces humidity in the winds. This results in little rainfall East of Western Ghats.This region of low rainfall is known as **rain-shadow area**.

(b) The second branch strikes the coast North of Mumbai and moving along Narmada and Tapi river valley. These winds cause rainfall in Central Highlands. The Chotanagpur plateau gets 15 cm of rainfall from this branch. The amount goes on decreasing towards East and then enters the Ganga plain to mingle with the Bay of Bengal branch.

(c) The third branch of these winds strike the Saurashtra Peninsula and the Kachchh and then move further towards Rajasthan, Punjab and Haryana. It causes little rain in Rajasthan, as the Aravalis are parallel to these winds. In Punjab and Haryana, it too joins the Bay of Bengal branch. These two branches reinforce each other and cause rain in the Western Himalayas.

(ii) Monsoon Winds of the Bay of Bengal

The Bay of Bengal branch also blows in the South-West direction and strikes the coast of Myanmar and part of South-East Bangladesh. It is deflected by the Arakan mountains along the coast of Myanmar towards Indian sub-continent. Thus, it blow into West Bengal and Bangladesh as South Easterly monsoon winds. From here, this branch splits into two under the influence of the Himalayas and thermal low in the North-West. One branch moves Westward along the Ganga plain upto the Punjab plains.

The other branch moves up to the Brahmaputra valley in the North and North-East causing widespread rain. They cause heavy rainfall (more than 1000 cm) in Cherrapunji and Mawsynram lying on the windward sides of the Garo and the Khasi hills.

---

4 **Loo** Hot, dry and oppressing winds blowing in the Northern plains from Punjab to Bihar with higher intensity between Delhi and Patna.

5 **Mango Shower** Towards the end of summer, there are pre-monsoon showers which are a common phenomena in Kerala and coastal areas of Karnataka. Locally, they are known as mango showers, since they help in the early ripening of mangoes.

6 **Blossom Shower** With this shower, coffee flowers blossom in Kerala and nearby areas.

Mawsynram receives the highest average annual rainfall in the world. Tamil Nadu coast remains dry during this season. There are two factors responsible for it. They are

(a) Tamil Nadu coast is situated parallel to the Bay of Bengal branch of South-West monsoon.

(b) It lies in the rain shadow area of the Arabian Sea branch of South-West monsoon.

Characteristics of Monsoonal Rainfall

- Rainfall received from the South-West monsoons is seasonal in nature as it occurs between June to September.

- It is mainly governed by relief or topography, therefore it is orographic or relief type of rainfall in which windward slopes receive heavy rainfall over 250 cm (Western Ghats) and leeward sides register low to scanty rain. In the same way, North-Eastern states receive heavy rainfall because of being located on windward side of Eastern Himalayas and hill ranges.

- Its spatial distribution is uneven. It means some areas get more than 250 cm of rainfall and some areas receive only 12-15 cm of rainfall.

- The rainfall received by the Bay of Bengal branch of monsoon wind is more in North-East parts and declines towards the West due to increasing distance from the sea. For example, 119 cm in Kolkata, 105 cm in Patna, 76 cm in Allahabad and 56 cm in Delhi.

- It is erratic in nature. It means some year it is early and sometime delayed. Thus causing great damage to standing crops and making the sowing of winter crops difficult. The total amount of annual rainfall also varies from year to year.

- There is 'burst of monsoon' and breaks in rainfall. When there is sudden and continuous rains, it is known as burst of monsoon. These wet spells are interspersed with rainless interval known as break in monsoon.

- Monsoon plays a pivotal role in the agrarian economy as over three-fourth of the total rain in the country is received during South-West monsoon season.

4. Season of Retreating Monsoon

The months of October and November are known for **retreating monsoons**. By the end of September, the pressure conditions start changing in the Northern India due to the apparent movement of sun towards South. The South-West monsoon winds becomes weak as the low pressure trough of the Ganga plain moves towards South India.

The monsoon retreats from the Western Rajasthan by the first week of September and from Rajasthan, Gujarat, Western Ganga plain and Central Highlands by end of month.

The low pressure moves to Northern part of Bay of Bengal by beginning of October and to Karnataka and Tamil Nadu by early November. The low pressure is completely removed from the Peninsula by mid of December.

The retreating season is marked by clear skies, rise in temperature and high humidity. This makes the weather oppressive commonly known as the **October heat**. This season is dry in North India but the Eastern part of the Peninsula gets most of its rain in these months. October and Novermber are the rainiest months of the year in these regions. It is also marked by cyclonic depression or tropical cyclones which originate over the Andaman Sea.

These depressions are dragged by the Easterly jet streams towards the coasts of Bangladesh, Myanmar, West Bengal, deltas of Godavari, Krishna and Kaveri and cause destruction in these areas. Every year cyclones cause disasters here. Majority of rainfall of Coromandal coast is derived from these depressions and cyclones. Such cyclonic storms are less frequent in Arabian Sea.

Traditional Indian Seasons

In the Indian tradition, a year is divided into six two-monthly seasons. This cycle of seasons, which the common people in North and Central India follow is based on their practical experience and age-old perception of weather phenomena. In South India, there is little variations in seasons. Traditional Indian seasons are discussed in given table

Seasons	Months (According to the Indian Calendar)	Months (According to the Gregorian Calendar)
Vasanta	Chaitra-Vaisakha	March-April
Grishma	Jyaistha-Asadha	May-June
Varsha	Sravana-Bhadra	July-August
Sharada	Asvina-Kartika	September-October
Hemanta	Margashirsa-Pausa	November-December
Shishira	Magha-Phalguna	January-February

Distribution of Rainfall

The average annual rainfall in India is about 125 cm, but it has following spatial variations

- **Areas of Heavy Rainfall** More than 200 cm rainfall is received along West coast, on windward side of Western Ghats, in sub-Himalayan areas, in the North-East and hills of Meghalaya. In some parts of Khasi and Jaintia hills the rainfall exceeds 1,000 cm. In the Brahmaputra valley and the adjoining hills, the rainfall is less than 200 cm.

- **Areas of Medium Rainfall** These regions get rainfall between 100 to 200 cm. It includes the North Ganga Plain along the Sub-Himalayas and Cachar valley and Manipur, the East coast of Tamil Nadu, the Southern part of Gujarat and North-Eastern Peninsula covering Odisha, Jharkhand, Bihar and Eastern Madhya Pradesh.
- **Areas of Low Rainfall** These areas receive rainfall between 50 to 100 cm. The regions are Western Uttar Pradesh, Eastern Rajasthan and Gujarat, Delhi, Haryana, Punjab and Jammu and Kashmir and Deccan Plateau.
- **Areas of Scanty/Inadequate Rainfall** The amount of rainfall received in these regions is below 50 cm. These include part of Peninsula, especially in Andhra Pradesh, Karnataka and Maharashtra, Western Rajasthan and Ladakh.
  Snowfall is restricted to the Himalayan region

Variability of Rainfall

Variability is characteristic feature of rainfall in India. The amount of rainfall in India is not fixed every year. It varies from year to year and the variability deviates from 20 to 50 per cent.

The variability of rainfall is computed with the help of the following formula

$$CV = \frac{\text{Standard Deviation}}{\text{Mean}} \times 100$$

Where, CV is the coefficient of variation.

The values of coefficient of variation show variability of rainfall in India.

The areas which receive over 100 cm of annual rainfall, such as Western coasts, Western Ghats, North-Eastern Peninsula, Eastern plains of Ganga, North-Eastern India, Uttarakhand and Himachal Pradesh and South-Western part of Jammu and Kashmir show the variablity of less than 25%.

The larger part of India where annual rainfall is 50-100 cm, the variability is 25-50%. The areas where annual rainfall is less than 50 cm, such as Western part of Rajasthan, Northern part of Ladakh and interior parts of Deccan plateau, the variability is 50%.

Climatic Regions of India

A **climatic region**[7] has a homogeneous climatic condition which is the result of a combination of two factors i.e. temperature and rainfall. They play an important role in classification of climate. Therefore, according to the **Koeppen's scheme** which is based on monthly values of temperature and precipitation, India has five major types of climate

(i) **Tropical Climate** Where the mean monthly temperature is above 18°C throughout the year.

(ii) **Dry Climate** Where temperature is high and rainfall is low. If dryness is less, it is semi-arid (S), if it is more, the climate is arid (W).

(iii) **Warm Temperate Climate** Where the mean temperature of the winter months varies between 18° C to minus 3° C.

(iv) **Cool Temperate Climate** Where temperature of warme st month is over 10° C and of coldest month is under minus 3° C.

(v) **Ice Climate** Where the mean temperature of the warmest month is under 10° C.

Koeppen used capital and small letter symbols to denote climatic types and sub-types, respectively. S and W are used to denote semi-arid and arid, respectively.

The sub-types include **f** (sufficient precipitation), **m** (rain forest despite a dry monsoon season), **w** (dry season in winter), **h** (dry and hot), **c** (less than four months with mean temperature over 10°C), and **g** (Gangetic plain). Accordingly, India can be divided into eight climatic regions

Climatic Regions of India According to Koeppen's Scheme

Type of Climate	Areas
Amw — Monsoon with short dry season.	West coast of India, South of Goa.
As — Monsoon with dry summer.	Coromandal coast of Tamil Nadu.
Aw — Tropical Savannah.	Most of the Peninsular plateaus, South of the Tropic of Cancer.
BShw — Semi-arid Steppe climate.	North-Western Gujarat, some parts of Western Rajasthan and Punjab.
BWhw — Hot desert.	Extreme Western Rajasthan.
Cwg — Monsoon with dry winter.	Ganga Plain, Eastern Rajasthan, Northern Madhya Pradesh, most of North-East India.
Dfc — Cold humid winter with short summer.	Arunachal Pradesh.
E — Polar type.	Jammu and Kashmir, Himachal Pradesh and Uttarakhand.

---

7 Climatic Region It has a homogeneous climatic condition which is the result of a combination of factors like temperature, rainfall, etc.

Monsoon and the Economic Life in India

India's 64% of population depends on agriculture which is largely based on South-West monsoon. Thus, the entire agricultural cycle of India depends on monsoon.

The entire country except Himalayas has optimum temperature conditions to grow the crops or plants throughout the year. Regional variations helps in growing a variety of crops, providing livelihood to a large number of people. This regional climatic variation in India is reflected in vast variety of food, clothes and house types.

Agricultural prosperity of India depends on timely and adequately distributed rainfall. Failure in timely and adequate rainfall adversely affects those regions where means of irrigations are not well developed. Variability of rainfall results in floods and droughts which causes damage to crops and affect the life of people.

Global Warming

The temperature of the world is significantly rising. Carbon dioxide in the atmosphere is increasing gradually with some other gases like methane, nitrous oxide, CFCs, etc that absorb more heat and cause global warming.

These gases are known as **greenhouse gases**. Methane, Chlorofluorocarbons (CFCs) and Nitrous oxide are better absorbers of long wave radiations than Carbon dioxide and thus, are more effective at enhancing greenhouse effect.

The factors that cause global warming are **natural** (volcanic eruption, forest fire, etc) and as well as **human activities** such as large scale industrialisation, burning of fossil fuels for various purposes, etc. A little rise in global temperature of the atmosphere will result in large number of problems such as

- Rise in sea level due to melting of glacier and icebergs.
- Increase the incidence of annual flooding and spread water and insect borne diseases.
- Climate boundaries will shift making some region wetter and other drier.
- Affect the agricultural pattern, ecosystem and human population and their economic status.

Chapter Practice

Objective Questions

• Multiple Choice Questions

1. Which of the following phenomena happens during winter season in India?
   (a) Low pressure condition over Northern part of India
   (b) Withdrawal of jet stream
   (c) Inflow of Western cyclonic disturbances
   (d) Shift of ITCZ towards North

Ans. (c) During winter season in India, the inflow of Western Cyclonic disturbances occur in the North-Western India.

2. Which of the following is correct about ITCZ?
   (a) Low pressure zone located at equator.
   (b) Zone of convergence of westerlies and trade wind
   (c) In winter, ITCZ is located around 20°N-25°N
   (d) All of the above

Ans. (a) The Inter Tropical Convergence Zone (ITCZ) is a low pressure zone located at the equator where trade winds converge and so, it is a zone where air tends to ascend.

3. Which of the following drives tropical depression in India?
   (a) Northerly jet stream   (b) Easterly jet stream
   (c) Westerly jet stream   (d) None of these

Ans. (b) The Easterly Jet stream drives the tropical depressions in India. These depressions play a significant role in the distribution of monsoon rainfall over the Indian subcontinent.

4. Which of the following is a consequence of El-Nino?
   (a) Presence of cold Humbolt current along Peru coast
   (b) Distortion of equatorial atmospheric circulation
   (c) Increase in amount of plankton
   (d) Early onset of monsoon in India

Ans. (b) El-Nino is responsible for droughts, floods, the distortion of the equatorial atmospheric circulation, irregularities in the evaporation of sea water on the Pacific and the Indian oceans.

5. Which one of the following phenomena happens when the Sun shines vertically over the Tropic of Capricorn in the Southern Hemisphere?   **(NCERT)**
   (a) High pressure develops over North-Western India due to low temperature.
   (b) Low pressure develops over North-Western India due to high temperature.
   (c) No changes in temperature and pressure occur in North-Western India.
   (d) 'Loo' blows in the North-Western India.

Ans. (a) When the Sun's position is over the Tropic of Capricorn on 22nd December in the Southern hemisphere, high pressure is formed over North and slightly low pressure in South due to low temperature.

6. Which of the following is not a fact regarding South India?   **(NCERT)**
   (a) Temperatures are high throughout the year.
   (b) Annual range of temperature is less here.
   (c) Diurnal range of temperature is less here.
   (d) Extreme climatic conditions are found here.

Ans. (d) The South India does not experience any extreme climatic condition due to the moderating effect of the sea.

7. Which of the following regions receives rainfall in winter season from North-East monsoon?
   (a) Punjab
   (b) Western Uttar Pradesh
   (c) Southern Andhra Pradesh
   (d) All of the above

Ans. (c) The coast of Tamil Nadu, Southern Andhra Pradesh, South-East Karnataka and South-East Kerala get torrential rainfall during winter season from the North-East monsoon.

8. Which of the following pairs is not correctly matched?

   (a) Loo – Opressing wind
   (b) Mango Shower – Helps in early ripening of mangoes
   (c) Blossom Shower – Important for Coffee flowers
   (d) Nor Westers – Important for wheat crop

Ans. (d) Nor Westers are evening thunderstorms in Bengal and Assam. These are useful for tea, jute and rice cultivations not wheat crop.

9. Which of the following pairs is not correctly matched?

(a)	Areas of heavy rainfall	– North-East and hills of Meghalaya
(b)	Areas of medium rainfall	– Manipur
(c)	Areas of low rainfall	– Bihar
(d)	Areas of scanty/ inadequate rainfall	– Karnataka

Ans. (c) Bihar is not an area of low rainfall. Areas of low rainfall include Western Uttar Pradesh, Eastern Rajasthan, Gujarat, Delhi, Haryana, Punjab and Jammu and Kashmir and Deccan Plateau.

10. Match the following.

	List I (Traditional Seasons)		List II (Months)
A.	Vasanta	1.	September-October
B.	Grishma	2.	March-April
C.	Sharada	3.	November-December
D.	Hemanta	4.	May-June

Codes

	A	B	C	D			A	B	C	D
(a)	4	2	3	1		(b)	2	4	1	3
(c)	4	3	2	1		(d)	3	2	4	1

Ans. (b)

11. Match the following.

	List I (Symbols)		List II (Denotes)
A.	f	1.	Dry season in winter
B.	h	2.	Sufficient precipitation
C.	m	3.	Rainforest despite dry monsoon season
D.	w	4.	Dry and hot
E.	g	5.	Gangetic plain
F.	e	6.	Polar type climate

Codes

	A	B	C	D	E	F
(a)	4	3	2	1	5	6
(b)	2	4	3	1	5	6
(c)	1	4	3	2	5	6
(d)	3	2	1	4	5	6

Ans. (b)

12. Consider the following statements and choose the correct option from the given options:

I. India with the rest of South-East Asia has the tropical monsoon climate.

II. A large area of India lies in the tropical zone and largely affected by the monsoon winds which emphasises the unity of the region.

Codes

(a) Only statement I is correct

(b) Only statement II is correct

(c) Both the statements are incorrect

(d) Both the statements are correct and statement II correctly explains the statement I.

Ans. (d) India with rest of the South-East Asia has the Tropical monsoon climate, because a large area of it lies in the tropical zone and largely affected by the monsoon winds which emphasies the unity of the region.

13. Consider the following statements and choose the correct option for the same

I. Rainfall received from South-West monsoon is seasonal in nature.

II. South-West monsoon occurs between June to September.

(a) Only statement I is correct

(b) Both the statements are correct

(c) Only statement II is correct

(d) Both are incorrect

Ans. (b) Both the statements are correct.

14. Arrange the following areas in ascending order according to the rainfall received by them.

I. Bihar

II. Khasi Hills

III. Andhra Pradesh

IV. Western Uttar Pradesh

Codes

(a) I, II, III, IV

(b) IV, III, II, I

(c) III, IV, I, II

(d) IV, I, II, III

Ans. (c) The correct ascending order of the areas according to the rainfall received by them is Andhra Pradesh, Western Uttar Pradesh, Bihar and Khasi Hills.

15. Arrange the following events of onset of monsoon in correct order.

I. ITCZ shifts Northwards

II. South-East trade blows as South-West monsoon.

III. Sun shines vertically over Tropic of Cancer.

IV. South-East trade winds cross the Equator.

Codes

(a) I, II, III, IV		(b) III, I, IV, II
(c) IV, III, II, I		(d) IV, I, II, III

Ans. (b) The correct order of the events of onset of monsoon is the Sun shines vertically over the Tropic of Cancer during summer months of April and May, the ITCZ shifts northwards, the South East trade winds cross the equator and South-East trade winds blow as South-West monsoon.

• Case Based MCQs

16. Read the case/source given and answer the questions that follow by choosing the correct option.

Surface Pressure and Winds : As the summer sets in and the sun shifts Northwards, the wind circulation over the subcontinent undergoes a complete reversal at both, the lower as well as the upper levels. By the middle of July, the low pressure belt nearer the surface [termed as Inter Tropical Convergence Zone (ITCZ)] shifts northwards, roughly parallel to the Himalayas between 20°N and 25°N. By this time, the westerly jet stream withdraws from the Indian region. In fact, meteorologists have found an interrelationship between the Northward shift of the equatorial trough (ITCZ) and the withdrawal of the westerly jet stream from over the North Indian Plain. It is generally believed that there is a cause and effect relationship between the two. The ITCZ being a zone of low pressure, attracts inflow of winds from different directions. The Maritime Tropical Airmass (mT) from the Southern hemisphere, after crossing the equator, rushes to the low pressure area in the general Southwesterly direction. It is this moist air current which is popularly known as the South-West monsoon.

Jet Streams and Upper Air Circulation : The pattern of pressure and winds as mentioned above is formed only at the level of the troposphere. An easterly jet stream flows over the southern part of the Peninsula in June, and has a maximum speed of 90 km per hour. In August, it is confined to 15°N latitude, and in September up to 22°N latitudes. The easterlies normally do not extend to the north of 30° N latitude in the upper atmosphere.

(i) Which of the following mountain ranges plays a major role for climate of India?
(a) The Aravalis   (b) The Nilgiris
(c) The Himalayas   (d) Jawadi Hills

Ans. (c) The Himalayan mountain range plays a major role for climate of India.

(ii) According to a general view, which of the following have cause and effect relationship between them?
(a) ITCZ + South-West monsoon winds
(b) Maritime tropical airmass + Southwest monsoon winds
(c) ITCZ + Westerly Jet Stream
(d) Easterly jet stream + Maritime tropical airmass

Ans. (c) According to a general view, ITCZ and westerly jet stream have cause and effect relationship between them.

(iii) Which of the following atmospheric layers is significant for the pattern of pressure and winds?
(a) Mesosphere   (b) Exosphere
(c) Stratosphere   (d) Troposphere

Ans. (d) The troposphere is significant for the pattern of pressure and winds.

(iv) In which month the easterly jet stream flows over states like Maharashtra, Chhattisgarh, Odisha, etc?
(a) June   (b) August
(c) September   (d) October

Ans. (c) In the month of September the easterly jet stream flows over peninsular states like Maharashtra, Chhattisgarh and Odisha, etc. which lie almost on 22°N latitudes.

12. Study the table given below and answer the questions that follow by choosing the correct option.

Climate Regions of India According to Koeppen's Scheme

Type of Climate	Areas
Amw–Monsoon with short dry season	West coast of India South of Goa
As–Monsoon with dry summer	Coromandel coast of Tamil Nadu
Aw–Tropical savannah	Most of the Peninsular plateaus, South of the Tropic of Cancer
Bshw–Semi–arid steppe climate	North-Western Gujarat, some parts of Western Rajasthan and Punjab
Bwhw–Hot desert	Extreme Western Rajasthan
Cwg–Monsoon with dry winter	Ganga plain, Eastern Rajasthan, Northern Madhya Pradesh, most of North-East India
Dfc–Cold humid winter with short summer	Arunachal Pradesh
E–Polar type	Jammu and Kashmir, Himachal Pradesh and Uttarakhand

(i) The capital letter 'S' denotes which of the following types of climate?
(a) Summer season   (b) South-West Monsoon
(c) Short dry season   (d) Semi arid climate

Ans. (d) The capital letter 'S' denotes semi-arid climate which is found in the North Western Gujarat, some parts of Western Rajasthan and Punjab.

(ii) The Gangetic plains experience which type of climate?
(a) Tropical savannah type
(b) Monsoon with dry summer
(c) Monsoon with dry winter
(d) Polar type

Ans. (c) The Gangetic plains experience Cwg type of climate which means monsoon with dry winter.

(iii) Which of the following regions is associated with dry winter?
(a) Ganga Plain
(b) Madhya Pradesh
(c) Most of North-East India
(d) All of the above

Ans. (c) All the given regions are associated with dry winter.

(iv) Which of the following regions does not experience polar type of climate?
(a) Meghalaya
(b) Uttarakhand
(c) Himachal Pradesh
(d) Jammu and Kashmir

Ans. (a) Meghalaya does not experience polar type of climate.

PART 2
Subjective Questions

• Short Answer (SA) Type Questions

1. Explain the spatial temperature variations in India.

Ans. The spatial temperature variations in India are
- In Western Rajasthan, the temperature rises to 55° C in summer and drops down to – 45° C in winters in Leh region in Jammu and Kashmir.
- Churu in Rajasthan may record a temperature of 50° C or more on a day in June, while the mercury hardly touches 19° C in Tawang in Arunachal Pradesh on the same day.
- On a December night, the temperature in Drass in Jammu and Kashmir may drop to –45° C, while Chennai or Thiruvananthapuram records 20°C or 22° C.
- The difference between day and night temperature in Kerala and Andaman islands is low, may be 7° C or 8° C, whereas the difference in day and night in the Thar desert may be 30° C to 35° C.

2. Discuss the mechanism of weather in the winter season.

Ans. In winter months, at lower level of atmosphere near surface of Earth, the weather conditions over India are influenced by distribution of pressure in Central and Western Asia. A high pressure centre in the region lying to the North of Himalayas develops during winter which gives rise to flow of air at low level from North towards Indian sub-continent, South of mountain range. These surface winds are in form of dry continental air mass and come in contact with trade winds over North-Western India.

Higher up in lower troposphere, jet streams blow over all of Western and Central Asia. These jet streams are bifurcated by Tibetan highlands and one branch blows North of Tibetan highlands while another blows South of Himalayas. This Southern branch drives Western cyclonic disturbances originating over Mediterranean Sea to Indian subcontinent.

3. What are jet streams ? How do they influence the climate of India?

Ans. The high velocity winds blowing in the upper troposphere are known as jet streams. They blow at a higher altitude as compared to the winds near the surface. The variations in the atmospheric pressure closer to the surface of Earth have no role in formation of these jet streams.

Jet streams influence the climate of India in the following ways
- The Westerly jet streams bring Western disturbances or cyclonic depressions in the North-Western parts of India.
- The Easterly jet streams bring the tropical cyclones fromed over the Andaman sea and Eastern Indian Ocean towards the East coast of India.

4. Monsoon connotes the seasonal reversal in the direction of winds. What causes the reversal of winds?

Ans. Monsoon type of climate is prevalent in South and South-East Asia. The monsoon winds shift their directions seasonally. This seasonal shift is accompanied by changes in the patterns of rainfall. The main causes of seasonal reversal of winds are
- Formation of low pressure Inter Tropical Convergence Zone (ITCZ) during the summer season over the Northern Ganga plains.
- Formation of high pressure zone at 20°S latitude over the Indian Ocean in the Arabian Sea.
- There is replacement of subtropical Westerly jet stream by the Easterly jet stream.

Thus, there is reversal of winds from North-East to South and South-West direction and vice-versa.

5. What is El Nino ? Describe the effects of El Nino.

Ans. El Nino means child christ. It is a complex weather system that appears every three to seven years and brings drought, floods and other weather extremes to different parts of the world.

El Nino is an extension of the warm equatorial Pacific current which gets replaced temporarily by the cold Peruvian current or Humboldt current. The system of El Nino involves the atmospheric and weather phenomenon with the appearance of warm currents on the Peru coast and Eastern Pacific.

The effects of El Nino include

- It affects weather in many parts of India and the world.
- It raises the temperature of water on the Peruvian coast by 10°C.
- It results in distortion of equatorial atmospheric circulation.
- Results in irregularities in sea water evaporation and reduction in Planktons, which reduces the amount of fish in the sea.

6. What is the cause of dry spells during rainy season in different parts?

Ans. During the South-West monsoon, after the rain occurs for a few days, the rain fails to occur for one or more weeks. These dry spells or breaks are common in rainy season in the different regions due to different reasons which are

- In Northern India, rains are likely to fail if rain bearing storms are not very frequent along the monsoon trough or ITCZ over this region.
- On the West coast, the dry spells are associated with days when winds blow parallel to the coast.
- According to a research, the dry spells may also occur due to large scale of deforestation for various purposes, this ultimately results in longer breaks in monsoon.

7. What are the main reasons for excessive cold in North India during winters as compared to the Peninsular region?

Ans. The reasons for excessive cold in North India during winters are

- Punjab, Haryana and Rajasthan being far away from the moderating influence of sea experience continental climate.
- The snowfall in the nearby Himalayan ranges creates cold wave situation.
- The cold waves come from the Caspian Sea and Turkmenistan cause frost and fog over North-Western parts of India. Whereas, in the Peninsular region, there is no well defined cold season. There is no variation in seasons due to the moderating effect of the sea and proximity to the equator.

8. "The climate of India is best described in terms of an annual cycle of seasons". Describe the characteristics of the hot weather season of India.

Ans. The climate of India is characterised by a rhythm of seasons. The hot weather season starts from the months of March-April. The characteristics of hot weather season are

- **Temperature** April, May and June are the months of summer in North India where temperature ranges between 35° C to 45° C due to the apparent movement of the sun towards the Tropic of Cancer. In South India, it is not so intense, as the surrounding water bodies keep the temperature low between 26° C to 32° C.
- **Pressure and Winds** High temperature in North India leads to low pressure condition and the ITCZ moves Northwards at 25° N in July. This elongated low pressure trough extends from Thar desert decent to Patna and Chotanagpur plateau.
- **Local Storms** The dry conditions prevail in the larger part of North but temporary storms or the local winds bring a welcome respite from the oppressing heat. 'Loo' which are hot, dry and oppressing winds blow in the Northern plains from Punjab to Bihar and with higher intensity between Delhi and Patna.

9. How are temperature and pressure shown on the maps? Where do you notice the high and low temperature in India during winter months?

Ans. On maps, temperatures are shown through isotherms. These are lines that join the places of same temperature.

Pressure is shown through isobars which join the places of same pressure.

During winters, the isotherm of 10° C passes through the lower Himalayan region, while isotherm of 25° C passes South-Western coast and South India.

The highest isobar of 1019 mb is seen in the North-Western part of India, whereas isobar of 1013 mb passes through extreme South and over the Bay of Bengal. Thus, the Isobar and Isotherm maps clearly indicate the temperature and pressure condition over the Indian sub continent during winters.

10. Why do Chennai receive more rainfall during winters than in summers?

Ans. Chennai receives more rainfall during winters than in summers as lies on the Eastern coastal plain on the coromandal coast. This region is located on the rainshadow zone of the Western Ghats and that is why the rainfall received in the summers is very less.

During October, November, the Sun shifts over the Tropic of Capricorn in the Southern Hemisphere. There is high pressure above the Northern plains and in the South, the air pressure is very low. The 1019mb and 1013mb isobars pass through North and South India respectively. Due to this pressure gradient, the North-East monsoon winds blow and pick up moisture from the Bay of Bengal and cause torrential rainfall near the Coromandal coast. Thus, Chennai receives most of its rainfall during the winter season.

11. Briefly describe the South-West monsoon season in India.

Ans. South-West monsoon season begins in June and ends in September. The low pressure condition over the North-Western plains get further intensified and are powerful enough to attract the trade winds of the Southern hemisphere.

The South-East trade winds cross the equator and are deflected towards the right due to the coriolis force and blow into the Indian landmass as South-West monsoon winds. Due to the tapering shape of Peninsular India, the South-West monsoon winds get divided into two branches

(i) The Arabian Sea branch

(ii) The Bay of Bengal branch

12. The monsoon winds flowing in the South-Westerly direction approach the landmass of India in two branches. Describe how the Arabian sea branch of the monsoon causes rainfall in various regions.

Ans. The monsoon winds of the Arabian Sea branch split into three branches and cause rainfall in following regions

- One branch is obstructed by Western Ghats. As the winds climb the slopes of Western Ghats from 900-1200m, the winds become cool. This results in heavy rainfall on the windward side of Sahyadris and Western coastal plain. After crossing the Western Ghats, these winds descend and get heated up which reduces humidity in the winds. This results in little rainfall East of Western Ghats.

- The second branch strikes the coast North of Mumbai and cause rainfall in Central Highlands. The Chotanagpur plateau gets 15 cm of rainfall from this branch. The amount goes on decreasing towards East and then enters the Ganga plain to mingle with the Bay of Bengal branch.

- The third branch of these winds strike the Saurashtra Peninsula and the Kachchh and move further towards Rajasthan, Punjab and Haryana. It causes little rain in Rajasthan, as the Aravalis are parallel to these winds. In Punjab and Haryana, it too joins Bay of Bengal branch. These two branches reinforce each other and cause rain in Western Himalayas.

13. Explain how the economic life in India is dependent on monsoons?

Ans. Economic life in India is dependent on monsoons in the following ways

- Monsoon is the axis around which the entire agricultural cycle of India revolves.
- Regional variations in monsoon climate help in growing various types of crops.
- Variability of rainfall brings drought or floods every year in one or the other parts of the country affecting the economic condition of the farmers.
- Sudden and heavy monsoon creates problem of soil erosion over large areas affecting the productivity of crops.
- Winter rainfall in the Northern part of India is highly beneficial for rabi crops.

14. What do you understand by global warming? What are the causes of global warming?

Ans. The increase in the overall temperature of the earth due to the presence of greenhouse gases in the atmosphere is known as global warming.

The major causes of global warming are

- **Deforestation** The forests have been cut down for various developmental activities. This leads to increase in levels of carbon dioxide.
- **Use of ACs and Refrigerators** With the excessive use of ACs and refrigerators, human beings are adding chloroflouro carbons in the atmosphere which causes warming of earth.
- **Volcanoes** The ash and smoke which is emitted out of the volcanoes goes into the atmosphere and increases the temperature of atmosphere.

15. What can be the possible effects of global warming on the earth's surface?

Ans. The effects of global warming on the earth's surface are

- Rise in sea level, as glacier and sea ice melt in response to warming.
- Submergence of vast coastal areas, mega cities and ports along it.
- Increase the incidence of annual flooding.
- Agriculture pattern would shift due to changing pattern of temperature and rainfall.
- Climate change would promote insect-borne diseases like malaria, dengue, etc.
- Shift in climatic boundaries will make some regions wetter and other drier.

• Long Answer (LA) Type Questions

1. Notwithstanding the broad climatic unity, the climate of India has many regional variations. Elaborate this statement giving suitable examples.

Ans. Though, India has the tropical monsoon climate, but it has many regional variations in temperature and rainfall that can be explained by the following examples

- On a summer day, Churu in Rajasthan may record a temperature of 50° C or more but Tawang in Arunachal Pradesh hardly touches 19° C on the same day.
- On winter night, temperature at Drass (Ladakh) may drop down to -45° C, while the places on the coasts in South India record 20° C to 22° C temperature.
- Annual range of temperatures may be hardly 7° C to 8° C in Kerala and Andaman islands whereas, Thar desert experiences more than 20° C annual range of temperature.
- High mountains of Himalayas receive snowfall, while rest of the country gets rainfall.
- Meghalaya gets more than 400 cm of rainfall, while Western Rajasthan receives 20 cm of rainfall.

- Most part of country gets rainfall during June to September, while coastal plains of Tamil Nadu receives rainfall in beginning of winter season.
- North India experiences continental or extreme climate, while South India has maritime climate.

2. Explain any five factors related to location and relief that affect the climate of India.

Ans. Five factors which are related to location and relief that affect the climate of India are

(i) **Latitude** The angular distance of a location from the equator in the North-South direction is called latitude. The tropical zone being nearer to the equator, experiences high temperatures throughout the year with small daily and annual range. Area North of the Tropic of Cancer being away from the equator experiences extreme climate with high daily and annual range of temperature.

(ii) **The Himalayan Mountains** The entire stretch of the mountains acts as climatic divide. It saves India from being a cold desert as it stops the cold Northern winds which originate near the Arctic circle and blow across Central and Eastern Asia. The Himalayas trap the monsoon winds and force them to shed moisture which saves the subcontinent from being a dry region.

(iii) **Distribution of Land and Water** Landmass and water heat up and cool down at different rate because water heats up or cools down slowly than the landmasses. This differential heating and cooling of land and sea creates difference in air pressure in different seasons which further causes reversal in the direction of monsoon winds.

(iv) **Distance from the Sea** The areas near the coast have an equable climate (neither very hot nor very cold) due to the moderating effect of the sea. The areas far away from the sea experience extremes of temperature or seasonal contrast as they are not affected by moderating influence of sea.

(v) **Altitude** Temperature decreases with height due to lapse rate. Air is thick near the sea level and the density of air decreases with height. Therefore, due to thin air, places in the mountains are cooler than plains.

3. How do temperate and tropical cyclones influence seasons of India that is the winter and summer?

Ans. The temperate and tropical cyclones influence the winter and summer seasons in the following ways

- **During Winter Season** The Western cyclonic disturbances or temperate cyclones that originate over the Mediterranean Sea are dragged by the Westerly jet streams towards the Indian subcontinent and cause rainfall in the North-Western part of India. An increase in the night temperature generally indicates the arrival of cyclonic disturbances. Tropical cyclones originate over the Bay of Bengal and the Indian Ocean. They move towards the East coast of India causing destruction due to high wind velocity and torrential rain on the coast of Tamil Nadu, Andhra Pradesh and Odisha.

- **During Summer** The Easterly jet stream steers the tropical depressions into India. These depressions play a significant role in the distribution of monsoon rainfall over the Indian subcontinent. The tracks of these depressions are the areas of highest rainfall in India. The frequency at which these depressions visit India, their direction and intensity, all go a long way in determining the rainfall pattern during the South-West monsoon period.

4. Describe in details the process of onset of monsoon season during the summer months in India.

Ans. The process of onset of monsoon season during the summer months is

- The Sun shines vertically over the Tropic of Cancer during summer months and the large landmass in the North of the Indian Ocean gets intensely heated. This causes an intense low pressure in the North-Western part of the subcontinent. The pressure in the Indian Ocean is high due to slow heating of water.

- The ITCZ shifts Northwards and the South-East trade winds cross the equator due to the intense low pressure cell formed over the Northern part.

- The shift of ITCZ is also related to the phenomenon of the withdrawal of the Westerly jet streams from the Northern plain and South of the Himalayas. Then, the Easterly jet streams sets in along 15° N latitude from the eastern coast and held responsible for the 'burst of monsoon' which means continuous heavy rainfall for few days.

- The South-East trade winds are deflected towards the subcontinent between 40° E to 60° E longitudes. The direction of the winds change due to coriolis force and start blowing from South-West and are known as South-West monsoons.

- The monsoon sets in over the Kerala coast by 1st June, Mumbai by 10th, Kolkata by 13th June and by mid-July it engulfs the entire subcontinent.

5. Explain the characteristics of cold weather season.

Ans. The characteristics of cold weather season are

- **Temperature** In the Northern hemisphere, the cold weather season begins in mid-November upto the month of February. In the North parts of India, mean daily temperature remains below 21° C. This region is excessively cold because it is away from the moderating influence of sea, the snowfall occurs on the high mountain ranges of the Himalayas and the cold waves caused by the winds coming from the Caspian Sea and Turkmenistan.

- **Pressure and Winds** Due to the sun's position over the Tropic of Capricorn and low temperature conditions in Northern plains and the Central Asia, a feeble high pressure is formed over North and slightly low pressure in South. As a result, wind start blowing from North-Western high pressure zone to low pressure zone over the Indian Ocean. Winds direction is influenced by the topography. They are North-Westerly down the Ganga valley, become Northerly in the Ganga-Brahmaputra delta and North-Easterly over the Bay of Bengal.

- **Rainfall** Winter monsoons do not cause rainfall because they have little humidity and also due to anti-cyclonic circulation on land. So, most parts of India do not have rainfall in winter season except central parts of India and Northern parts of Southern Peninsula which gets rainfall occasionally. Arunachal Pradesh and Assam in the North-Eastern parts of India also gets rainfall between 25 mm and 50 mm during winter season.

  The temperate cyclones from the Mediterranean Sea cause rainfall in Punjab, Harayana, Delhi and Western Uttar Pradesh. Though the amount is not enough but highly beneficial for rabi crops. The precipitation is in the form of snowfall in the lower Himalayas and it goes on decreasing from West to East in the plains and from North to South in the mountains.

6. How do monsoon winds of the Bay of Bengal branch blow and affect the rainfall pattern in different parts?

Ans. The monsoon winds of the Bay of Bengal branch blow and affect the rainfall pattern in different parts in the following ways

The Bay of Bengal branch strikes the coast of Myanmar and part of South-East Bangladesh. Instead of the South-West direction, it is deflected by the Arakan mountains along the coast of Myanmar and then blow into West Bengal and Bangladesh as South Easterly monsoon winds. From here, this branch splits into two under the influence of the Himalayas and thermal low pressure in the North-West.

- One branch moves Westward along the Ganga plain upto the Punjab plains. The other branch moves up the Brahmaputra valley in the North-East causing widespread rain.
- They cause heavy rainfall (more than 1000 cm) in Cherrapunji and Mawsynram lying on the windward sides of the Garo and the Khasi hills.
- The Tamil Nadu or Coromandal coast remains dry because it is parallel to the Bay of Bengal branch of South-West monsoon and it also lies in the rain shadow area of the Arabian Sea branch of South-West monsoon.

7 Give an account of the phenomenon of the Indian monsoon.

Ans. The phenomenon of the Indian monsoon is

- **Onset of the Monsoon** When the sun shines vertically over the Tropic of Cancer during summer months, the large landmass in the North of the Indian Ocean gets intensely heated. This causes an intense low pressure in the North-Western part of the subcontinent. The pressure in the Indian Ocean is high due to slow heating of water. The ITCZ shifts northwards and the South-East trade winds cross the equator due to the intense low pressure cell formed over the Northern part of India.

- **Rain-bearing System and Rainfall Distribution** There are two rain bearing systems of monsoon due to the Peninsular shape of the country. First originate in the Bay of Bengal causing rainfall over the plains of the north. Second is the Arabian Sea branch of South-West monsoon which brings heavy rain to the West coast of India. The amount of rainfall decreases from West to East on the West coast.

- **Break in Monsoon** After having rains for a few days during the monsoon period, the rain fails to occur for one week or more, this dry spell is known as Break in the Monsoon which are quite common during rainy reason. This break can be seen on the West coast when winds blow parallel to the coast. In the Northern part of India, the break in the monsoon occur when rain bearing storms are not very frequent along the monsoon trough or low pressure zone or ITCZ.

8. Explain the characteristics of monsoonal rainfall.

Ans. Characteristics of monsoonal rainfall are

- It is seasonal in nature as it occurs between June to September.
- It is mainly governed by topography, therefore it is orographic or relief type of rainfall in which windward slopes receive heavy rainfall over 250 cm (Western Ghats) and leeward sides register low to scanty rain.
- Its spatial distribution is uneven. It means some areas get more than 250 cm of rainfall and some areas receive only 12-15 cm of rainfall.
- The rainfall received by the Bay of Bengal branch of monsoon wind is more in North-East parts and declines towards the West (Kolkata 119 cm, Patna 105 cm, Allahabad 76 cm and Delhi 56 cm).
- It is erratic in nature. It means some year its early and sometime it is delayed. The total amount of annual rainfall also varies from year to year.
- It has burst of monsoon and breaks in rainfall. When there is sudden and continuous rains, it is known as 'burst of monsoon.' These wet spells are interspersed with rainless interval known as 'break in monsoon.'
- It causes flood in some areas when the rainfall is above average and droughts in other parts when the rainfall is below average.
- Monsoon plays a pivotal role in the agrarian economy agriculture is dependent on the rainfall received during South-West monsoon season.

9. Describe the season of retreating monsoon, conditions associated with it and distribution of rain.

Ans. The monsoon winds start retreating in the months of October and November from the Indian subcontinent. The low air pressure over the Northern India is replaced by the high pressure and the monsoon retreats from Western Rajasthan, Gujarat, Western Ganga plains and Cultural highlands first.

The conditions associated with this season are

- Clear skies and rise in temperature.
- Oppressive weather due to high humidity.
- In second half of October, temperature falls rapidly in North India.
- Dry weather in North India region.
- Rainfall in Eastern part of Peninsula.

Ditribution of rain in this season is

- The rain in this season is associated with cyclonic depressions originating over Andaman Sea.
- These depressions manage to cross the Eastern coast and the Indian Peninsula, causing rain.
- Majority of the rainfall on the East coast is due to these cyclonic depressions.
- These cyclones cause very heavy rainfall which is very destructive in the highly populated regions of Godavari, Krishna and Kaveri deltas.
- Every year, the cyclonic depressions bring disasters here due to their high rainfall and thunderstorms.

10. How there is variability in rainfall in India? Mention the spatial variations of rainfall in India.

Ans. There is variability in rainfall in India because the amount of rainfall is not fixed or definite in India. It varies from year to year and place to place. It can be calculated by the following formula

$$CV = \frac{\text{Standard Deviation}}{\text{Mean}} \times 100$$

Where, CV is the Coefficient of variation.

The average annual rainfall in India is about 125 cm, but it has following spatial variations

- **Areas of Heavy Rainfall** In these areas, rainfall exceeds more than 200 cm. It includes the Western Coast Plains, the windward slopes of Khasi and Jaintia hills. In the Brahmaputra valley and the adjoining hills, the rainfall is less than 200 cm.
- **Areas of Medium Rainfall** These regions get rainfall between 100 to 200 cm. It includes the North Ganga plain along the Sub-Himalayas and Cachar valley and Manipur, the East coast of Tamil Nadu, the Southern part of Gujarat and North-Eastern parts of Odisha, Madhya Pradesh, Jharkhand and Bihar.
- **Areas of Low Rainfall** These areas receive rainfall between 50 to 100 cm. The regions are Western Uttar Pradesh, Eastern Rajasthan and Gujarat, Delhi, Punjab and Jammu and Kashmir.
- **Areas of Scanty/Inadequate Rainfall** The amount of rainfall received in these regions is below 50 cm. They include the central part of the Deccan plateaus (parts of Andhra Pradesh, Karnataka and Maharashtra), Western Rajasthan and Ladakh.

• Case Based Questions

1. Read the case/source given and answer the following questions.

Towards the end of the nineteenth century, it was believed that the differential heating of land and sea during the summer months is the mechanism which sets the stage for the monsoon winds to drift towards the subcontinent. During April and May when the sun shines vertically over the Tropic of Cancer, the large landmass in the North of Indian Ocean gets intensely heated. This causes the formation of an intense low pressure in the North-Western part of the subcontinent. Since the pressure in the Indian Ocean in the South of the landmass is high as water gets heated slowly, the low pressure cell attracts the South-East trades across the Equator. These conditions help in the Northward shift in the position of the ITCZ. The South-West monsoon may thus, be seen as a continuation of the South-East trades deflected towards the Indian subcontinent after crossing the Equator. These winds cross the Equator between 40°E and 60°E longitudes. The shift in the position of the ITCZ is also related to the phenomenon of the withdrawal of the westerly jet stream from its position over the North Indian plain, South of the Himalayas. The easterly jet stream sets in along 15°N latitude only after the Western jet stream has withdrawn itself from the region. This easterly jet stream is held responsible for the burst of the monsoon in India.

There seem to be two rain-bearing systems in India. First originate in the Bay of Bengal causing rainfall over the plains of North India. Second is the Arabian Sea current of the South-West monsoon which brings rain to the West coast of India. Much of the rainfall along the Western Ghats is orographic as the moist air is obstructed and forced to rise along the Ghats. The frequency of the tropical depressions originating from the Bay of Bengal varies from year to year. Their paths over India are mainly determined by the position of ITCZ which is generally termed as the monsoon trough.

(i) Due to which mechanism the monsoon winds drift towards the Indian subcontinent?

Ans. The differential heating of land and sea during the summer months is the mechanism which sets the stage for the monsoon winds to drift towards the subcontinent.

(ii) The ITCZ is responsible for the South-West monsoon in India. Explain in brief.

Ans. Inter-Tropical Convergence Zone (ITCZ) is a low pressure zone located at the equator where trade winds converge. It is responsible for the South-West monsoon in India as when the ITCZ shifts northwards (toward the Tropic of Cancer), the South-East trade winds cross the equator due to the intense low pressure cell formed over the Northern part. These winds deflect towards the subcontinent due to coriolis force and start blowing from South-West to North-East and known as South-West Monsoons.

(iii) Mention the factors related to intensity of rainfall in West cost of India.

Ans. The intensity of rainfall over the West Coast of India is related to two factors

   (i) The offshore meteorological conditions.

   (ii) The position of equatorial jet stream along the Eastern Coast of Africa.

2. Read the case/source given and answer the following questions that follows.

Latitude : Northern part of the India lies in sub-tropical and temperate zone and the part lying South of the Tropic of Cancer falls in the tropical zone. The tropical zone being nearer to the equator, experiences high temperatures throughout the year with small daily and annual range. Area North of the Tropic of Cancer being away from the equator, experiences extreme climate with high daily and annual range of temperature.

The Himalayan Mountains: The lofty Himalayas in the North along with its extensions act as an effective climatic divide. The towering mountain chain provides an invincible shield to protect the subcontinent from the cold Northern winds.

These cold and chilly winds originate near the Arctic Circle and blow across central and Eastern Asia. The Himalayas also trap the monsoon winds, forcing them to shed their moisture within the subcontinent.

Distribution of Land and Water: India is flanked by the Indian Ocean on three sides in the South and girdled by a high and continuous mountain-wall in the North. As compared to the landmass, water heats up or cools down slowly. This differential heating of land and sea creates different air pressure zones in different seasons in and around the Indian subcontinent. Difference in air pressure causes reversal in the direction of monsoon winds.

(i) Which parallel of latitude divides India into subtropical, and temperate zone and tropical zone?

Ans. The Tropic of Cancer which passes through the central part of India, divides India into subtropical and temperate zones (North of it) and tropical zone (South of it).

(ii) How do the Himalayas act as effective climatic divide for India? Explain in brief.

Ans. The entire stretch of the Himalayas acts as climatic divides as it saves India from being a cold desert by stopping the cold Northern winds which originate near the Arctic Circle and blow across Central and Eastern Asia. The Himalayas trap the monsoon winds and force them to shed moisture which saves the subcontinent from being a dry region.

(iii) What is the influence of the sea on the areas close to and far from sea? Explain in brief.

Ans. The areas near the sea have an equable climate (neither very hot nor very cold) due to the moderating effect of the sea. The areas far away from the sea experience extremes of temperature or seasonal contrast as they are not affected by moderating influence of sea.

3. Read the case source given below and answer the questions that follows

Temperature : Usually, the cold weather season sets in by mid-November in Northern India. December and January are the coldest months in the Northern plain. The mean daily temperature remains below 21°C over most parts of Northern India. The night temperature may be quite low, sometimes going below freezing point in Punjab and Rajasthan. There are three main reasons for the excessive cold in North India during this season

   (i) States like Punjab, Haryana and Rajasthan being far away from the moderating influence of sea experience continental climate.

   (ii) The snowfall in the nearby Himalayan ranges creates cold wave situation.

   (iii) Around February, the cold winds coming from the Caspian Sea and Turkmenistan bring cold wave along with frost and fog over the North-Western parts of India.

The Peninsular region of India, however, does not have any well-defined cold weather season. There is hardly any seasonal change in the distribution pattern of the temperature in coastal areas because of moderating influence of the sea and the proximity to equator. Pressure and Winds: The weather in this season is characterised by feeble high pressure conditions over the Northern plain.

In South India, the air pressure is slightly lower. Due to low pressure gradient, the light winds with a low velocity of about 3-5 km per hour begin to blow outwards. By and large, the topography of the region influences the wind direction. They are westerly or northwesterly down the Ganga Valley. They become northerly in the Ganga-Brahmaputra delta. Free from the influence of topography, they are clearly northeasterly over the Bay of Bengal. During the winters, the weather in India is pleasant.

The pleasant weather conditions, however, at intervals, get disturbed by shallow cyclonic depressions originating over the East Mediterranean Sea and travelling eastwards across West Asia, Iran, Afghanistan and Pakistan before they reach the North-Western parts of India. On their way, the moisture content gets augmented from the Caspian Sea in the North and the Persian Gulf in the South.

(i) Why is there no well-defined cold season in the Peninsular region?

Ans. In the Peninsular region, there is no well-defined cold season because this region has sea on three sides and a close proximity to the equator.

(ii) How do high pressure form over north and low pressure over South?

Ans. Due to the Sun's position over the Tropic of Capricorn on 22nd December and low temperature conditions in Northern plains and the Central Asia, a feeble high pressure form over North and slightly low pressure in South. As a result, winds start blowing from North-Western high pressure zone to low pressure zone over the Indian ocean in South.

(iii) Why regions in North India experience extreme cold during winter season?

Ans. The reasons which are responsible for the extreme cold in North India during winter season are
  (i) States like Punjab, Haryana and Rajasthan being far away from the moderating influence of sea experience continental climate.
  (iii) Cold waves caused by the winds coming from the Caspian sea and Turkmenistan bring cold wave along with frost and fog over the North-Western parts of India.

• Map Based Questions

1. Locate and label the following on the map of India.
   (i) Two areas of winter rain.
   (ii) Areas having variability of rainfall over 50%.
   (iii) Wind direction over the Arabian Sea and the Bay of Bengal in summer season.
   (iv) Areas of low temperature during winter.
   (v) The direction of Westerly jet streams.

Ans.

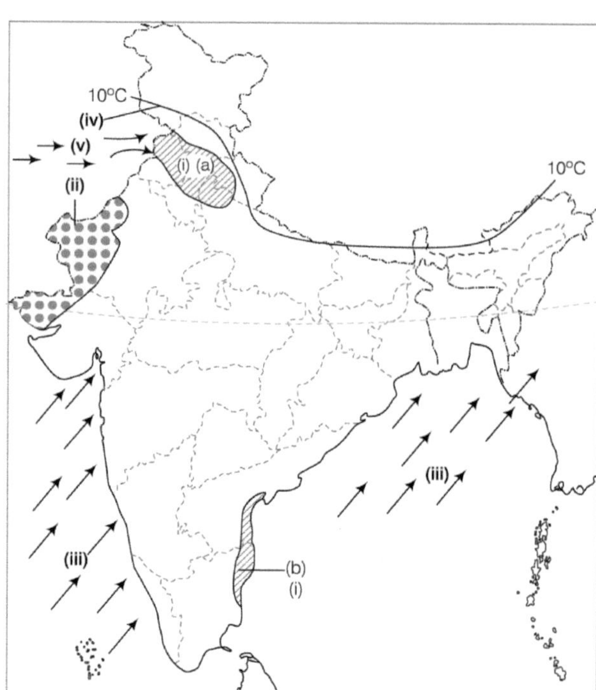

2. Locate and label the following on the map of India.
   (i) Two areas of heavy rainfall.
   (ii) A region of equable or maritime climate.
   (iii) The rain shadow area of the Western Ghats.
   (iv) The direction of the Easterly jet streams.
   (v) The areas that receive 100-200 cm of rainfall.

Ans.

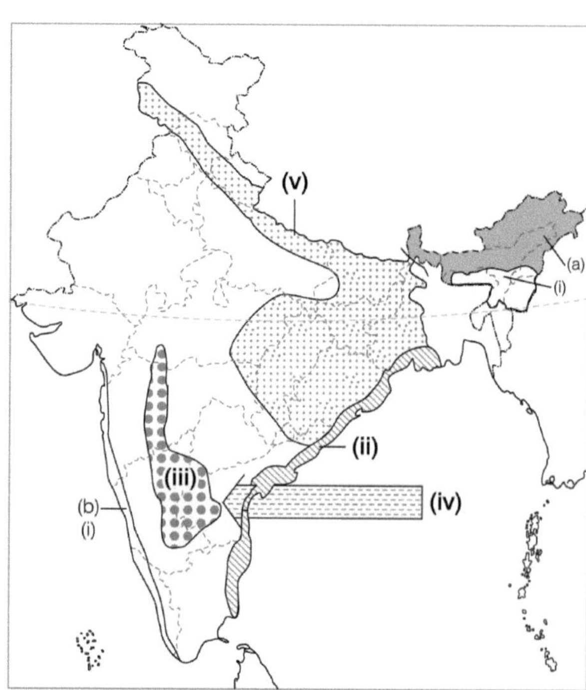

Chapter Test

Objective Questions

1. Which of the following factors affect climate of India?
   - (a) Latitude
   - (b) Distance from sea
   - (c) Relief
   - (d) All of these

2. The monsoon sets the earliest in which of the following states?
   - (a) Delhi
   - (b) Kerala
   - (c) Haryana
   - (d) Tamil Nadu

3. Break in monsoon in Northern India occurs due to
   - (a) low frequency of rain bearing storms
   - (b) presence of ITCZ over the region
   - (c) Both (a) and (b)
   - (d) None of these

4. El-Nino occurs in which month?
   - (a) September
   - (b) March
   - (c) December
   - (d) June

5. The local storm which helpful in rice cultivation is
   - (a) Loo
   - (b) Nor Wester
   - (c) Mango shower
   - (d) Blossom shower

Short Answer Type Questions

6. Distinguish between weather and climate.

7. What do you understand by range of temperature? In which part of India do you find higher range of temperature and why?

8. Write the important features of retreating monsoon season.

9. Explain the role of Westerly and Easterly jet streams in the climate of India.

10. What are monsoon burst and breaks?

Long Answer Type Questions

11. Write the important features of the winter monsoon season.

12. Discuss the mechanism of monsoon in summer season.

13. Describe the climatic types in India on the basis of Koeppen's scheme.

14. Describe the pattern of rainfall distribution in India.

Answers

1. (d) All of these
2. (b) Kerala
3. (c) Both (a) and (b)
4. (c) December
5. (b) Nor Wester

Natural Vegetation

In this Chapter...

- Types of Forest
- Forest Cover in India
- Forest Conservation
- Wildife
- Biosphere Reserves

Natural vegetation refers to a plant community that has been left undisturbed over a long time. India is a land of great variety of natural vegetation due to large variation in latitude, altitude, topography, temperature, rainfall, soil, etc.

Depending upon the variation in climate and soil, the vegetation of India changes from one region to other. The Himalayan region is marked with temperate vegetation, the Western Ghats and Andaman and Nicobar Islands have tropical rain forests, the deltaic region has tropical forests and mangroves, the desert and semi-desert area has cactii, a wide variety of bushes and thorny vegetation.

Types of Forest

On the basis of certain common features such as predominant vegetation type and climatic regions, Indian forests can be divided into the following groups

(i) Tropical Evergreen and Semi-Evergreen Forests

(ii) Tropical Deciduous Forests

(iii) Tropical Thorn Forests

(iv) Montane/Mountain Forests

(v) Littoral and Swamp Forests

Tropical Evergreen and Semi-Evergreen Forests

Tropical Evergreen Forests

Climatic Condition These are found in warm and humid areas with average annual precipitation of over 200 cm and mean temperature above 22°C.

Region They are found on the Western slope of the Western Ghats, hill of the North-Eastern region and the Andaman and Nicobar Islands.

Species Species found in the forests include rosewood, mahogony, aini ebony, etc.

Characteristics The main characteristic of Tropical Evergreen Forests are

- There is no definite or fixed time for trees to shed their leaves, flowering and fruition. Therefore, they appear green all the year round.
- In these forests, trees reach great heights upto 60 m or above.
- Forests are well stratified, with layers closer to the ground and are covered with shrubs and creepers, with short structured trees followed by tall variety of trees.

Semi-Evergreen Forests

Climatic Condition The semi-evergreen forest are found in the less rainy parts of the regions having rainfall between 150-200 cm and temperature of 26 degree celcius.

Regions The are located on the Western Ghats, lower slopes of Eastern Himalayas and Andaman and Nicobar Islands, etc.

Species Main species are white cedar, hollock and kail.

Characteristics The main characteristics of Semi Evergreen Forest are

- Such forests have mixture of evergreen and moist deciduous trees and they are less dense than the evergreen forests.
- The undergrowing climbers provide an evergreen character or feature to these forests.

Exploitation of Forests by Britishers

The British were aware of the economic value of these forests in India hence, large scale exploitation of forests was started according to their need.

The oak forests in Garhwal and Kumaon were replaced by pine or chirs which was needed to lay railway lines. Forests were cleared for plantation (agriculture) of tea, rubber and coffee.

Timber was also used for construction activities because it acts as insulator of heat. Thus, the protectional use of forests was replaced by commercial use.

Tropical Deciduous Forests

These are most widespread forests in India, also known as the **monsoon forests**. They spread over regions which receive rainfall between 70-200 cm. On the basis of the availability of water (moisture), these forests are further divided into the following categories

Moist Deciduous Forests

Climatic Conditions These are found in the areas which receive rainfall between 100-200 cm.

Regions These are found in the North-Eastern states along the foothills of Himalayas, Eastern slopes of the Western Ghats and Odisha.

Species The main species of these forests are teak, sal, shisham, hurra, mahua, amla, semul, kusum, sandalwood, etc.

Characteristics These forests are mixture of trees and grases. Large open grass patches are found in these forests.

Dry Deciduous Forests

Climatic Conditon They cover vast areas of the country, where rainfall ranges between 70-100 cm.

Regions They are found in rainier areas of the Peninsula and the plains of Uttar Pradesh and Bihar. Southern and Western Rajasthan have scanty vegetation due to low rainfall and overgrazing.

Species The common trees of these forests are tendu, palas, amaltas, bel, khair, axlewood, etc.

Characteristics The main charecteristics of Dry Deciduous Forest are

- These forests have a parkland landscape with open stretches in which teak and other trees interspersed with patches of grass are common.
- As the dry season begins, the trees shed their leaves completely and the forest appears like a vast grassland with naked trees all around.
- On the wetter margins, it has a transition to the moist deciduous while on the drier margins, it has the thorn forests.

Tropical Thorn Forests

Climatic Condition These forests occur in the areas which receive rainfall less than 50 cm.

Regions These forests are found in semi-arid areas of Punjab, Haryana, Rajasthan, Gujarat, Madhya Pradesh and Uttar Pradesh.

Species Important species found are babool, ber, khair, neem, khejri, palas wild date etc.

Characteristics The main characteristics of tropical thorn forests are

- These consist of a variety of grasses and shrubs.
- Plants remain leafless for most parts of the year and give an expression of scrub vegetation.
- Tussocky grass grows upto a height of 2 m in these areas.

Montane/Mountain Forests

In mountainous areas, natural vegetation changes because of the change in temperature conditions with changing height. As the temperature decreases with increasing altitude, the Himalayan ranges result in a succession of vegetation from the **tropical** to the **tundra**. Mountain Forests can be classified into the following categories:

The Northern Mountain Forests

The Northern mountain forests can be divided into three types of vegetation viz. Wet temperate forests, Alpine forest and pasture and tundra vegetation.

Wet Temperate Forests

Deciduous forests are found in the foothills of the Himalayas which are succeeded by the wet temperate forests that are found between an altitude of 1000-2000 m.

In the higher hill ranges of North-Eastern India, hilly areas of West Bengal and Uttarakhand, evergreen broad leaf trees such as oak and chestnut are predominant. Pine forests are well developed between 1,500-1,700 m.

Alpine Forests and Pastures

At the height of 3000-4000m, there is a transition to Alpine to forests and pastures. Temperate grassland are also found at many places in this zone.

Common trees in alpine forests are silver firs, junipers, pines, birch and rhododendrons. Blue Pine and spruce also appear at altitudes of 2,225-3,048 m. These pastures are used for **transhumance**[1] by tribes like the Gujjars, Bakarwals, the Bhotiyas and the Gaddis.

Tundra Vegetation

At higher altitude, mosses and lichens form a part of tundra vegetation. Trees are not found in this region as it is permafrost region.

Generally, the North-facing slopes of Himalayas are drier and do not have thicker vegetation cover. The Southern slopes carry a thicker cover of vegetation because of relatively higher precipitation.

Commercial Usage of Montane Forests

Chir Pine, deodar (endemic species), chinar and walnut are useful commercial trees, used for construction, furniture, handicrafts, etc. Deodar is a durable wood and is mainly used in construction activity. Kashmir handicrafts are mainly sustained by the chinar and walnut species.

The Southern Mountain Forests

These forests are found in three distinct areas of Peninsular India i.e. the Western Ghats, the Vindhyas and the Nilgiris and are also found in the Satpura and Maikal ranges.

These forests are near the tropics and only 1,500 m above sea level, vegetation is **temperate** in the higher regions and **sub-tropical** in the lower regions of the Western Ghats especially in Kerala, Tamil Nadu and Karnataka.

The temperate forests are called **Sholas**[2] in the Nilgiris, Anaimalai and Palani hills. Important species from economic point of view are magnolia, laurel, cinchona, wattle, etc.

Littoral and Swamp Forests

India has a rich variety of wetland habitats. About 70% of this comprises areas under paddy cultivation. In India, 3.9 million hectares of the total wetland has been grouped into eight categories i.e

(i) The reservoirs of the Deccan plateau with lagoons and other wetlands of Southern-West coast.

(ii) The vast saline area of Rajasthan, Gujarat and the Gulf of Kachchh.

(iii) The freshwater marshes of the Gangetic Plains.

(iv) The flood plains of Brahmaputra marshes and swamps in hills of North-East India and Himalayan foothills.

(v) The reservoirs, lakes and rivers of the montane region in Kashmir and Ladakh.

(vi) The Mangrove forest and other wetlands of the island arcs of the Andaman and Nicobar Islands.

(vii) Delta wetlands and lagoons of **Chilika lake** (India's East coast).

(viii) Fresh water lakes and reservoirs from Gujarat Eastwards through Rajasthan (**Keoladeo National Park**[3] in Bharatpur) and Madhya Pradesh.

Chilika lake (Odisha) and Keoladeo National Park (Bharatpur) are protected as water fowl (birds which can swim in water) habitats under the Convention of Wetlands of International Importance, also known as **Ramsar Convention**.

Mangroves

Climatic Condition These grow along the coasts in the salty marshes, tidal creeks, mud flats and estuaries.

Regions They are highly developed in the Andaman and Nicobar Islands and the Sunderbans of West Bengal. They are also found in the Mahanadi, the Godavari and the Krishna deltas.

Species Rhizophora and Avicennia are main species of mangroves.

These forests give shelter to a large variety of birds. These forests need **conservation**[4] as these are too being encroached upon.

1　**Transhumance** It refers to a type of pastoralism or nomadism where there is a seasonal movement of livestock between the summers and winter seasons. The nomads move towards the mountains in summers and towards valleys in winters.

2　**Sholas** Sholas is a local name for temperate montane forests located in Nilgiris, Anaimali and Palni hills.

3　**National Park** It is an area which is strictly reserved for the protection of the wildlife and where activities such as forestry, grazing or cultivation are not allowed.

4　**Conservation** The protection of natural environment and natural resources for the future is called conservation.

Characteristics The main characteristics of Mangroves forests are

- They consist a number of salt-tolerant species of plants.
- In India, the mangrove forests are spread over 6,740 sq km i.e. 7% of the world's mangrove forests.

Forest Cover in India

It is important to note that the forest area and the actual forest cover are not same.

Forest Area

The forest area is the area notified and recorded as the forest irrespective of the existence of trees. The State Revenue Department has the record of the forest land of each state. It covers 23.28% of the total land area of the country. Lakshadweep has 0% forest area and Andaman and Nicobar Islands have 86.93% forest area.

North and North-Western states i.e. Rajasthan, Gujarat, Punjab, Haryana, and Delhi have less than 10% of forest area. Tamil Nadu and West Bengal have 10-20% of forest area. In Peninsular India, excluding Tamil Nadu, Dadra and Nagar Haveli and Goa, all the Peninsular states have 20-30% of forest cover e.g. Maharashtra, Andhra Pradesh, Karnataka, Telangana and Kerala. North-Eastern states have more than 30% of the forest area.

Actual Forest Cover

It is the area occupied by forests with canopy. It is based on the aerial photographs and satellite images. According to India State of Forest Report, 2019, India has 21.67% of actual forest cover out of which 12.41% is dense forest and 9.26% is open forests.

In Jammu and Kashmir, the forest cover is 9.56 % and in Andaman and Nicobar Islands, it is 84.01%. In a state, forest cover should be one-third of the total area to maintain the ecological balance and 15 states of India fulfil this criteria. Hilly topography and areas of heavy rainfall are good for forest growth.

The states have been grouped into four regions on the basis of the percentage of the actual forest cover

	Region	Percentage Cover of the Forest
(i)	The region of high concentration	> 40
(ii)	The region of medium concentration	20-40
(iii)	The region of low concentration	10-20
(iv)	The region of very low concentration	< 10

Forest Conservation

Forests have a complex relationship with life and environment. Conservation of forest is important for survival and prosperity of humankind. The Government of India proposed to have a nation wide forest conservation policy, adopted in 1952 and further modified in 1988.

According to the New Forest Policy, the government will emphasise sustainable forest management in order to conserve and expand forest reserve and to meet the needs of local people because forests provide numerous direct and indirect advantages to our economy and society.

The forest policy aimed at

- Bringing 33% of the geographical area under forest cover.
- Maintaining environmental stability and to restore forests where ecological balance was disturbed.
- To conserve natural heritage of the country, its biological diversity and genetic pool.
- To check soil erosion, extension of desertlands and reduction of floods and droughts.
- To increase forest cover through social forestry and afforestation on degraded land.
- To increase the productivity of forests to make timber, fuel, fodder and food available to rural population dependent on forests and to encourage the substitution of wood.
- To create people's movement involving women to encourage planting of trees and stop felling of trees.

Based on the Forest Conservation Policy, the following steps were initiated

Social Forestry

It means the management and protection of forests and afforestation on barren lands for environmental, social and rural development. The **National Commission on Agriculture (1976)** has classified social forestry into the following categories

(i) **Urban Forestry** It means growing and managing trees on public and private lands in and around urban centres such as green belts, residential, industrial and commercial green belts, parks and along roadside.

(ii) **Rural Forestry** It lays emphasis on promotion of agro forestry and **community forestry**.

(a) **Agro-Forestry** It combines forestry with agriculture. It is raising of trees and agricultural crops on the same land including the waste patches so that the production of food, fodder, fuel, timber, fruits, etc can be done at the same time.

(b) **Community Forestry** It involves the raising of trees on public or community land such as the village pasture, temple land, roadside, canal bank, river bank, strips along railway lines and schools. It aims at providing benefits to community as a whole. It provides a means under which the people of landless class can associate themselves in cultivating trees for their own benefits.

Farm Forestry

It is the process under which farmers grow trees for commercial and non-commercial purposes on their farmlands. The government distribute seedlings free of cost to small and medium farmers. Several lands such as margins of agricultural lands, grasslands and pastures, land around homes and cow sheds can be used to grow trees under non-commercial farm forestry.

Forests and Life

Forests are source of sustenance and livelihoods for tribal communities. It provides them food, fruits, edible leaves, honey, nourishing roots, wild game, construction material and items for practicing their arts. Out of total of 593 districts, 188 have been identified as tribal districts. Tribal districts are rich in forest cover. These 188 tribal districts forming only 33.63% of total geographical area of country account for about 59.61% of total forest cover of country.

The knowledge of tribals regarding forestry can be used in development of forests, rather than treating them as only minor forest produce collectors, tribals should be made growers of minor forest produce and encouraged to participate in conservation.

Wildlife

Wildlife of India is a great natural heritage. Due to diverse ecosystem which the country has preserved and supported through ages, there is a remarkable diversity of life forms. About 4-5% of all known plant and animal species on earth are found in India. But their numbers have reduced significantly due to human activities and certain species are about to get extinct.

Some of the important reasons for the decline in wildlife are

- Forests have been exploited on a large scale due to industrial and technological advancement that has affected the habitat of animals.
- To fulfil the needs of the growing population, forests have been cleaned for agriculture, human settlement, roads, mining, industries, reservoirs, etc.

- Pressure on forests increased when trees are cut for fuel, fodder and timber by local people.
- Hunting and overgrazing has caused adverse effect on wildlife and its habitat. Now, the commercial poaching is rampant.
- Forest fire disturbs wildlife as well.

Wildlife Conservation in India

The protection of wildlife has a long tradition in India. So, certain steps have been taken by the government for the conservation of it. In **1972**, a comprehensive **Wildlife Act** was enacted, which provides the legal framework for conservation of wildlife. The two main objectives of the Act are

(i) To provide protection to the endangered species listed in schedule of the Act.

(ii) To provide legal support to the conservation areas of the country classified as **National Parks, Wildlife Sanctuaries** and **Closed Areas**.

This act has been amended in 1991 to include the following changes

- Making punishments more stringent against **hunting** and **poaching**.
- Making provisions for the protection of specified plant species and endangered species of wild animals.

For the purpose of effective conservation of plants and animals 101 National Parks and 553 Wildlife Sanctuaries have been established and special steps have been initiated by Government of India in collaboration with **UNESCO's 'Man** and **Biosphere** (MAB) **Programme'** for the purpose of effective conservation of flora and fauna.

The Government of India's special schemes like **Project Tiger** (1973), **Project Elephant** (1992) have been launched to conserve these species and their habitat in a sustainable manner.

Project Tiger has been implemented since 1973 with following objectives

- To ensure maintenance of viable population of tigers in India for scientific, aesthetic, cultural and ecological values.
- To preserve areas of biological importance as natural heritage for benefit, education and enjoyment of people.

Initially the Project Tiger was launched in 9 tiger reserves covering an area of 16,339 sq km which has increased to (now, 50) tiger reserves covering an area of 71027.10 sq km of core tiger habitats distributed in 18 states. The tiger population has increased significantly from 1411 in 2006 to 2697 in 2020 which is 70% of the global tiger population.

Project Elephant was launched in 1992 to assist states having free ranging population of wild elephants. Its objective is to ensure long-term survival of identified viable population of elephants in their natural habitat. The project is implemented in 16 states. Apart from this, some other projects such as **Crocodile Breeding Project, Project Hangul** and **Conservation of Himalayan Musk Deer** have also been launched by the Government of India.

Biosphere Reserves

A Biosphere Reserve is a unique representative ecosystem of terrestrial and coastal areas which are internationally recognised within framework of UNESCO's Man and Biosphere (MAB) programme. It aims at achieving three objectives

(i) **Conservation** Conservation of **biodiversity**[5] and ecosystem.
(ii) **Development** Development of the area in the associated environment.
(iii) **Logistics** The area should be linked internationally for research and monitoring.

There are 18 biosphere reserves in India. Out of these 11 Biosphere Reserves of India have been recognised by the UNESCO on World Network of Biosphere Reserves.

Nilgiri Biosphere Reserve (NBR)

It is the **first biosphere reserve** established in India in September 1986 covering the area of 5,520 sq km. It covers the complex of Wyanad, Nagarhole, Bandipur, upper Nilgiri plateau, Silent Valley hill, slopes of Nilambur, Mudumalai and Siruvani hills. Its topography is extremely varied, ranging from an altitude of 250 m to 2650 m.

It has a variety of natural vegetation from dry scrubs, dry and moist deciduous, semi-evergreen and wet evergreen forests, evergreen sholas, grasslands and swamps.

It includes the largest known population of two endangered animal species namely the **Nilgiri Tahr** and the **Lion-tailed macaque**. The largest south Indian Population of elephants, tigers, gaur, sambar, chital and various endemic and endangered plants are also found in good numbers in this reserve.

About 80% of the flowering plants of the Western Ghats occur in this Biosphere reserve. It is also known for the habitat of tribal groups remarkable for traditional mode of harmonious use of environment.

Nanda Devi Biosphere Reserve

It is situated in Uttarakhand and includes parts of Chamoli, Almora, Pithoragarh and Bageshwar districts. The major forest types of reserve are temperate. Important species found in this biosphere reserve are silver weed and orchids like latifolie and rhododendron.

It has a rich fauna, for example, snow leopard, black bear, brown bear, musk dear, golden eagle and black eagle. Major threats to the ecosystem are the collection of endangered plants for medicinal use, forest fire and poaching.

Sunderbans Biosphere Reserve

It extends over a vast area of 9,630 sq km in the swampy delta of the river Ganga in West Bengal. It consists of mangrove forests, swamps and forested islands. The mangrove trees provide safe homes to a large number of species from fish to shrimp (a type of fish) and more than 170 bird species. The mangrove forests are characterised by **Heritiera fomes**, a species valued for its timber.

It is the home of nearly 200 **Royal Bengal Tigers**. The tigers at the park have adapted itself to saline and freshwater environment. They are good swimmers and they hunt scarce preys such as chital deer, barking deer, wild pig and even macaques.

Gulf of Mannar Biosphere Reserve

It covers 105,000 sq km of area on the South-East coast of India and is one of the world's richest marine biodiverse region. It covers 21 islands with estuaries, beaches, coral reefs, salt marshes, mangrove, etc. Around 3,600 plants and animals species of this reserve are endangered, e.g. sea cow (Dugong dugon) and six mangrove species, endemic to Peninsular India are also endangered.

---

5 Biodiversity It is the variety of plants and animals life in the world or in a particular habitat, a high level of which is usually considered to be important and desirable.

List of Biosphere Reserves

Name of the Biosphere Reserve and Total Geographical Area (km)	Date of Designation	Location in the States/UT
Nilgiri (5520)	01.08.1986	Part of Wyanad, Nagarhole, Bandipur and Mudumalai, Nilambur, Silent Valley and Siruvani Hills (Tamil Nadu, Kerala and Karnataka).
Nanda Devi (5860.69)	18.01.1988	Part of Chamoli, Pithoragarh and Almora Districts in Uttarakhand.
Nokrek (820)	01.09.1988	Part of East, West and South Garo Hill Districts in Meghalaya.
Manas (2837)	14.03.1989	Part of Kokrajhar, Bongaigaon, Barpeta, Nalbari, Kamrup and Darrang Districts in Assam.
Sunderban (9630)	29.03.1989	Part of delta of Ganga and Brahamaputra river system in West Bengal.
Gulf of Mannar (10500)	18.02.1989	Indian part of Gulf of Mannar extending from Rameswaram island in the North to Kaniyakumari in the South of Tamil Nadu.
Great Nicobar (885)	06.01.1989	Southern most island of Andaman and Nicobar Islands.
Similipal (4374)	21.06.1994	Part of Mayurbhanj District in Odisha.
Dibru-Saikhowa (765)	28.07.1997	Part of Dibrugarh and Tinsukia Districts in Assam.
Dehang Debang (5111.5)	02.09.1998	Part of Upper Siang, West Siang and Dibang Valley Districts in Arunachal Pradesh.
Pachmarhi (4981.72)	03.03.1999	Part of Betul, Hoshangabad and Chhindwara Districts in Madhya Pradesh.
Kangchenzonga (2619.92)	07.02.2000	Part of North and West Districts in Sikkim.
Agasthyamalai (3500.36)	12.11.2001	Part of Thirunelveli and Kaniyakumari Districts in Tamil Nadu and Thiruvananthapuram, Kollam and Pathanmthitta districts in Kerala.
Achanakmar-Amarkantak (3835.51)	30.03.2005	Part of Anuppur and Dindori Districts of Madhya Pradesh (3835.51) and Bilaspur district of Chhattisgarh.
Kachchh (12454)	29.01.2008	Part of Kachchh, Rajkot, Surendranagar and Patan Districts in Gujarat.
Cold Desert (7770)	28.08.2009	Pin Valley National Park and surroundings; Chandratal and Sarchu and Kibber Wildlife sanctuary in Himachal Pradesh.
Seshachalam (4755.997)	20.09.2010	Sechachalam hill ranges in Eastern Ghats encompassing part of Chittoor and Kadapa Districts in Andhra Pradesh.
Panna (2998.98)	25.08.2011	Part of Panna and Chhattarpur Districts in Madhya Pradesh.

Source : *Annual Report 2018-19, Ministry of Environment and Forests, Government of India*

Chapter Practice

Objective Questions

• Multiple Choice Questions

1. Which of the following trees do not belong to tropical evergreen forests?
- (a) Rosewood
- (b) Kusum
- (c) Aini
- (d) None of these

Ans. (b) Kusum do not belong to tropical evergreen forest.

2. Which of the following were the reasons for the exploitation of forest resources by Britishers?
- (a) To lay railway lines
- (b) To introduce plantations
- (c) For construction activities
- (d) All of the above

Ans. (d) The reasons for the exploitation of forest resources by Britishers were to lay railway lines, to introduce plantations and for construction activities, etc.

3. Tropical deciduous forests are found in the regions which receive rainfall between
- (a) 100-600 cm
- (b) 70-200 cm
- (c) 90 - 100 cm
- (d) 100 - 200 cm

Ans. (b) Tropical deciduous forests are found in the regions which receive rainfall between 70-200 cm.

4. Which of the following is an example of tree species found in the dry deciduous forests?
- (a) Climbers
- (b) White cedar
- (c) Kail
- (d) Khair

Ans. (d) Khair, tendu, palas, amaltas, bel, axlewood, etc are examples of tree species which are found in the dry deciduous forests.

5. Which of the following types of forests are found in semi-arid areas of Punjab, Haryana, Rajasthan and Gujarat?
- (a) Dry deciduous forests
- (b) Tropical thorn forests
- (c) Moist deciduous forests
- (d) Semi-evergreen forests

Ans. (b) Tropical thorn forests are found in semi-arid areas of Punjab, Haryana, Rajasthan, Gujarat, Madhya Pradesh and Uttar Pradesh.

6. Which of the following species grows upto height of 2 m as undergrowth in tropical thorn forest?
- (a) Khair
- (b) Khejri
- (c) Tussocky grass
- (d) All of these

Ans. (c) Tussocky grass grows upto a height of 2 m in the tropical thorn forests.

7. Which of the following is not a part of the northern mountain forests?
- (a) Alpine forests
- (b) Tundra vegetation
- (c) Wet Temperate forests
- (d) Moist deciduous forests

Ans. (d) Moist deciduous forests are not a part of the northern mountain forests.

8. Which of the following pairs is not correctly matched?

(a) Tropical Evergreen Forests	–	Well stratified
(b) Semi-Evergreen Forests	–	Undergoing climbers provide an evergreen feature to these forests
(c) Tropical Deciduous Forests	–	Semi-deciduous is a type of these forest
(d) Dry Deciduous Forests	–	These have a parkland landscape

Ans. (c) Semi-deciduous is not a type of tropical deciduous forest. They are divided into two types; moist deciduous forests and dry deciduous forests.

9. Which of the following pairs is not correctly matched?

(a) Region having forest area less than 10%	–	Rajasthan
(b) Region having forest area between 10-20%	–	Tamil Nadu
(c) Region having forest area between 20-30%	–	Goa
(d) Region having forest area more than 30%	–	North-Eastern States

Ans. (c) In Peninsular India, excluding Tamil Nadu, Dadra and Nagar Haveli and Goa, all the Peninsular states have 20-30% of forest cover. For example, Maharasthra, Andhra Pradesh, Karnataka, Telangana and Kerala.

10. Match the following.

List I (Biosphere Reserve)		List II (Location)	
A.	Panna	1.	Andhra Pradesh
B.	Similipal	2.	Madhya Pradesh
C.	Cold Desert	3.	Himachal Pradesh
D.	Seshachalam	4.	Odisha
E.	Manas	5.	Meghalaya
F.	Nokrek	6.	Assam

Codes

	A	B	C	D	E	F
(a)	1	3	2	4	5	6
(b)	2	4	3	1	6	5
(c)	3	2	1	4	6	5
(d)	1	4	2	3	5	6

Ans (b)

11. Match the following.

List I (Project/Policy)		List II (year)	
A.	Forest Policy	1.	1973
B.	Wildlife Act	2.	1952
C.	Project Tiger	3.	1992
D.	Project Elephant	4.	1972

Codes

	A	B	C	D
(a)	1	2	3	4
(b)	3	1	2	4
(c)	2	4	1	3
(d)	2	1	4	3

Ans (c)

12. Consider the following statements and choose the correct option from the given options

I. India is a land of great variety of natural vegetation.

II. It is due to large variation in latitude, altitude, topography, temperature, rainfall, soil, etc.

Codes

(a) Only statement I is correct

(b) Only statement II is correct

(c) Both the statements are incorrect

(d) Both the statements are correct and statement II correctly explains the statement I

Ans. (d) India is a land of great variety of natural vegetation due to large variation in latitude, altitude, topography, temperature, rainfall, soil, etc.

13. Consider the following statements and choose the correct option for the same

I. The Southern slopes of the Himalayas carry a thicker cover of vegetation.

II. The Southern slopes receives higher precipitation.

Codes

(a) Only statement I is correct

(b) Both statement I and II are correct

(c) Only statement II is correct

(d) Both the statements are incorrect

Ans. (b) Both the statements I and II are correct.

14. Arrange the following types of forests in ascending order as per the rainfall received by them

I. Dry deciduous forests

II. Moist deciduous forests

III. Tropical thorn forests

IV. Tropical Evergreen forests

Codes

(a) I, II, III, IV

(b) III, I, II, IV

(c) IV, III, II, I

(d) I, IV, III, II

Ans. (b) The correct ascending order of types of forests as per the rainfall received by them is tropical thorn forests, dry deciduous forests, moist deciduous forests and tropical evergreen forests.

15. Arrange the following biosphere reserves in correct sequence from north to south direction.

I. Nokrek Biosphere Reserve

II. Pachmarhi Biosphere Reserve

III. Similipal Biosphere Reserve

IV. Nilgiri Biosphere Reserve

Codes

(a) I, II, III, IV

(b) IV, III, II, I

(c) I, IV, III, II

(d) III, I, IV, II

Ans. (a) The correct sequence of biosphere reserves from north to South direction is Nokrek, Pachmarhi, Similipal and Nilgiri biosphere reserves.

• Case Based MCQs

16. Read the case/source given and answer the questions that follow by choosing the correct option.

Tropical deciduous forests are the most widespread forests in India. They are also called the monsoon forests. They spread over regions which receive rainfall between 70-200 cm. On the basis of the availability of water, these forests are further divided into moist and dry deciduous.

The Moist deciduous forests are more pronounced in the regions which record rainfall between 100-200 cm. These forests are found in the northeastern states along the foothills of Himalayas, eastern slopes of the Western Ghats and Odisha. Teak, sal, shisham, hurra, mahua, amla, semul, kusum, and sandalwood etc. are the main species of these forests. Dry deciduous forest covers vast areas of the country, where rainfall ranges between 70 -100 cm. On the wetter margins, it has a transition to the moist deciduous, while on the drier margins to thorn forests. These forests are found in rainier areas of the Peninsula and the plains of Uttar Pradesh and Bihar. In the higher rainfall regions of the Peninsular plateau and the northern Indian plain, these forests have a parkland landscape with open stretches in which teak and other trees interspersed with patches of grass are common. As the dry season begins, the trees shed their leaves completely and the forest appears like a vast grassland with naked trees all around. Tendu, palas, amaltas, bel, khair, axlewood, etc. are the common trees of these forests. In the western and southern part of Rajasthan, vegetation cover is very scanty due to low rainfall and overgrazing.

(i) The moist deciduous forests are found in which of the following rainfall regions?
(a) Areas of high rainfall
(b) Areas of medium rainfall
(c) Areas of low rainfall
(d) Areas of inadequate rainfall

Ans. (b) The moist deciduous forests are found in the medium rainfall regions which receive rainfall between 100-200 cm.

(ii) Moist deciduous forests are known for which of the following species of trees?
(a) Sal   (b) Palas
(c) Amaltas   (d) Bel

Ans. (a) Moist deciduous forests are known for sal, teak, shisham, hurra, mahua, amla, semul, kusum and sandalwood etc.

(iii) The dry deciduous forests are found in which of the following rainfall regions?
(a) Areas of high rainfall
(b) Areas of medium rainfall
(c) Areas of low rainfall
(d) Areas of inadequate rainfall

Ans. (c) The dry deciduous forests are found in the low rainfall regions which receive rainfall between 70-100 cm.

(iv) The dry deciduous forests have a transition to which of the following forests on the drier margins?
(a) Temperate forests
(b) Moist deciduous forests
(c) Tropical thorn forests
(d) Tropical evergreen forests

Ans. (c) The dry deciduous forests have a transition to tropical thorn forests on the drier margins.

PART 2

Subjective Questions

• Short Answer (SA) Type Questions

1. Why and how the British had exploited the forests in India?

Ans The British exploited the forests in India as they were aware of the economic value of forests in India and they wanted to get the valuable forest produce such as fuel, timber, wood, etc. The British needed all these resources for the development of their country, as raw materials.

They exploited the resources in the following ways

* They replaced the protectional use of forests to commercial use by changing the structure of these forests. They grew those plant species that can be used as raw materials in industries.
* Oak forests in Garhwal and Kumaon regions were replaced by pine, which could be used to lay down railway lines.
* Forests were cleared for plantation agriculture such as tea, coffee, rubber etc.
* The British also cut down the trees to obtain timber for construction activities as timber acts as a good insulator.

2. Distinguish between Moist Deciduous and Dry Deciduous Forests.

Ans Differences between Moist Deciduous Forests and Dry Deciduous Forests are

Basis	Moist Deciduous Forests	Dry Deciduous Forests
Rainfall	They are found in the regions where rainfall is between 100-200 cm.	They are found in the areas where rainfall ranges between 70-100 cm.
Species	Teak, sal, shisham, mahua, amla, semul, kusum, sandalwood, etc. are the main species of this forests.	Tendu, palas, bel, khair, axlewood, amaltas, etc. are found in this region.
Location	These forests are found in the North-Eastern states along the foothills of Himalayas, Eastern slopes of the Western Ghats.	These forests are found in rainier areas of the Peninsula and the plains of Uttar Pradesh and Bihar. As the dry season begins, the trees shed their leaves and forests appears like a vast grassland with naked trees all around.

3. The desert region of Rajasthan is known for a number of bushes and thorny vegetation. What are the characteristics of this type of vegetation?

Ans Thorny vegetation is mainly found in the desert region of Rajasthan. The important characteristics of this type of vegetation are

- These forests occur in the areas which receive rainfall less than 50 cm.
- These consist of a variety of grasses and shrubs. Plants remain leafless for most part of the year and gives an expression of scrub vegetation.
- Important species found in this region are babool, ber, khair, neem, khejri, palas, wild date palm, etc.
- Tussocky grass grows upto a height of 2 m in these areas.
- These forests are also found in semi-arid areas of Punjab, Haryana, Rajasthan, Gujarat, Madhya Pradesh and Uttar Pradesh.

4. What are Montane forests? Describe any one type of montane vegetation.

Ans Montane forests are those forests that are found in the mountain regions. In the mountain regions, because of change in the altitude, the temperature decreases and thus, the vegetation of the mountain region also changes from Tropical to Tundra.

Montane forests are classified into Northern and Southern Montane forests.

Northern Montane Forests

The characteristics of Northern Montane forests are

- In the Northern Montane forests, deciduous forests are found in the foothills of Himalayas.
- They are succeeded by wet temperate forests at an altitude of 1000-1200 m.
- Temperate grasslands are also found in many places in this zone.
- At much higher altitudes, Tundra vegetation is found which includes mosses and lichens.

5. What are mangrove forests? Explain how they form a unique type of vegetation. Where are they found in India?

Ans. Mangrove forests are forests of small tree or shrubs, that grow in coastal or saline areas. Mangroves occur in the tropical region having roots submerged under the water.

They form a unique type of vegetation because

- They grow along the coast in salty marshes, tidal creeks, mud flats or estuaries.
- They consist of plant species, which are salt tolerant and survive in saline water.
- These forests provide shelter to a wide variety of birds.
- They are adapted to low oxygen conditions as their roots are submerged under the water.

In India, Mangroves cover 6740 sq km of area. It is almost 7% of the world's mangroves. These are well developed in Andaman and Nicobar islands, and Sunderbans of West Bengal. They are also found between Mahanadi, Godavari and Krishna deltas.

6. What are the eight wetland groups in India?

Ans The eight wetland groups in India are

(i) The reservoirs of the Deccan plateau with lagoons and other wetlands of West coast.

(ii) The vast saline area of Rajasthan, Gujarat and the Gulf of Kachchh.

(iii) The fresh water marshes of the Gangetic Plains.

(iv) The flood plains of Brahmaputra; marshes and swamps in hills of North-East India and Himalayan foothills.

(v) The reservoirs, lakes and rivers of the montane region in Kashmir and Ladakh.

(vi) The mangrove forest and other wetlands of the island arcs of the Andaman and Nicobar Islands.

(vii) Delta wetlands and lagoons of Chilika lake (India's East coast).

(viii) Fresh water lakes and reservoirs from Gujarat Eastwards through Rajasthan (Keoladeo National Park in Bharatpur and Madhya Pradesh).

7. Explain the spatial variations in the forest area in various States of India.

Ans. There is spatial variation in the forest area in various States of India in the following ways according to their respective forest areas

- Rajasthan, Gujarat, Punjab and Haryana are the states with less than 10% of forest area.
- Tamil Nadu and West Bengal are the states with 10-20% of forest area.
- Maharashtra, Andhra Pradesh, Karnataka, Kerala, Telangana and all the Peninsular states excluding Tamil Nadu, Goa and Dadra and Nagar Haveli are the states with 20-30% of forest area.
- North- Eastern states of India have more than 30% of forest area.

8. Explain the reasons for declining wildlife.

Ans. Reasons for declining wildlife are

- Forests have been exploited on a large scale due to industrial and technological advancement that has affected the habitat of animals.
- To fulfil the needs of the growing population, forests have been cleared for agriculture, human settlement, roads, mining industries, reservoirs, etc.
- Pressure on forests increases when trees and their branches are cut for fuel, fodder and timber by local people. Hunting and overgrazing has caused adverse effect on wildlife and its habitat.
- Forest fire often in tropical forests disturbs wildlife as well.

9. Various measures have been taken by the government to protect and conserve wildlife in India. Explain the objectives of any two of these.

Ans. Government of India has taken various measures to conserve and protect wildlife. These includes Wildlife Protection Act, establishment of National Parks, Biosphere Reserves, special Projects like Project Tiger, Project Elephant etc.

Wildlife Protection Act, 1972

The main objectives of Wildlife Protection Act are

- To provide protection to endangered species listed in the Schedule of the Act.
- To provide legal support to the conservation areas of the country classified as National Parks and Wildlife Sanctuaries.

Biosphere Reserves

The main objectives of establishing the biosphere reserves are

- To conserve biodiversity and ecosystem.
- Development of area in an integrated manner.
- Area should be linked internationally for research and monitoring.

10. What were the main objectives of Project Tiger launched by the Government. Explain, how it has contributed to the protection of tiger.

Ans. Project Tiger was launched in 1973 by the Government of India with the aim of protecting the tiger species and preserving and conserving the population of tigers.

The main objectives of Project Tiger are

- To ensure that there is a viable population of tigers in India for scientific, aesthetic, cultural and ecological values.
- To preserve areas of biological importance as natural heritage for the benefit, education and enjoyment of the people.
- Eliminating all forms of human exploitation and disturbance from habitat of tigers.

It has contributed to protection of tiger in the following ways

- The area under Tiger Reserves have increased from earlier 16,339 sq km to 36,988 sq km.
- The total number of tiger reserves have increased from earlier 9 to 50.
- The tiger population has significantly increased from 1,411 to 3,642.

11. How should we contribute in conservation of forests and wildlife?

Ans We should contribute in conservation of forests and wildlife in following ways

- For effective conservation, we should plant as many trees as we can by participating in programs like Van Mahotsav.
- We should take pledge never to kill any animal, neither for fun or food and convince others to do so.
- Hunting by greedy hunters for commercial purposes should be stopped at all cost.
- Reckless cutting of forests to bring land under cultivation and inhabitation should be minimised.
- Pollution due to chemical and industrial wastes should be checked.

12. When was 'Nanda Devi' declared as a biosphere reserves. Mention characteristic features of the Nanda Devi Biosphere Reserve.

Ans The 'Nanda Devi' was declared as a biosphere reserve in the year 1988. The characteristic features of Nanda Devi Biosphere Reserve are

- It covers total area of 5860 sq km. Nanda Devi Biosphere Reserve is situated in Uttarakhand.
- It includes parts of Chamoli, Almora, Pithoragarh and Bageshwar districts.
- The major forest types of the reserve are temperate. The important species include silver weed and orchids like latifolie and rhododendron.
- It has rich fauna such as snow leopard, black bear, brown bear, musk deer, snow-cock, golden eagle and black eagle.

13. Briefly describe a marine Biosphere Reserve of India.

Ans The Gulf of Mannar is the first Marine Biosphere Reserve in India. It is situated along the South-East coast of Tamil Nadu. It is one of the richest biosphere reserves from the marine biodiversity perspective.

The features of this reserve are

- It covers total 10,500 sq km of area on the South-East coast of India.
- The Biosphere Reserve comprises 21 islands with estuaries, beaches, forests, sea grasses, corals, salt marshes and mangroves.
- Various endangered plant and animal species are found in this biosphere reserve. These are seacow (Dugong), and various mangrove species that are endemic to Peninsular India.
- It is included under the Man and Biosphere Reserve Program of UNESCO.

• Long Answer (LA) Type Questions

1. Differentiate between the tropical evergreen and semi-evergreen forests.

Ans **Tropical Evergreen Forests**

Conditions These are found in warm and humid areas having an average annual rainfall of over 200 cm and mean annual temperature of 22 degrees celcius.

Regions They are found on the Western slopes of Western Ghats, hill of North-East region and the Andaman and Nicobar Islands.

Features There is no definite time for the trees to shed their leaves, flowering and fruition. They appear green all the year round. In these forests, the trees reach great height upto 60m or above. Forests are well stratified and creepers, short structured trees followed by tall variety of trees.

Species Species in this region are rosewood, mahogany, aini, ebony etc.

Semi-Evergreen Forests

Conditions The semi evergreen forests are found in the less rainy parts of these regions having rainfall between 150-200 cm and temperature of 26 degree celcius.

Regions They are located on the western coast, lower slopes of Eastern Himalayas, Assam, Odisha etc.

Features Such forests have a mixture of evergreen and moist deciduous trees and they are less dense than the evergreen forests. The undergrowing climbers provide an evergreen character to these forests.

Species Main species are white cedar, hollock and kail.

2. "The Himalayan ranges show a succession of vegetation from the tropical to the tundra." Justify.

Ans. The Himalayan ranges show a succession of vegetation from the tropical to the tundra due to the following features

- Deciduous forests are found in the foothills of the Himalayas which are succeeded by the wet temperate forest. These forests are found between on altitude of 1,000-2,000m.

- Evergreen broad leaf trees such as oak and chestnut are predominant in these areas. Pine forest are well developed between 1,500-1,000 m.

- At the height of 3,000-4,000 m, there is a transition to alpine forests and pastures. Temperate grasslands are also found at many places in this zone.

- Blue pine and spruce appear at altitudes of 2,225-3,048m. Common trees in Alpine forests are silver firs, junipers, pines, birch and rhododendrons.

- At the higher altitudes, mosses and lichens form a part of tundra vegetation. In this region, trees and scrubs are mainly absent, they cannot survive in the permafrost region.

3. What steps have been taken up to conserve forests? (NCERT)

Ans. In order to conserve forests, Forest Policy was adopted by government in 1952 which was modified in 1988. Based on the Forest Conservation Policy, social forestry was initiated. Social forestry means the management and protection of forests and afforestation on barren lands for environmental, social and rural development. The National Commission on Agriculture (1976) has classified social forestry into the following categories:

- **Urban Forestry** It means growing and managing trees on public and private lands in and around urban centres such as green belts, residential, industrial and commercial green belts, parks and along roadside.

- **Rural Forestry** It lays emphasis on promotion of agro forestry and community forestry. Agro-forestry combines forestry with agriculture. It is raising of trees and agricultural crops on the same land including the waste patches so that the production of food, fodder, fuel, timber, fruits, etc. can be done at the same time. Community forestry involves the raising of trees on public or community land such as the village pasture, temple land, roadside, canal bank, river bank, strips along railway lines and schools. It aims at providing benefits to community as a whole. It provides a means under which the people of landless class can associate themselves in cultivating trees for their own benefits.

4. Discuss the usefulness of forest and wildlife for human beings and explain the institutional efforts made by the government for protection and conservation of biodiversity.

Ans. The usefulness of forest and wildlife for human beings is

- Large number of medical plants are grew in forests. They are used as a mode for recreational activities. They provide lot of ecological services such as foods, prevent soil erosion etc.

- Wildlife of India is a great natural heritage. Almost 4-5% of all known plant and animal species are found in India. Wildlife also plays an important role in maintaining the ecological balance in nature. Efforts made by government to protect and conserve biodiversity are

- In 1972, a comprehensive Wildlife Act was enacted, which provides a legal framework for conservation and protection of wildlife in India. It provides protection to the endangered species.

- 101 National parks and 553 Wildlife sanctuaries have been constructed to protect the wildlife.

- For the purpose of conservation of biodiversity, special steps have been initiated by the Government in collaboration with the UNESCO's Man and Biosphere Reserve program.

- Special schemes such as Project Tiger (1973) and Project Elephant (1992) have been launched to conserve these species and habitats in a sustainable manner.
- Other projects like Crocodile Breeding Project, Project Hangul and Conservation of Himalayan musk dear have been launched by the Government.

5. What do you understand by biosphere reserve and explain the first of the 18 biosphere reserves of India?

Ans A Biosphere Reserve is a unique representative ecosystem of terrestrial and coastal areas which are internationally recognised within framework of UNESCO's Man and Biosphere (MAB) programme.

The Nilgiri Biosphere Reserve is the first biosphere reserve established in 1986. If features are

- It is the first biosphere reserve established in India in 1986 covering the area of 5,520 sq km including the hills of Nilgiri ranging from an altitude of 250 m to 2,650 m.
- It covers the complex of Wyanad, Nagarhole, Bandipur, upper Nilgiri plateau, Silent Valley, hill slopes of Nilambur, Mudumalai and Siruvani hills.
- It has a variety of natural vegetation from dry scrubs, moist deciduous grassland, semi-evergreen and evergreen forests.
- It includes the largest known population of two endangered animal species namely the Nilgiri Tahr and the Lion-tailed macaque. Other animals like elephants, tigers, gaur, sambar, chital are also found in good numbers in this reserve.
- About 80% of the flowering plants of the Western Ghats occur in this biosphere reserve.

6. What are the characteristics of Sunderbans Biosphere Reserve?

Ans. The characteristics of Sunderbans Biosphere Reserve are

- It extends over a vast area of 9,630 sq km in the swampy delta of the river Ganga in West Bengal.
- It consists of mangrove forests, swamps and forested islands. The mangrove trees provide safe homes to a large number of species from fish to shrimp (a type of fish) and more than 170 bird species. The mangrove forests are characterised by **Heritiera fomes**, a species valued for its timber.
- It is the home of nearly 200 Royal Bengal Tigers. The tigers at the park have adapted itself to saline and freshwater environment. They are good swimmers and they hunt scarce preys such as chital deer, barking deer, wild pig and even macaques.

• Case Based Questions

1. Read the given case/source and answer the following questions.

Tropical evergreen forests are found in the Western slope of the Western Ghats, hills of the North-Eastern region and the Andaman and Nicobar Islands. They are found in warm and humid areas with an annual precipitation of over 200 cm and mean annual temperature above 22°C. Tropical evergreen forests are well stratified, with layers closer to the ground and are covered with shrubs and creepers, with short structured trees followed by tall variety of trees. In these forests, trees reach great heights up to 60 m or above. There is no definite time for trees to shed their leaves, flowering and fruition. As such these forests appear green all the year round. Species found in these forests include rosewood, mahogony, aini, ebony, etc. The semi evergreen forests are found in the less rainy parts of these regions. Such forests have a mixture of evergreen and moist deciduous trees. The undergrowing climbers provide an evergreen character to these forests. Main species are white cedar, hollock and kail.

The British were aware of the economic value of the forests in India, hence, large scale exploitation of these forests was started. The structure of forests was also changed. The oak forests in Garhwal and Kumaon were replaced by pine (chirs) which was needed to lay railway lines. Forests were also cleared for introducing plantations of tea, rubber and coffee. The British also used timber for construction activities as it acts as an insulator of heat. The protectional use of forests was, thus, replaced by commercial use.

(i) What are the climatic features of the tropical evergreen forests?

Ans. The climatic features of tropical evergreen forests are that these forests are grown in warm and humid areas with an annual precipitation of over 200 cm and mean annual temperature above 22°C.

(ii) The tropical thorn forests are found in which regions?

Ans. Tropical thorn forests are found in semi-arid areas of Punjab, Haryana, Rajasthan, Gujarat, Madhya Pradesh and Uttar Pradesh.

(iii) Mention any two features of tropical thorn forests.

Ans. Two features of these forests are

(i) These consist of a variety of grasses and shrubs

(ii) Plants remain leafless for most parts of the year and give an expression of scrub vegetation.

2. Read the given case/source and answer the following questions.

Social forestry means the management and protection of forests and afforestation on barren lands with the purpose of helping in the environmental, social and rural development. The National Commission on Agriculture (1976) has classified social forestry into three categories. These are urban forestry, rural forestry and farm forestry. Urban forestry pertains to the raising and management of trees on public and privately owned lands in and around urban centres such as green belts, parks, roadside avenues, industrial and commercial green belts, etc.

Rural forestry lays emphasis on promotion of agro-forestry and community-forestry. Agro-forestry is the raising of trees and agriculture crops on the same land inclusive of the waste patches. It combines forestry with agriculture, thus, altering the simultaneous production of food, fodder, fuel, timber and fruit. Community forestry involves the raising of trees on public or community land such as the village pasture and temple land, roadside, canal bank, strips along railway lines, and schools etc. Community forestry programme aims at providing benefits to the community as a whole. Community forestry provides a means under which the people of landless classes can associate themselves in tree raising and thus, get those benefits which otherwise are restricted for landowners.

(i) How social forestry led to development?

Ans. Social forestry led to development as it manage and protect the forests and led to afforestation on barren lands for environmental, social and rural development.

(ii) What is farm forestry?

Ans. Farm forestry is the process under which farmers grow trees for commercial and non-commercial purposes on their farmlands.

(iii) State two features of farm forestry.

Ans. Two features of farm forestry are

    (i) In this forestry, the government distribute seedlings free of cost to small and medium farmers.

    (ii) Several lands such as margins of agricultural lands, grass lands and pastures, land around homes and cow sheds can be used to grow trees under non-commercial farm forestry.

3. Read the given case/ source and answer the following questions.

The Nanda Devi Biosphere Reserve situated in Uttarakhand includes parts of Chamoli, Almora, Pithoragarh and Bageshwar districts. The major forest types of the reserve are temperate. A few important species are silver weed and orchids like latifolie and rhododendron. The biosphere reserve has a rich fauna, e.g., the snow leopard, black bear, brown bear, musk deer, snowcock, golden eagle and black eagle. Major threats to the ecosystem are the collection of endangered plants for medicinal use, forest fires and poaching.

The Nilgiri Biosphere Reserve (NBR), the first of the fourteen biosphere reserves of India, was established in September 1986. It embraces the sanctuary complex of Wyanad, Nagarhole, Bandipur and Mudumalai, the entire forested hill slopes of Nilambur, the Upper Nilgiri plateau, Silent Valley and the Siruvani hills. The total area of the biosphere reserve is around 5,520 sq. km. The Nilgiri Biosphere Reserve possesses different habitat types, unspoilt areas of natural vegetation types with several dry scrubs, dry and moist deciduous, semi-evergreen and wet evergreen forests, evergreen sholas, grasslands and swamps.

It includes the largest known population of two endangered animal species, namely the Nilgiri Tahr and the Lion-tailed macaque.

(i) Nanda Devi Biosphere Reserve is extended to which places of India?

Ans. The Nanda Devi Biosphere Reserve is located in Uttarakhand. It extended to the parts of Chamoli, Almora, Pithoragarh and Bageshwar districts of Uttarakhand.

(ii) Which features make the Nilgiri Biosphere Reserve an important reserve in India?

Ans. Three features which make the Nilgiri Biosphere Reserve an important reserve in India are as follows

    (i) The Nilgiri Biosphere Reserve is the first of the eighteen biosphere reserves of India. It was established in September, 1986.

    (ii) It includes the largest known population of two endangered animal species, namely the Nilgiri Tahr and the Lion-tailed macaque.

(iii) Nanda Devi Biosphere Reserve is a home of which species of flora and fauna?

Ans. Nanda Devi Biosphere Reserve is a home of many types of species of flora and fauna. For example, the major forest types of the reserve are temperate forests. A few important species are silver weed and orchids like latifolie and rhododendron. It also has a rich fauna like the snow leopard, black bear, brown bear, musk deer, snowcock, golden eagle and black eagle.

• Map Based Questions

1 Locate and label the following on the map of India.
 (i) Areas of Mangrove forests
 (ii) Thorn and scrub forests
 (iii) Nanda Devi Biosphere Reserve
 (iv) Simlipal Biosphere Reserve
 (v) The forests that grow on mountain slope

Ans

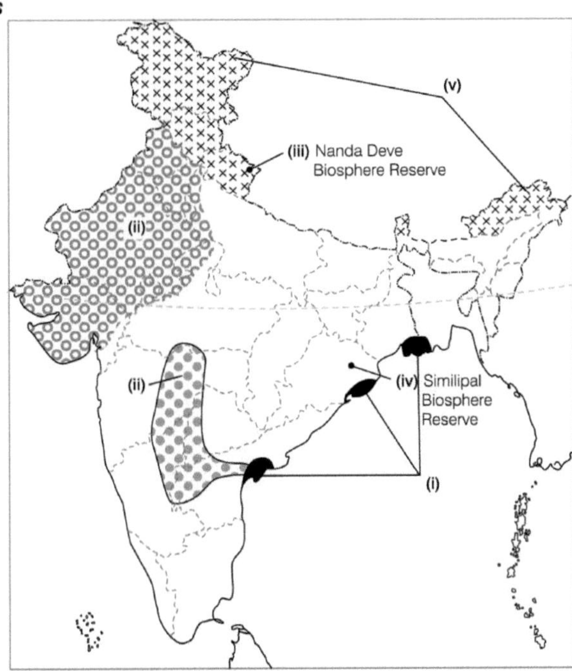

2 Locate and label the following on the map of India.
 (i) The type of forests where rainfall is above 200 cm
 (ii) The most widespread forest of India
 (iii) Sunderban Biosphere Reserve
 (iv) Gulf of Mannar Biosphere Reserve
 (v) Nilgiri Biosphere Reserve

Ans

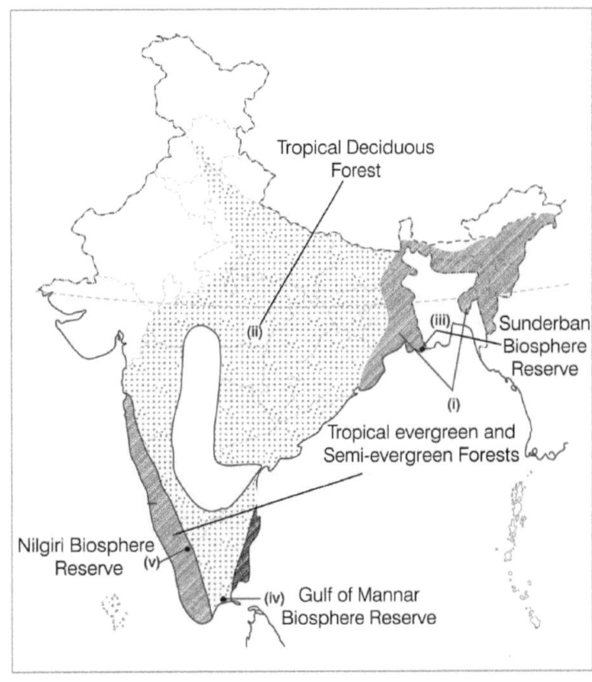

Chapter Test

Objective Questions

1. Kail is a species found in
   - (a) tropical evergreen forest
   - (b) semi-evergreen forest
   - (c) moist deciduous forest
   - (d) tropical thorn forest

2. Which of the following species is found in tropical thorn forest?
   - (a) Semul
   - (b) Neem
   - (c) Deodar
   - (d) Cinchona

3. When was Wildlife Act, 1972 amended?
   - (a) 1973
   - (b) 1992
   - (c) 1991
   - (d) 2019

4. Consider the following statements and choose correct ones.
   I. Mangroves are highly developed in sunderbans of West Bengal.
   II. Chilika lake is protected under Ramsar convention.

   Codes
   - (a) Only I
   - (b) Only II
   - (c) Both I and II
   - (d) None of these

Short Answer Type Questions

5. What steps have been taken by the government to protect wildlife in India?

6. Distinguish between forest cover and forest area.

7. Why do tribals live in harmony with nature and protect forests?

8. India is a land of great variety of natural vegetation. Justify.

9. What measures can be taken to increase the forest cover of the country?

10. Differentiate between tropical evergreen and decidous forests.

Long Answer Type Questions

11. Describe the evergreen, deciduous and thorn forests of India.

12. Vegetation changes with change in altitude. Justify.

13. Write a short note on littoral and swamp forests.

14. Describe the rich flora and fauna of India.

Answers

1. (b) semi-evergreen forest   **2.** (b) Neem
3. (c) 1991   **4.** (c) Both I and II

CHAPTER 03

Soils

In this Chapter...

- Importance of Soil
- Soil Profile
- Classification of Soils
- Soil Degradation
- Soil Erosion
- Soil Conservation

Soil is the mixture of rock debris (an accumulation of fragments of rock) and organic materials which develop on the Earth's surface. Components of the soil are mineral particles, **humus**[1], water and air. The amount of each component varies from one soil to the other soil. The soil on the surface of Earth has evolved over a thousand of years.

Various agents of weathering and gradation have acted upon **parent rock**[2] material to produce a thin layer of soil. Soil consists of the mineral particles, humus, water and air. The amount of each of these depend upon the type of soil. These are present in different soils in varied combinations.

The major factors affecting formation of soil are relief, vegetation and other life forms, parent material, time and climate. Besides these, human activities also influence the formation of soil to a large extent.

Importance of Soil

Soil is the most important layer of the Earth's crust as

- It supports trees, grasses, crops and numerous life forms over the Earth's surface.
- It is a valuable resource, as the bulk of food and much of our clothing is derived from land-based crops that grow in the soil.
- It provides shelter to variety of micro-organisms that help to maintain the fertility of soil.

- Aquatic plants and organisms derive nutrients from soil through water.
- Soils are living systems like any other organism, they too develop, decay, get degraded and respond to proper treatment, if administered in time.

Soil Profile

The layers of soil are called horizons. The arrangement of these layers in known as soil profile. The three layers of soil are

(i) **Horizon-A** It is the topmost zone where organic materials have got incorporated with the mineral matter, nutrients and water which are necessary for growth of plants.

(ii) **Horizon-B** It is a transition zone between 'Horizon A' and 'Horizon-C'. It has some organic matter in it and the mineral matter is noticeably weathered.

(iii) **Horizon-C** It is composed of loose parent material. It is the first stage in the soil formation process and eventually leads to the formation of horizon A and horizon B.

Below these three horizons is the rock which is known as **parent rock** or the **bedrock**.

---

1 **Humus** The dead organic content of the soil.
2 **Parent Rock** The rock underneath three horizons is known as the parent rock or the bedrock.

Classification of Soils

In ancient times, soils were classified on the basis of its fertility into two main groups, **Urvara** (fertile) and **Usara** (sterile).

In 16th century AD, soils were classified on the basis of their inherent characteristics and external features such as texture, colour, slope of land and moisture content in the soil. On the basis of texture, soils were identified as sandy, clayey, silty and loamy.

On the basis of colour, soils were known as red, yellow and black. Since Independence, a number of scientific surveys have been conducted on soils. For example, the Soil Survey of India, established in 1956 selected the Damodar Valley for comprehensive studies of soils. In the similar way, an institute under Indian Council of Agricultural Research (ICAR), namely the National Bureau of Soil Survey and the Land Use Planning did the comparable study on Indian soils.

ICAR's Classification of Soils

In order to make the study of soil comparable at the international level, ICAR has classified the Indian soil on the basis of their nature and character as per the United States Department of Agriculture (USDA) Soil Taxonomy in following order

Order	Area (in Thousand Hectares)	Percentage
Inceptisols	130372.90	39.74
Entisols	92131.71	28.08
Alfisols	44448.68	13.55
Vertisols	27960.00	8.52
Aridisols	14069.00	4.28
Ultisols	8250.00	2.51
Mollisols	1320.00	0.40
Others	9503.10	2.92
Total		**100**

Source : Soils of India, National Bureau of Soil Survey and Land Use Planning, Publication Number 94

India has varied relief features like landforms, climatic zones and vegetation types. These have contributed in the development of various types of soils in India.

The soils of India are classified on the basis of genesis, colour, composition and location into the following types:

- Alluvial Soils
- Black Soils
- Red and Yellow Soils
- Laterite Soils
- Arid Soils
- Saline Soils
- Peaty Soils
- Forest Soils

Alluvial Soils

This soils are widespread in the Northern plains and river valleys. It covers 40% of the total area of the country. It is depositional soil formed by sediments brought and deposited by rivers and streams.

Through a narrow corridor in Rajasthan, they extend into plains of Gujarat. These soils are found in deltas of East coast and in river valleys in the Peninsular region.

Characteristics of alluvial soils are

- These soils vary in nature from **sandy loam** to **clay**. The colour also varies from light grey to ash grey, depending on the depth of deposition, texture of material and time taken for attaining maturity.
- They are **rich in potash** and lime but **poor in phosphorous**.
- Two different types of Alluvial soil have developed in upper and middle Ganga Plain i.e. **Bhangar** and **Khadar**. Khadar is the new alluvium and more fertile, as it is deposited by floods annually. This, alluvium enriches the soils by depositing fine silt.
- Bhangar is older alluvium, deposited in the upper valleys away from the flood plains. Both Khadar and Bhangar contain more calcareous concretions (Kankars).
- These soils are more loamy and clayey in lower and middle Ganga valley and Brahmaputra valley. The sand content decreases from West to East.
- These soils are intensively cultivated in India.

Black Soils

These soils covers most of the Deccan Plateau which includes Maharashtra, Madhya Pradesh, Gujarat, Andhra Pradesh and some parts of Tamil Nadu.

Characteristics of black soils are

- They are generally clayey, deep and impermeable . It is very deep in the upper reaches of Godavari and Krishna and North-Western part of Deccan Plateau.
- Black soil swell and becomes sticky when wet and shrink when dried. Thus, they develop wide cracks during dry season. This results in **self ploughing** of soil.
- They can retain moisture for a very long time due to slow absorption and less loss of moisture. This helps the crops, especially rain fed ones to sustain during dry season.
- They are rich in lime, potash, iron, magnesia and alumina but lack in phosphorous, nitrogen and organic matter.
- The colour ranges from **deep black** to **grey**.
- They are also known as **Regur** or **Black** cotton soils.

Red and Yellow Soils

Red soil develops on crystalline igneous rocks in areas of low rainfall in Eastern and Southern part of Deccan Plateau. A long stretch of area along the Piedmont zone of Western Ghat is occupied by Red loamy soil. Red and Yellow soils are found in parts of Odisha and Chhattisgarh and in Southern parts of middle Ganga plain.

Characteristics of red and yellow soils are

- The soil develops a reddish colour due to a wide diffusion of iron in **crystalline** and **metamorphic** rocks.
- It looks yellow when it occurs in a hydrated form.
- It is generally poor in nitrogen, phosphorous and humus.
- The fine-grained Red and Yellow soils are fertile and coarse grained soils in dry upland areas are poor in fertility.

Laterite Soils

Laterite has been derived from the Latin word *'later'* which means brick. These develop in areas of high temperature and heavy rainfall. These soils are formed as the result of intense leaching due to tropical rains. Leaching is washing off of the top layer of soil due to excessive rains.

These soils have mainly developed in higher areas of Peninsular Plateau. These are commonly found in the hilly areas of Odisha and Assam, Madhya Pradesh, Andhra Pradesh, Tamil Nadu, Karnataka and Kerala.

Characteristics of laterite soils are

- With rain, lime and silica are leached away and soils which are rich in **iron-oxide** and **aluminium** compound are left behind.
- They are deficient in phosphate, calcium, nitrogen and organic matter.
- Iron oxide and potash are in excess in this soil.
- Humus content of soil is removed fast by bacteria that thrives well in high temperature.
- These soils are not suitable for cultivation but can be made fertile by use of manures and fertilizers.
- Red laterite soil in Tamil Nadu, Andhra Pradesh and Kerala are suitable for crops like cashewnut.
- They are widely cut as bricks for use in house construction.

Arid Soils

These soils are characteristically developed in Western Rajasthan which exhibit characteristic arid topography.

Characteristics of arid soils are

- Arid soils range from red to brown in colour.

- They are sandy in structure and saline in nature. In some areas salt content is so high that common salt is obtained by evaporating saline water.
- They lack **moisture** and **humus** due to dry climate, high temperature and accelerated evaporation.
- They are poor in nitrogen and organic matter and phosphate content is normal.
- They have **kankar** layers in the bottom horizons due to increasing calcium content downwards that restricts infiltration of water.
- When irrigation is made available, soil moisture is readily available for a sustainable plant growth.

Saline Soils

These soils are also known as **Usara** soils. These soils have more salt due to dry climate and poor drainage. Saline soils occur in arid and semi-arid regions and in waterlogged and swampy areas. They are more widespread in Western Gujarat, deltas of Eastern coast and in Sunderban areas of West Bengal. In Rann of Kuchchh, South-West monsoon brings salt particles which gets deposited as a crust. These soil are formed in delta regions due to seawater intrusions.

Characteristics of saline soils are

- Saline soils contain a larger proportion of **sodium**, **potassium** and **magnesium**.
- They are sandy to loamy in structure and lack in nitrogen and calcium.
- They are infertile and do not support any vegetative growth.
- The fertile soils are becoming saline due to intensive cultivation and excessive irrigation. For example, in areas of Green Revolution.
- In dry climate regions where excessive irrigation are in practice, the fertile soils have become saline due to capillary action as salt is deposited on the top layer of soil. Thus, farmers are advised to add gypsum to solve the problem of salinity, e.g. in Punjab and Haryana.

Peaty Soils

These soils are found in the areas of heavy rainfall and high humidity, where there is a good growth of vegetation. It widely occurs in Northern part of Bihar, Southern part of Uttarakhand and the coastal areas of West Bengal, Odisha and Tamil Nadu.

Characteristics of peaty soils are

- They have large amount of dead organic matter which accumulates in these areas and gives rich **humus** and **organic** content to soil.

- Organic matter in these soils may go even upto 40-50%.
- These are heavy and black in colour.
- They are **alkaline** in nature.

Forest Soils

These soils are formed in forest areas where sufficient rainfall is available, also depending on mountain environment where they are formed. Characteristics of forest soils are

- These soils vary in **structure** and **texture**.
- They are loamy and silty on valley sides and coarse-grained in the upper slopes. They are fertile in the lower valleys.
- On higher altitudes and snow bound areas of Himalayas, they experience denudation and are **acidic** in nature with low **humus content**.

Soil Degradation

When the nutritional status of the soil declines and depth of the soil goes down due to erosion and misuse, there is decline in soil fertility. This is known as soil degradation.

The degree of soil degradation varies from place to place according to the **topography, wind velocity** and **amount of rainfall**. Soil degradation is the main factor leading to the depleting soil resource base in India. According to estimates, about half of the total land of India is under some dergee of degradation.

Soil Erosion

The destruction of soil cover or top layer is described as soil erosion. Generally, the soil forming processes and the erosional processes of running water and wind goes on simultaneously and there is a balance between these two processes. The rate of removal of fine particles from the surface is same as rate of addition of particles to soil layer.

But sometimes, such a balance is disturbed by natural or human factors, leading to a greater rate of removal of soil.

India losses millions of tonnes of soil and also looses about 8000 hectares of land to ravines and agents of its degradation every year, which adversely affects our national productivity.

Soil erosion leads to formation of more eroded materials. These eroded materials are carried down to rivers and they lower down their carrying capacity and cause frequent floods and damage to agricultural lands.

Soil erosion is mainly caused by two factors

(i) Human Factors

With increasing population, the demand on the land is also increasing, therefore forests and other natural vegetation is removed for settlement, cultivation, grazing animals, etc. which leads to soil erosion. Some human factors that lead to soil erosion are

- **Deforestation** It is one of the major causes of soil erosion as roots of plants binds soil and prevent erosion. Plants also add humus to soil by shedding leaves and twigs. Its effect is more in hilly regions.
- **Over-irrigation** It makes the arable land saline. The salt deposited in lower profiles of soil comes up to the surface and destroys its fertility.
- **Use of Chemical fertilisers** In the absence of organic manures, chemical fertilisers are harmful to the soil. Unless the soil gets enough humus, chemicals harden the soil and reduce its fertility. This problem is common in command areas of river valley projects which were first beneficiaries of Green Revolution.

(ii) Natural Factors

Wind and water are powerful agents of soil erosion because of their ability to remove soil and transport it. Wind erosion is significant in **arid** and **semi-arid** regions. Water erosion is more serious and occurs extensively in different parts of India mainly in the form of sheet and **gully erosion**[3]. In regions with heavy rainfall and steep slopes, erosion by running water is more significant.

Types of Soil Erosion by Water

Two types of soil erosion by water are

(i) **Sheet Erosion** It takes place on level lands after heavy shower and the soil removal is not easily noticeable. It is harmful, since it removes the finer and more fertile top soil.

(ii) **Gully Erosion** It is common on steep slopes. The gullies deepen with rainfall, cut the agriculture lands into small fragments and make them unfit for cultivation. A region with a large number of deep gullies or ravines is called a badland topography. Ravines are widespread in Chambal basin and are also found in Tamil Nadu and West Bengal.

---

3 Gully Erosion It is the erosion of the soil and rock by the concentration of runoff into gullies.

Soil Conservation

Soil conservation is a methodology to maintain soil fertility, prevent soil erosion and exhaustion and improve the degraded condition of the soil.

Steps or measures for soil conservation are

- Lands with a slope gradient of 15-25% should not be used for cultivation. Terraces should carefully be made if the land is to be used for agriculture.
- Over-grazing and shifting cultivation should be regulated and controlled by educating villagers about the consequences.
- In arid and semi-arid areas, efforts should be made to protect cultivable land from encroachment by sand dunes through developing shelter belts of trees and agro-forestry.
- Lands not suitable for cultivation should be converted into pastures for grazing.
- Finger gullies can be eliminated by terracing. Headward extension of gullies can be controlled by gully plugging, terracing or by planting over vegetation.
- Adoption of remedial measures for soil conservation which includes contour bunding, contour terracing, regulated forestry, cover cropping, mixed farming, constructing check dams and crop rotation.

The above measures help to reduce soil erosion but these plans should be adopted according to the climatic conditions, configuration of land and the social behaviour of people. Central Arid Zone Research Institute (CAZRI) has made experiments to stabilise sand dunes in Western Rajasthan.

The Central Soil Conservation Board, set up by Government of India, has prepared a number of plans for soil conservation in different parts of the country. However, these plans are fragmental in nature. Thus, for proper soil conservation following techniques should be adopted

- Integrated land use planning
- Classification of land according to their capability
- Preparation of land use maps
- Put land to right uses

However, the final responsibility for achieving the conservation of land will rest on the people who operate on it and receive the benefits.

Chapter Practice

Objective Questions

• Multiple Choice Questions

1. Which of the following is not a component of soil?
  (a) Mineral particles   (b) Humus
  (c) Water   (d) Atmosphere

Ans. (d) Atmosphere is not a component of soil.

2. What was the factor which formed basis of soil classification in ancient times?
  (a) Color   (b) Texture
  (c) Fertility   (d) All of these

Ans. (c) Fertility was the factor which formed basis of soil classification in ancient times.

3. Which one of the following is the most widespread and most productive category of soil?
  (a) Alluvial soil   (b) Black soil
  (c) Laterite soil   (d) Forest soil

Ans. (a) Alluvial soils are the most widespread and most productive category of soils in India.

4. Which of the following is the characteristic of Alluvial soils?
  (a) Rich in phosphorous.
  (b) Vary in nature from sandy loam to clay.
  (c) Colour varies from light grey to ash grey.
  (d) Both (b) and (c)

Ans. (d) Alluvial soils vary in nature from sandy loam to clay and their colour varies from light grey to ash grey. They are poor in phosphorous.

5. Which soil is known as regur soil?
  (a) Black soil
  (b) Red soil
  (c) Saline soil
  (d) Peaty soil

Ans. (a) Black soils are also known as regur or black cotton soils.

6. Which of the following is true about red and yellow soil?
  (a) Rich in nitrogen, phosphorous and humus.
  (b) Coarse grained Red soil is fertile.
  (c) Soil develops reddish color due to diffusion of iron in crystalline and metamorphic rocks.
  (d) All of the above

Ans. (c) Red and Yellow soils develop reddish color due to diffusion of iron in crystalline and metamorphic rocks.

7. The soil formed as a result of intense leaching due to tropical rains is
  (a) Peaty soil
  (b) Laterite soil
  (c) Arid soil
  (d) Red and Yellow soil

Ans. (b) Laterite soils are formed as a result of intense leaching due to tropical rains.

8. Which of the following pairs is not correctly matched

  (a) Soil Horizon – Topmost zone of soil
  (b) Soil Horizon – Transition zone between Horizon - A and Horizon C
  (c) Soil Horizon – first stage in the soil formation process
  (d) Parent rock – middle zone

Ans. (d) Parent rock is below the three horizons (A, B, C) not in the middle zone.

9. Which of the following pairs is not correctly matched?
  (a) Classification of soil on the basis of fertility - Urvara
  (b) Classification of soil on the basis of inherent characteristic and texture - Peaty and texture
  (c) Classification of soil on the basis of colour - Black
  (d) Classification of soil on the basis of genesis, colour, composition and location - Alluvial

Ans. (b) Sandy, clayey, silty and loamy (not peaty) are the types of soils which are classified on the basis of inherent characteristics and texture.

10. Match the following.

List I (Types of soils)		List II (Lack in chemical composition)
A.	Alluvial soils	1. Humus
B.	Black soils	2. Phosphorous
C.	Red and yellow soils	3. Calcium
D.	Laterite soils	4. Nitrogen
E.	Arid soils	5. Nitrogen and Calcium
F.	Saline soils	6. Nitrogen and organic matter

Codes

	A	B	C	D	E	F
(a)	2	4	1	3	6	5
(b)	1	2	3	4	5	6
(c)	6	5	4	3	2	1
(d)	1	3	4	5	6	2

Ans. (a)

11. Match the following.

Soil		Associated with
A.	Black soil	1. Cut as bricks
B.	Alluvial soil	2. Regur soil
C.	Laterite soil	3. Normal phosphate content
D.	Arid soil	4. Bhangar

Codes

	A	B	C	D
(a)	2	4	1	3
(b)	1	2	3	4
(c)	2	1	4	3
(d)	2	4	3	1

Ans (a)

12. Consider the following statements and choose the correct option.
  I. Black soil helps the crops, especially rainfed ones to sustain during dry season.
  II. Black soil can retain moisture for a very long time.

Codes
(a) Only I is correct
(b) Only II is correct
(c) Both are incorrect
(d) Both statements are correct and statement II correctly explains statement I

Ans. (d) Black soil helps the crops especially rainfed ones to sustain during dry season. It is due to the fact that black soil can retain moisture for a very long time.

13. Consider the following statements and choose the correct option from the given options.
  I. Soils are living systems.
  II. Soils develop, decay, get degraded and respond to proper treatment, if administered in time.

Codes
(a) Only I is correct
(b) Only II is correct
(c) Both statements are correct
(d) Both statements are incorrect

Ans. (c) Soils are living systems like any other organisms. Soils too develop, decay, get degraded and respond to proper treatment, if administered in time.

14. Arrange the following soil orders in ascending order in terms of their percentage share in India.
  I. Inceptisols   II. Mollisols
  III. Alfisols   IV. Entisols

Codes
(a) I, II, III, IV   (b) IV, I, II, III
(c) II, III, IV, I   (d) III, I, II, IV

Ans. (c) The correct ascending order of soil in terms of their percentage share in India is Mollisols, Alfisols, Entisols and Inceptisols.

15. Arrange the following types of soils found in the North-Eastern states in correct order from North to South direction.
  I. Red and yellow soils   II. Forest soils
  III. Laterite soils   IV. Alluvial soils

Codes
(a) I, II, III, IV   (b) II, I, IV, III
(c) IV, III, II, I   (d) I, IV, III, II

Ans. (b) The correct order of types of soils found in the North-Eastern States from North to South direction is forest soils, red and yellow soils, alluvial soils and laterite soils.

• Case Based MCQs

16. Read the case/source given and answer the questions that follow by choosing the correct option.

Laterite has been derived from the Latin word 'Later' which means brick. The laterite soils develop in areas with high temperature and high rainfall. These are the result of intense leaching due to tropical rains. With rain, lime and silica are leached away and soils rich in iron oxide and aluminium compound are left behind. Humus content of the soil is removed fast by bacteria that thrives well in high temperature. These soils are poor in organic matter, nitrogen, phosphate and calcium, while iron oxide and potash are in excess. Hence, laterites are not suitable for cultivation. However, application of manures and fertilisers are required for making the soils fertile for cultivation.

Red laterite soils in Tamil Nadu, Andhra Pradesh and Kerala are more suitable for tree crops like cashewnut. Laterite soils are widely cut as bricks for use in house construction. These soils have mainly developed in the higher areas of the peninsular plateau.

(i) The term leaching is associated with which of the following events?
(a) Very high temperature
(b) Humidity
(c) Excessive rains
(d) Cloudiness

Ans. (c) Leaching is associated with excessive rains as it wash off the top layer of soil due to excessive rain.

(ii) Which of the following is not a part of chemical composition of laterite soil?
(a) Potash   (b) Phosphate
(c) Phosphorous   (d) Aluminium

Ans. (c) Phosphorous is not a part of chemical composition of laterite soil.

(iii) Laterite soil is mainly used for which of the following purposes?
(a) Cultivation of rice (paddy)
(b) Cultivation of cashewnut
(c) Use for bricks
(d) Both (a) and (c)

Ans. (d) Laterite soil is mainly used for growing cashewnut and as bricks for construction purpose.

(iv) Laterite soil is not found in which of the following States?
(a) Assam
(b) Tamil Nadu
(c) Gujarat
(d) Karnataka

Ans. Laterite soil is not found in Gujarat.

17. Study the table given below and answer the questions that follows by choosing the correct option.

ICAR has classified the soils of India into the following order as per the USDA soil taxonomy

Sl. No.	Order	Area (in Thousand Hectares)	Percentage
(i)	Inceptisols	130372.90	39.74
(ii)	Entisols	92131.71	28.08
(iii)	Alfisols	44448.68	13.55
(iv)	Vertisols	27960.00	8.52
(v)	Aridisols	14069.00	4.28
(vi)	Ultisols	8250.00	2.51
(vii)	Mollisols	1320.00	0.40
(viii)	Others	9503.10	2.92
Total			**100**

(i) As per the USDA soil taxonomy, which of the following soils covers larger area of India?
(a) Aridisols   (b) Vertisols
(c) Mollisols   (d) Inceptisols

Ans. (d) As per the USDA soil taxonomy, Inceptisols covers larger area of India, i.e 39.74%.

(ii) As per the ICAR, what is the area (in thousand hectares) of the second largest soil of India?
(a) 27960.00   (b) 30102.61
(c) 80321.78   (d) 92131.71

Ans. (d) As per the ICAR, the area (in thousand hectares) of the second largest soil of India is 92131.71

(iii) Which type of soil covers least area in India as per the ICAR?
(a) Vertisols   (b) Ultisols
(c) Mollisols   (d) Entisols

Ans. (c) As per the ICAR, Mollisols covers least area in India i.e. 1320.00 thousand hectares.

(iv) What is the total percentage of the seven soil orders given by ICAR?
(a) 99.1%   (b) 97.08%
(c) 95.61%   (d) 99.00%

Ans. (b) The total percentage of the seven soil orders given by ICAR is 97.08%.

Subjective Questions

• Short Answer (SA) Type Questions

1. What are the nutrients required by the soil to maintain its fertility. How can we improve the fertility of soil?

Ans. A large number of elements such as carbon, hydrogen, oxygen, calcium, iron, magnesium zinc and sulphur etc are required by the soil as nutrients to maintain its fertility.

We can improve the fertility of soil by the following methods

- Mixed cropping and crop rotation.
- Addition of manure and chemical fertilisers.
- Contour bunding and terracing to prevent erosion.
- Regulated forestry and controlled grazing.
- Cropping and nutrient management cover.

Besides this, a large number of micro organisms like bacteria, fungi, earthworm, ants etc. also play an important role in maintaining the fertility of soil.

2. 'The layers of soil are called horizons'. Mention the three horizons of soil profile.

Ans. Three horizons of soil profile are

(i) **Horizon A** It is the topmost layer or zone where organic materials have got incorporated with the mineral matter, nutrients and water, which are necessary for the growth of plants.

(ii) **Horizon B** It is the middle layer between A and C and contains matter derived from below as well as from above. It has some organic matter in it, although mineral matter is noticeably weathered.

(iii) **Horizon C** It is composed of the loose parent material. This layer is the first stage in the soil formation process and eventually forms the above two layers.

3. Why are soil surveys important? Write a few agencies that have been involved in conducting scientific surveys of soils in India.

Ans. Soil surveys are important to get information about the kinds of soil, their shapes, colour, nutrient composition etc. It helps in planning cropping pattern, irrigation requirements, classification and management of soils.

The agencies that have conducted scientific surveys of soils are

(i) The Soils Survey of India made comprehensive studies of soils in the Damodar Valley.

(ii) The National Bureau of Soil Survey and the Land Use Planning an Institute under the control of Indian Council of Agriculture Research (ICAR) did a lot of studies on Indian soils.

(iii) ICAR has studied Indian soils and classified them on the basis of their nature and character as per USDA (United States Department of Agriculture) Soil Taxonomy.

4. How are red and yellow soils formed? Write main features of it.

Ans. Red and yellow soils are formed by weathering of crystalline, igneous and metamorphic rocks in areas of low rainfall.

Features of red and yellow soils are

- The soil develops a reddish colour due to a wide diffusion of iron in crystalline and metamorphic rocks.
- It looks yellow when it occurs in a hydrated form.
- They are generally poor in nitrogen, phosphorous and humus.
- The fine-grained soils are fertile and coarse grained soils in dry upland areas are poor in fertility.

5. Where are the arid soils found in India? Why are they less fertile as compared to other soils?

Ans. The arid soils are mainly found in the Western Rajasthan region having arid topography.

These soils are less fertile as compared to other soils because

- They have high salt content and the salinity of soil reduces it fertility.
- Due to dry climate, high temperature and accelerated evaporation, they are deficient in moisture and humus, which also reduces its fertility.
- The quantity of Nitrogen required for crops is insufficient.
- Lower horizons of soil are occupied by Kankar formations because of increasing calcium content downwards.
- Kankar formation decreases the infiltration of water and reduces fertility. However, with proper irrigation, these soils can be made fertile.

6. What are forest soils? How are they different from peaty soils?

Ans. Forest soils are the soils formed in forest areas where there is availability of sufficient rainfall.

They are different from peaty soils in the following ways

- Peaty soils are found in areas of heavy rainfall and very high humidity.
- Peaty soils have high organic and humus content.
- These soils are alkaline in nature.
- The crops grown here include rice as they are submerged during rains.

7. Distinguish between laterite soils and saline soils.

Ans Differences between laterite soils and saline soils are

Basis	Laterite Soil	Saline soil
Climate	They occur in areas with high temperature, high rainfall.	They occur in arid and semi-arid regions and in water logged and swampy areas.
Nature	They contain a large proportion of sodium, potassium and magnesium and they are infertile.	They are poor in organic matter, nitrogen, phosphate and calcium but iron oxide and potash are in excess.
Formation	They are a result of intense leaching due to tropical rains. With rains, lime and silica are leached away.	The fertile soil becomes saline due to capillary action as salt is deposited on the top layer of the soil.

8. How do you know that a particular type of soil is fertile or not? Differentiate between naturally determined fertility and culturally induced fertility.

Ans. The methods for determining whether a particular type of soil is fertile or not varies for farmers and pedologists

- **Farmers** They understand the fertility of soil by cultivating crops and yield of crops per hectare.
- **Pedologists** They determine the fertility of soil by its composition. A soil rich in iron, potash, lime, humus etc is considered fertile. For example, alluvial soil, black soil, while soil lacking these are considered infertile e.g., Saline soil, laterite soil etc.

Naturally determined and culturally induced fertility can be differentiated as

Naturally Determined Fertility	Culturally Induced Fertility
Soil which supports cultivation without much help of fertilisers is said to have naturally determined fertility.	The soil which supports cultivation by addition of fertilisers is said to have culturally induced fertility.
It may decrease if soils are not monitored and treated regularly.	It may decrease if chemical fertilisers and manures are not supplied to the soil regularly.

9. How soil erosion takes place by water?

Ans. Soil erosion takes place by water in the following ways

- **Sheet Erosion** It takes place on level lands after heavy shower and the soil removal is not easily noticeable. It is harmful, since it removes the finer and more fertile top soil.
- **Gully Erosion** It is common on steep slopes. The gullies deepen with rainfall, cut the agriculture lands into small fragments and make them unfit for cultivation. A region with a large number of deep gullies or ravines is called a **badland topography**. Ravines are widespread in Chambal basin and are also found in

Tamil Nadu and West Bengal.

Thus, India losses millions of tonnes of soil and also looses about 8000 hectares of land to ravines and agents of its degradation every year, which adversely affects our national productivity.

10. Explain the human factors which are responsible for reducing the fertility of soil.

Ans. Human factors which are responsible for reducing the fertility of soil are

- **Deforestation** It is one of the major causes of soil erosion due to which soil losses its fertility. Roots of plants help to bind soil, prevent erosion and also add humus to soil by shedding leaves and twigs. The effect of deforestation is more in hilly regions.
- **Over - irrigation** It makes the arable land saline. The salt deposited in lower profiles of soil comes up to the surface and destroys its fertility.
- **Use of Chemical Fertilisers** In the absence of organic manures, chemical fertilisers are harmful to the soil. Unless the soil gets enough humus, chemicals harden the soil and reduce its fertility. This problem is common in cultural command areas of river valley projects which were first beneficiaries of Green Revolution.

11. Explain the need for soil conservation in India.

Ans. There is a need for soil conservation in India as

- Soil is necessary for plants growth as it binds the roots, hold water and nutrients.
- Soils are home to various micro-organisms that fix nitrogen and decompose organic matter.
- Soil protects the groundwater from pollutants.
- Soils provide us with essential construction and manufacturing materials.
- Soil helps in regulating carbon dioxide in the atmosphere by acting as a carbon store.

• Long Answer (LA) Type Questions

1 Explain the formation of alluvial soils. Where are they found? What are their characteristics?

Ans The Alluvial soils are formed by sediments brought down by the rivers and streams into the plain areas. These sediments in the forms of sand, silt and clay gets deposited as there is reduction in the speed of the river as it descends from the mountain to the plains.

It is widespread in the Northern plains and river valleys. Through a narrow corridor in Rajasthan, they extend into plains of Gujarat. These soils are found in deltas of East coast and in river valleys in the Peninsular region. It covers 40% of the total area of the country.

Characteristics of Alluvial soils are

- These soils vary in nature from sandy loam to clay.
- The colour also varies from light grey to ash grey, depending on the depth of deposition, texture of material and time taken for attaining maturity.

- They are rich in potash and lime but poor in phospho-rous. Two different types of Alluvial soils are found in upper and middle Ganga plain i.e. Bhangar and Khadar.
- These soils are more loamy and clayey in lower and middle Ganga plain and Brahmaputra valley. The sand content decreases from West to East.

2. What are Black soils? Describe their formation and characteristics.

Ans. Black soil also known as 'regur soil', is a type of soil made up of the lava flows. It is most suitable soil for cotton cultivation. Black soils are mainly found in the Deccan Plateau which includes parts of Maharashtra, Madhya Pradesh, Gujarat, Andhra Pradesh and parts of Tamil Nadu.

They have been formed by weathering of igneous rocks which have been formed by the solidification of lava spread over large areas during volcanic activities over thousands of years ago.

Characteristics of Black soils are

- They are deep black to grey in colour.
- They are generally clayey, deep and impermeable. It is very deep in the upper reaches of Godavari and Krishna and North-Western part of Deccan Plateau.
- They can retain moisture for a very long time due to slow absorption and less loss of moisture. This helps the crops especially rain fed ones to sustain during dry season.
- They are rich in lime, potash, iron, magnesia and alumina but lack in phosphorous, nitrogen and organic matter.

3. What do you mean by soil degradation and soil erosion? Explain.

Ans. Soil Degradation

When there is decline in the soil fertility, nutritional status of soil and the depth of soil decreases, it is known as soil degradation. It is the result of erosion and misuse of soil.

Soil degradation is the main factor that is leading to the depletion of soil resources in India. The factors that affect the degree of degradation of soil include the topography, wind velocity and the amount of rainfall at the place.

Soil Erosion

The destruction of soil cover or top layer is described as soil erosion. Generally, the soil forming processes and the erosional processes of running water and wind goes on simultaneously and there is a balance between these two processes. The rate of removal of fine particles from the surface is the same as the rate of addition of particles to the soil layer.

But sometimes, such a balance is disturbed by natural or human factors, leading to a greater rate of removal of soil. Soil erosion leads to formation of more eroded materials.

These eroded materials are carried down to rivers and they lower down their carrying capacity and cause frequent floods and damage to agricultural lands.

4. What is soil conservation? Suggest some measures to conserve soil.

Ans. Soil conservation is a methodology to maintain soil fertility, prevent soil erosion and exhaustion and improve the degraded condition of the soil.

Some measures to conserve soil are

- **Sustainable Farming Practices**
  - To check open cultivable lands on slopes from farming. Lands with a slope gradient of 15-25 per cent should not be used for cultivation.Terraces should be carefully made on the land to be used for agriculture.
  - Over-grazing and shifting cultivation should be regulated and controlled by educating villagers about the ecological consequences of such practices.
- **Prevent Gully Erosion**
  - Eliminate Finger gullies by terracing.
  - Construct a series of check dams to reduce erosive velocity of water in bigger gullies.
- **Land Use Planning**
  - Lands not suitable for cultivation should be converted into pastures for grazing.
  - Integrated land use planning that should be adopted for proper soil conservation. Lands should be classified according to their capability; land use maps should be prepared and lands should be put to right uses.
  - Adopting remedial measures for soil conservation which includes contour bunding, contour terracing, regulated forestry, cover cropping, mixed farming, crop rotation and constructing check dams.

• Case Based Questions

1. Read the case/source given and answer the following questions.

Soil is the mixture of rock debris and organic materials which develop on the earth's surface. The major factors affecting the formation of soil are relief, parent material, climate, vegetation and other life-forms and time. Besides these, human activities also influence it to a large extent. Components of the soil are mineral particles, humus, water and air. The actual amount of each of these depend upon the type of soil. Some soils are deficient in one or more of these, while there are some others that have varied combinations. If we dig a pit on land and look at the soil, we find that it consists of three layers which are called horizons.

'Horizon A' is the topmost zone, where organic materials have got incorporated with the mineral matter, nutrients and water, which are necessary for the growth of plants.

'Horizon B' is a transition zone between the 'horizon A' and 'horizon C', and contains matter derived from below as well as from above. It has some organic matter in it, although the mineral matter is noticeably weathered.

'Horizon C' is composed of the loose parent material. This layer is the first stage in the soil formation process and eventually forms the above two layers. This arrangement of layers is known as the soil profile. Underneath these three horizons is the rock which is also known as the parent rock or the bedrock.

(i) Enlist the factors which are responsible for the formation of soil.

Ans. Important factors which are responsible for the formation of soil are relief, vegetation and other life forms, parent material, time and climate.

(ii) What are the significance of Horizons A and B of soils?

Ans. The significance of Horizon - **A** is that it is the topmost zone of soil, where organic materials have got incorporated with the mineral matter, nutrients and water, which are necessary for the growth of plants.

The significance of Horizon - **B** is that it is a transition zone between the Horizon A and Horizon C and contains matter derived from below as well as from above.

(iii) Which agencies are significant for conducting scientific surveys of soils?

Ans. The agencies that are significant in conducting scientific surveys of soils are
- The Soils Survey of India that made comprehensive studies of soils in the Damodar Valley.
- The National Bureau of Soil Survey and the Land Use Planning an Institute under the Control of India Council of Agriculture Research (ICAR) that had done a lot studies on India soils.

2 Read the case/source given and answer the following questions.

The alluvial soils vary in nature from sandy loam to clay. They are generally rich in potash but poor in phosphorous. In the Upper and Middle Ganga plain, two different types of alluvial soils have developed, i.e. Khadar and Bhangar. Khadar is the new alluvium and is deposited by floods annually, which enriches the soil by depositing fine silts.

Bhangar represents a system of older alluvium, deposited away from the flood plains. Both the Khadar and Bhangar soils contain calcareous concretions (Kankars). These soils are more loamy and clayey in the lower and middle Ganga plain and the Brahmaputra valley. The sand content decreases from the West to East. The colour of the alluvial soils varies from the light grey to ash grey. Its shades depend on the depth of the deposition, the texture of the materials and the time taken for attaining maturity. Alluvial soils are intensively cultivated.

Black soil covers most of the Deccan Plateau which includes parts of Maharashtra, Madhya Pradesh, Gujarat, Andhra Pradesh and some parts of Tamil Nadu. In the upper reaches of the Godavari and the Krishna, and the North-Western part of the Deccan Plateau, the black soil is very deep. These soils are also known as the 'Regur Soil' or the 'Black Cotton Soil'. The black soils are generally clayey, deep and impermeable.

(i) How alluvial soils are formed?

Ans. Alluvial soils are depositional soils which are formed by sediments brought and deposited by rivers and streams.

(ii) Differentiate between Khadar and Bangar soils

Ans. Differences between Khadar and Bhangar are

Basis	Khadar Soil	Bhangar Soil
Composition	It is composed of new alluvium and deposited by flood annually which enriches the soil by depositing fine silts.	It is composed of old alluvium and deposited away from the flood plains.
Fertility	It is fertile and suitable for agriculture.	It is less fertile and suitable for agriculture with the help of fertiliser.

(iii) How is black soil beneficial for farmers ? State any two reasons.

Ans. Black soil is beneficial for farmers in the following ways
- Black soil swell and becomes sticky when wet and shrink when dried. Thus, they develop wide cracks during dry season . This results in self-ploughing of soil.
- They can retain moisture for a very long time due to slow absorption and less loss of moisture. This helps the crops, especially rainfed ones to sustain during dry season.

3 Read the case/source given and answer the following questions.

The soil forming processes and the erosional processes of running water and wind go on simultaneously. But generally, there is a balance between these two processes. The rate of removal of fine particles from the surface is the same as the rate of addition of particles to the soil layer. Sometimes, such a balance is disturbed by natural or human factors, leading to a greater rate of removal of soil. Human activities too are responsible for soil erosion to a great extent. As the human population increases, the demand on the land also increases. Forest and other natural vegetation is removed for human settlement, for cultivation, for grazing animals and for various other needs.

Wind and water are powerful agents of soil erosion because of their ability to remove soil and transport it. Wind erosion is significant in arid and semi-arid regions. In regions with heavy rainfall and steep slopes, erosion by running water is more significant. Water erosion which is more serious and occurs extensively in different parts of India, takes place mainly in the form of sheet and gully erosion. Sheet erosion takes place on level lands after a heavy shower and the soil removal is not easily noticeable. But it is harmful since it removes the finer and more fertile top soil. Gully erosion is common on steep slopes. Gullies deepen with rainfall, cut the agricultural lands into small fragments and make them unfit for cultivation. A region with a large number of deep gullies or ravines is called a bad land topography.

(i) What is soil erosion?

Ans. The destruction of soil cover or top layer is described as soil erosion.

(ii) Which natural factors are mostly responsible for soil erosion? State in brief.

Ans. Wind and water are mostly responsible for soil erosion because of their ability to remove soil and transport it. Wind erosion is significant in arid and semi-arid regions.

Water erosion is more serious and occurs extensively in different parts of India mainly in the form of sheet and gully erosion. In regions with heavy rainfall and steep slopes, erosion by running water is more significant.

(iii) What is Gully erosion? Mention the states where it is common.

Ans. Gully erosion is a type of soil and rock erosion which occurs due to concentration of runoff into gullies. It is common on steep slopes.

A region with a large number of deep gullies or ravines is called a badland topography. Ravine are widespread in Chambal basin and are also found in Tamil Nadu and West Bengal.

• Map Based Questions

1 On the outline map of India, shade and label the following soils.

  (i) The areas of forest soils in North-East.

 (ii) The region of arid soils.

(iii) The large patches of laterite soils.

(iv) Major parts where red soil occurs.

 (v) The areas of alluvial soils in North India.

Ans.

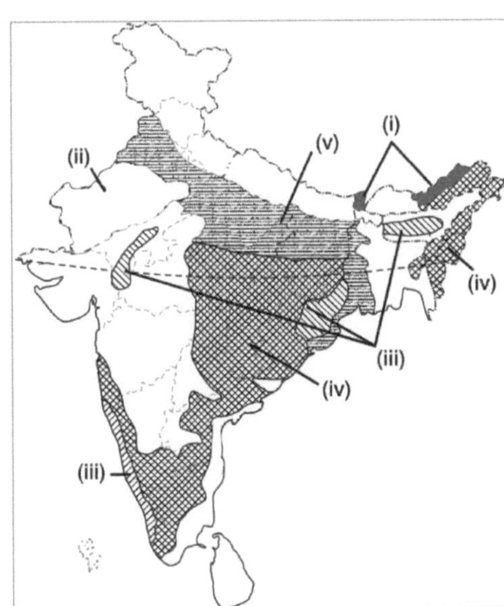

Chapter Test

Objective Questions

1. On the basis of nature and character as per US Department of Agriculture, the soil order which covers minimum area is ....

  (a) Mollisol   (b) Inceptisol
  (c) Entisol   (d) Aridisols

2. Which of the following soils is depositional soil?

  (a) Black soil   (b) Red soil
  (c) Laterite soil   (d) Alluvial soil

3. Wind erosion is very common in which of the following regions?

  (a) Arid   (b) Semi-arid
  (c) Plateau region   (d) Both (a) and (b)

4. Which of the following pairs is not correctly matched?

  (a) Black soils   —   Krishna valley
  (b) Laterite soils   —   Hilly areas of Odisha
  (c) Saline soils   —   Uttar Pradesh
  (d) Peaty soils   —   Tamil Nadu

5. Consider the following statements about Laterite soil and choose correct ones.

  I. They develop in area of high temperature.

  II. They are deficient in iron oxide and potash.

  III. These are suitable for cultivation.

  Codes
  (a) Only I   (b) Both II and III
  (c) Only III   (d) Both I and II

Short Answer Type Questions

6. Classify soils on the basis of origin, genesis, colour and location.

7. What factors make the soils of India infertile and depleted?

8. Write three characteristics of black soils.

9. How are peaty soils different from Saline soils?

10. Which areas are dominated by forest soils and why?

11. Soil is an indispensable resource. Justify.

12. Find out the reasons for such a large amount of loss of soils in India every year.

Long Answer Type Questions

13. Explain about the features of red and yellow soils.

14. Give the formation and types of alluvial soils.

15. Conserving soil is conserving life. Explain.

Answers

1. (a) Mollisol   **2.** (d) Alluvial soil
3. (d) Both (a) and (b)   **4.** (c) Saline soils — Uttar Pradesh
5. (a) Only I

Practice Paper 1*
(Solved)

Instructions
1. This question paper is divided into four sections A, B, C and D.
2. Section A has 1 question including case based multiple choice questions.
3. Section B has 5 questions including short answer questions with internal choice.
4. Section C has 2 questions including long answer questions with internal choice.
5. Section D has 1 question based on map.
6. Marks are mentioned against each question.
7. There is no negative marking.

■ **Time :** 2 Hours
■ **Max. Marks :** 35

** As exact Blue-print and Pattern for CBSE Term II exams is not released yet, so the pattern of this paper is designed by the author on the basis of trend of past CBSE Papers. Students are advised not to consider the pattern of this paper as official, it is just for practice purpose.*

Section A

This section consists of one case based question.

Case Based MCQs

1. Read the case/source given and answer the questions that follow by choosing the correct option.

   Carbon dioxide is meteorologically a very important gas as it is transparent to the incoming solar radiation but opaque to the outgoing terrestrial radiation. It absorbs a part of terrestrial radiation and reflects back some part of it towards the earth's surface. It is largely responsible for the green house effect. The volume of other gases is constant but the volume of carbon dioxide has been rising in the past few decades mainly because of the burning of fossil fuels. This has also increased the temperature of the air. Ozone is another important component of the atmosphere found between 10 and 50 km above the earth's surface and acts as a filter and absorbs the ultra-violet rays radiating from the sun and prevents them from reaching the surface of the earth. $(1 \times 5 = 5)$

   (i) Which among the following gases is the most abundant gas in atmosphere?
   (a) Oxygen
   (b) Carbon dioxide
   (c) Ozone
   (d) Nitrogen

   (ii) Ozone is an important component of atmosphere. Where is ozone layer present ?
   (a) Troposphere
   (b) Stratosphere
   (c) Thermosphere
   (d) Exosphere

   (iii) Carbon dioxide is transparent to the incoming solar radiation which is also known as
   (a) terrestrial radiation
   (b) insolation
   (c) conduction
   (d) None of these

(iv) Oxygen contributes .... in atmosphere.
    (a) 20.94%   (b) 10.94%
    (c) 20.49%   (d) 10.49%

(v) Which of the following is not a Greenhouse gas ?
    (a) Water vapour   (b) Carbon dioxide
    (c) Oxygen   (d) Methane

Section B

This section consists of 5 questions of Short Answer Type.

Short Answer Type Questions

2. What are the factors that control temperature distribution on the surface of the earth? What do you mean by inversion of temperature? (3)

3. Explain the types of tides based on frequency. (3)

4. What do you understand by 'hotspots' (3)

Or

How biodiversity is essential for ecosystem? Explain.

5. North India experience excessive cold during winters as compared to Peninsular region. Explain by giving reasons. (3)

Or

India have great spatial variations in its rainfall distribution. Discuss.

6. The carbon cycle is mainly the conversion of carbon dioxide. Define the carbon cycle. (3)

Or

Write and explain about oxygen cycle.

Section C

This section consists of 2 questions of Long Answer Type.

Long Answer Type Questions

7. "Forests and tribals are very closely related." Justify the statement. (5)

Or

Mangrove forests are unique in their own way. Explain.

8. Explain the spatial variation in the rainfall throughout the country. (5)

Or

The cold weather season in Northern India sets in by mid-November. Explain the characteristics of cold weather season.

Section D

Map Based Question

9. (i) On the map of India locate the following. (3)
    (a) Nandadevi Biosphere Reserve
    (b) Simlipal Biosphere Reserve
    (c) Gulf of Mannar Biosphere Reserve

(ii) On the map of the world given below the distribution of surface air temperature in the month of January is shown by lines as A and B. Identify the temperature shown over these lines.

Answers

1. (i) (d) The most abundant gas in atmosphere is nitrogen.

(ii) (b) Ozone layer is present in stratosphere.

(iii) (b) Incoming solar radiation is known as insolation.

(iv) (a) Oxygen contributes 20.94% in atmosphere.

(v) (c) Oxygen is not a greenhouse gas.

2. The factor that control temperature at any place are

- The latitude of the place
- The altitude of the place
- Distance from the sea, the air- mass circulation
- The presence of warm and cold ocean currents
- Local aspects

If there is an increase of air temperature with increase in height, it is known as inversion of temperature.

It occurs near the earth's surface or at greater height in the troposphere.

3. The types of tides on the basis of frequency are

- **Semi-diurnal tides** This is the most common tidal pattern, featuring two high tides and two low tides each day. The successive high tides or low tides are approximately of the same height.
- **Diurnal Tides** There is only one high tide and one low tide during each day. The successive high and low tides are approximately of the same height.
- **Mixed Tides** Tides having variations in height are known as mixed tides. These tides generally occur along the west coast of North America and on many islands of the Pacific Ocean.

4. Some areas are richer in species than others. Areas rich in species diversity are called hotspots of diversity. Hotspots are defined according to their vegetation. Plants are important because these determine the primary productivity of an ecosystem. Most of the hotspots rely on species-rich ecosystems for food, firewood, cropland, and income from timber.

In Madagascar, for example, about 85 per cent of the plants and animals are found nowhere else in the world. In order to concentrate resources on areas that are most vulnerable, the International Union for the Conservation of Nature and Natural Resources (IUCN) has identified certain areas as biodiversity hostspots. Some of the hotspots are Queensland, Melanesia, Western Ghats (India), Tropical Andes, Atlantic Forest (Brazil), etc.

Or Biodiversity is very essential for an ecosystem due to its following features

- Various functions performed by various species are essential for functioning of ecosystem. These functions include capture of energy, cycling of nutrients, fixing up gases etc.
- Greater the amount of diversity in an ecosystem, more the productive species will be.
- With more biodiversity, species ability to survive through adversities and attacks also increase.
- With greater diversity, ecosystem has greater chances of adaptation with environment.
- Biodiversity provides stability to the ecosystem.

5. The following are the reasons for excessive cold in North India during winters

- Punjab, Haryana and Rajasthan being far away from the moderating influence of sea experience continental climate.
- The snowfall in the nearby Himalayan ranges creates cold wave situation.
- The cold waves come from the Caspian Sea and Turkmenistan cause frost and fog over North-Western parts of India.

Whereas in the Peninsular region, there is no well defined cold season. There is no variation in seasons due to the moderating effect of the sea and proximity to the equator.

Or The average annual rainfall in India is about 125 cm, but it has great spatial variations in the following ways

- **Areas of High Rainfall** The highest rainfall occurs along the west coast, on the Western Ghats, as well as in the sub-Himalayan areas is the northeast and the hills of Meghalaya. Here the rainfall exceeds 200 cm.
- **Areas of Medium Rainfall** Rainfall between 100-200 cm is received in the Southern parts of Gujarat, East Tamil Nadu etc.
- **Areas of Low Rainfall** Western Uttar Pradesh, Delhi, Haryana, Punjab, Jammu and Kashmir, eastern Rajasthan, Gujarat and Deccan Plateau receive rainfall between 50-100 cm.
- **Areas of Inadequate Rainfall** Parts of the Peninsula, especially in Andhra Pradesh, Karnataka and Maharashtra, Ladakh etc.

6. The carbon cycle is mainly the conversion of carbon dioxide. This conversion is initiated by the fixation of carbon dioxide from the atmosphere through photosynthesis. Such conversion result in the production of carbohydrates, glucoses that may be converted to other organic compounds such as sucrose, starch, cellulose, etc. Here, some of the carbohydrates are utilised directly by the plant itself. During this process, more carbon dioxide is generated and is released through its leaves or roots during the day.

The remaining carbohydrates not being utilised by the plant become part of the plant tissue. Plant tissues are either being eaten by the herbivorous animals or get decomposed by the microorganisms. The herbivores convert some of the consumed carbohydrates into carbon dioxide for release into the air through respiration. The microorganisms decompose the remaining carbohydrates after the animal dies.

Or Oxygen is the main by-product of photosynthesis. It is involved in the oxidation of carbohydrates with the release of energy, carbon dioxide and water. The cycling of oxygen is a highly complex process. Oxygen occurs in a number of chemical forms and combinations. It combines with nitrogen to form nitrates and with many other minerals and elements to form various oxides such as the iron oxide, aluminium oxide and others.

Much of oxygen is produced from the decomposition of water molecules by sunlight during photosynthesis and is released in the atmosphere through transpiration and respiration processes of plants.

7. Forests and tribals are closely related in the following ways

- To a vast number of tribal people, forests are home and livelihood. It provides them food, fruits of all kinds, edible leaves, honey nourishing roots and wild game.
- It provides them with material to build their houses and items for practising their arts.
- The importance of forests in tribal economy is well-known as they are the source of sustenance and livelihood for tribal communities.
- The age old knowledge of tribals regarding forestry can be used in the development of forests. Thus, rather than treating tribals as minor forest produce collectors they should be made growers of minor forest produce and encouraged to participate in conservation.

Or Mangrove forests are unique due to their following features

- They are found in the swamp and marshy areas.
- They can survive both in fresh and salty water.
- The trees have stilt like breathing or support rots, sticking out of mud and water.
- They are exposed at low tides and get submerged at high tides.
- Hot and wet climate favours their dense growth.
- Sunderi is the well known Mangrove trees. The famous Sunderban deltas are named after these trees.

8. There is great variation in rainfall throughout the country as

- Cherrapunji and Mawsynram in the Khasi Hills of Meghalaya receive rainfall over 1,080 cm in a year while Jaisalmer in Rajasthan rarely gets more than 9 cm of rainfall during the same period.
- Tura situated in the Garo Hills of Meghalaya may receive an amount of rainfall in a single day which is equal to 10 years of rainfall at Jaisalmer. While the annual precipitation is less than 10 cm in the North-West Himalayas and the western deserts, it exceeds 400 cm in Meghalaya.
- The highest rainfall occurs along the west coast, on the western Ghats as well as in the sub-Himalayan areas in the North-West and the hills of Meghalaya, rainfall exceeding 200 cm. In some parts of Khasi and Jaintia hills, the rainfall exceeds 1,000 cm. In the Brahmaputra valley and the adjoining hills, the rainfall is less than 200 cm.
- Rainfall between 100-200 cm is received in Southern parts of Gujarat, east Tamil Nadu, North-Eastern Peninsular covering Orissa, Jharkhand, Bihar, eastern Madhya Pradesh, Northern Ganga Plain along the sub-Himalayas and the Cachar valley and Manipur.

- Western Uttar Pradesh, Delhi, Haryana, Punjab, Jammu and Kashmir, Eastern Rajasthan, Gujarat and Deccan Plateau receive rainfall between 50-100 cm.

Or The characteristics of cold weather season are

- **Temperature** In the North parts of India, mean daily temperature remains below 21° C. This region is excessively cold because it is away from the moderating influence of sea, the snowfall occurs on the high mountain ranges of the Himalayas and the cold waves caused by the winds coming from the Caspian Sea and Turkmenistan.
- **Pressure and Winds** Due to the sun's position over the Tropic of Capricorn and low temperature conditions in Northern plains and the Central Asia, a feeble high pressure is formed over North and slightly low pressure in South. As a result, wind start blowing from North-Western high pressure zone to low pressure zone over the Indian Ocean. Wind direction is influenced by the topography. They are North-Westerly down the Ganga valley, become Northerly in the Ganga-Brahmaputra delta and North-Easterly over the Bay of Bengal.
- **Rainfall** Winter monsoons do not cause rainfall because they have little humidity and also due to anti-cyclonic circulation on land. So, most parts of India do not have rainfall in winter season except central parts of India and Northern parts of Southern Peninsula which gets rainfall occasionally.

9. (i)

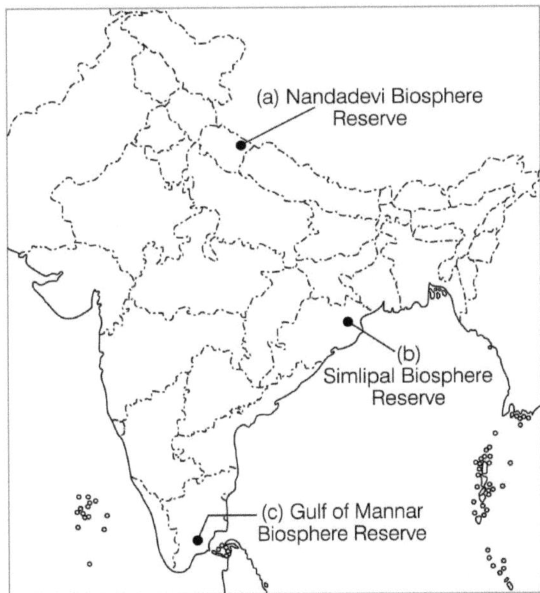

(ii)

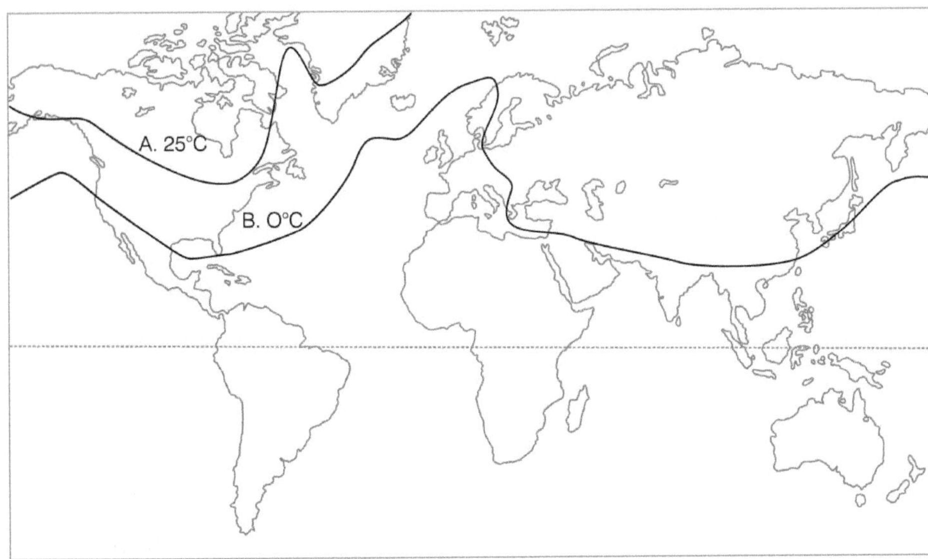

Practice Paper 2*
(Unsolved)

<table>
<tr><td>Instructions</td><td>■ Time : 2 Hours</td></tr>
</table>

Instructions ■ **Time** : 2 Hours ■ **Max. Marks** : 35

1. This question paper is divided into four sections A, B, C and D.
2. Section A has 1 question including case based multiple choice questions.
3. Section B has 5 questions including short answer questions with internal choice.
4. Section C has 2 questions including long answer questions with internal choice.
5. Section D has 1 question based on map.
6. Marks are mentioned against each question.
7. There is no negative marking.

** As exact Blue-print and Pattern for CBSE Term II exams is not released yet, so the pattern of this paper is designed by the author on the basis of trend of past CBSE Papers. Students are advised not to consider the pattern of this paper as official, it is just for practice purpose.*

Section A

This section consists of one case based question.

Case Based Question

1. Read the case/source given and answer the questions that follow by choosing the correct option.

To a vast number of tribal people, the forest is a home, a livelihood, their very existence. It provides them food, fruits of all kinds, edible leaves, honey, nourishing roots and wild game. It provides them with material to build their houses and items for practising their arts. The importance of forests in tribal economy is well-known as they are the source of sustenance and livelihood for tribal communities. It is commonly believed that the tribal communities live in harmony with nature and protect forests. Out of a total of 593 districts 188 have been identified as tribal districts. The tribal districts account for about 59.61 per cent of the total forest cover of the country whereas the geographical area of 188 tribal districts forms only 33.63 per cent of the total geographical area of the country. It demonstrates that tribal districts are generally rich in forest cover. Forest and tribals are very closely related. The age-old knowledge of tribals regarding forestry can be used in the development of forests. Rather than treating tribals as minor forest produce collectors they should be made growers of minor forest produce and encouraged to participate in conservation.

$(1 \times 5 = 5)$

(i) The National Commission on Agriculture (1976) has classified social forestry into

  (a) Three   (b) Four

  (c) Two   (d) One

(ii) The forest policy aimed at bringing .... per cent of the geographical areas under forest cover.

  (a) 32   (b) 31

  (c) 33   (d) 35

(iii) The Government of India proposed to have a nation-wide forest conservation policy and adopted a forest policy ....
    (a) 1950   (b) 1951
    (c) 1956   (d) 1952

(iv) When did the Indian forest policy further modified?
    (a) 1978   (b) 1988
    (c) 1998   (d) 1968

(v) What is the actual forest cover in India according to India State of Forest Report 2011?
    (a) 21.05 per cent   (b) 22.05 per cent
    (c) 23.05 per cent   (d) 24.05 per cent

Section B

This section consists of 5 questions of Short Answer Type.

Short Answer Type Questions

2. What would happen if there is no ozone in the atmosphere? (3)

Or

What is the role of dust particles in atmosphere?

3. 'Gulf Current is warm and Labrador Current is cold'. Explain why some currents are warm or cold? (3)

Or

What are under currents?

4. Differentiate between extinct, endangered, vulnerable and rare species with examples. (3)

5. Differentiate between the South-West monsoon and retreating monsoon. (3)

6. Green revolution is bringing salinity in the soil. How? (3)

Or

Is it right to say that different regions exhibit different types of erosion? If yes, then why?

Section C

The section consists of 2 questions of Long Answer Type.

Long Answer Type Questions

7. What kinds of steps have been taken by Central Soil Conservation Board, set up by the Government of India? (5)

Or

How were soils classified in ancient times?

8. Mangrove forests are unique in their own way. Explain. (5)

Or

Explain in short about four important biospheres of India.

Section D

Map Based Question

9. (i) On the map of India, locate the following. (3)

    (a) An area that receive 100-200 cm of rainfall.

    (b) One region of arid soil.

    (c) One region of red and yellow soil

(ii) Identify the distribution of pressure (in millibars) in January shown by the lines marked as A and B on the map of the world given below. (2)

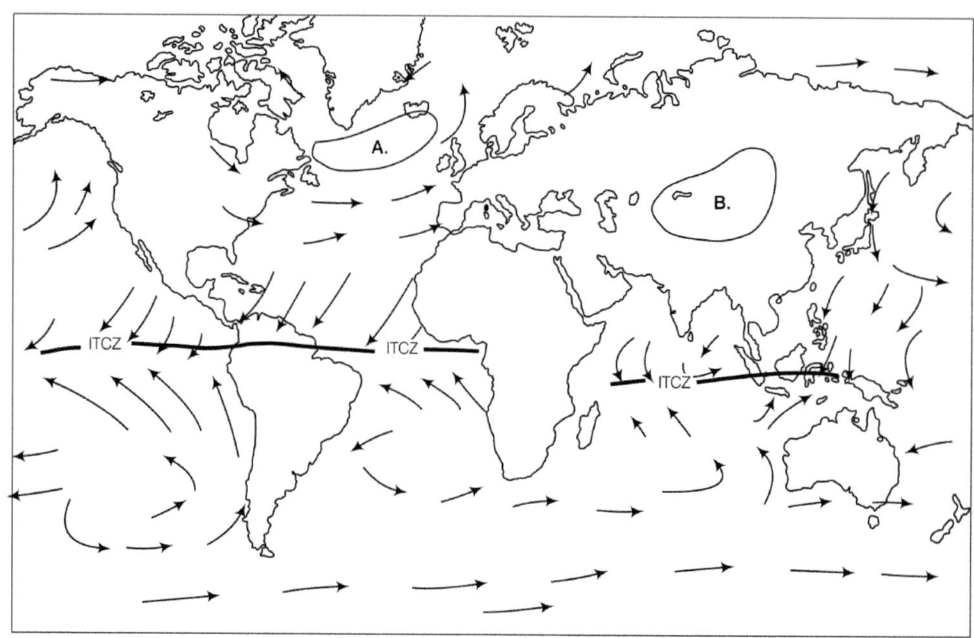

Answers

1. *(i) (b)*   *(ii) (c)*   *(iii) (d)*   *(iv) (b)*   *(v) (c)*

9. *(ii)* A. Low Pressure - 1000 mb

    B. High Pressure - 1030 mb

Practice Paper 3*
(Unsolved)

Instructions
- **Time :** 2 Hours
- **Max. Marks :** 35

1. This question paper is divided into four sections A, B, C and D.
2. Section A has 1 question including case based multiple choice questions.
3. Section B has 5 questions including short answer questions with internal choice.
4. Section C has 2 questions including long answer questions with internal choice.
5. Section D has 1 question based on map.
6. Marks are mentioned against each question.
7. There is no negative marking.

** As exact Blue-print and Pattern for CBSE Term II exams is not released yet, so the pattern of this paper is designed by the author on the basis of trend of past CBSE Papers. Students are advised not to consider the pattern of this paper as official, it is just for practice purpose.*

Section A

This section consists of one case based questions.

Case Based Question

1. Read the case/source given and answer the questions that follow by choosing the correct option.

   The ocean currents may be classified based on their depth as surface currents and deep water currents: (i) surface currents constitute about 10 per cent of all the water in the ocean, these waters are the upper 400 m of the ocean; (ii) deep water currents make up the other 90 per cent of the ocean water. These waters move around the ocean basins due to variations in the density and gravity. Deep waters sink into the deep ocean basins at high latitudes, where the temperatures are cold enough to cause the density to increase. Ocean currents can also be classified based on temperature: as cold currents and warm currents: (i) cold currents bring cold water into warm water areas. These currents are usually found on the West coast of the continents in the low and middle latitudes (true in both hemispheres) and on the East coast in the higher latitudes in the Northern Hemisphere; (ii) warm currents bring warm water into cold water areas and are usually observed on the east coast of continents in the low and middle latitudes (true in both hemispheres). In the Northern hemisphere they are found on the West coasts of continents in high latitudes.   (1 × 5 = 5)

   (i) Which of the following is warm current?
   - (a) California Current
   - (b) Humboldt (Peru)
   - (c) Labrador Current
   - (d) Gulf Current

   (ii) Which of the following is cold current?
   - (a) North Atlantic Drift
   - (b) North Pacific Drift
   - (c) Alaska Current
   - (d) Canaries Current

   (iii) Near the equator the ocean water is about .... cm higher in level than in the middle latitudes.
   - (a) 10
   - (b) 5
   - (c) 6
   - (d) 8

(iv) What is the speed of the currents?
   (a) Less than or equal to 5 knots
   (b) Less than 10 knots
   (c) More than 15 knots
   (d) Equal to 20 knots

(v) Due to the coriolis force, the warm currents from low latitudes tend to move to the .... in the Northern hemisphere.
   (a) left
   (b) right
   (c) parallel
   (d) None of these

Section B

This section consists of 5 questions of Short Answer Type.

Short Answer Type Questions

2. Explain the concept of food chain with the help of diagram. (3)

Or

How does an ecosystem work?

3. Differentiate between the direction of land breeze and sea breeze. (3)

4. Why ocean waves are important? Mention their role for the welfare of human beings. (3)

Or

Explain how do heating of solar energy, wind, gravitation and coriolis force affect the ocean currents.

5. "Monsoon is a gambling for Indian farmers". Explain. (3)

Or

"In spite of abundant rainfall, India is a water thirsty land". Why is it so?

6. Which soil is also called regur soil? Explain its features. (3)

Section C

This section consists of 2 questions of Long Answer Type.

Long Answer Type Questions

7. Write a detailed note on coriolis force. (5)

Or

What factors affect direction and velocity of winds?

8. According to the statistics received from state records, there are differences in forest area and actual forest cover. Explain. (5)

Or

Give an account of a marine biosphere reserve of India.

Section D

Map Based Question

9. (i) Locate the following on the map of India. (3)
   (a) Area receiving highest rainfall
   (b) An alluvial soil region
   (c) Mangrove forest region

(ii) Identify the currents marked as A and B on the map of the world given below. (2)

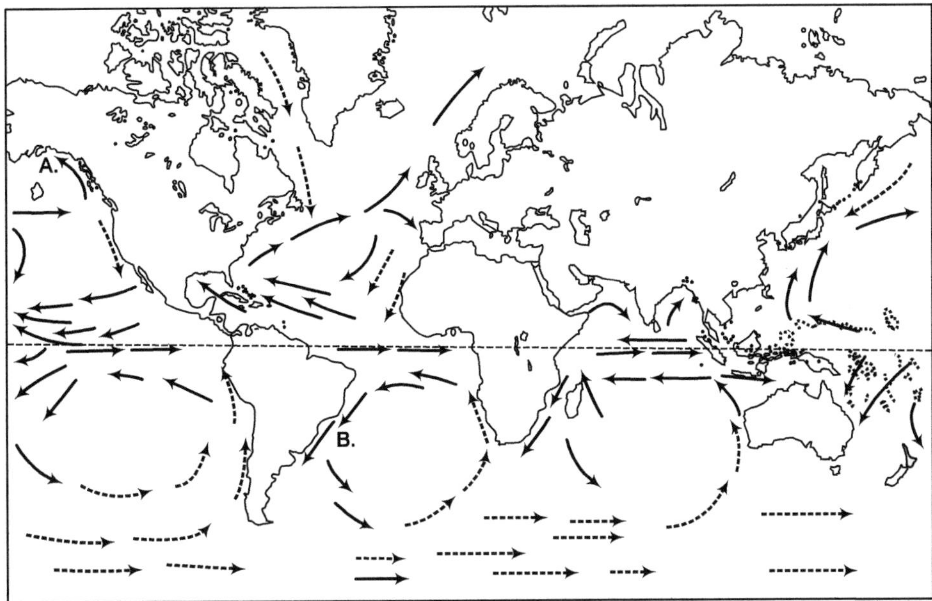

Answers

1. (i) (d) *(ii) (d)* *(iii) (d)* *(iv) (a)* *(v) (a)*

9. (ii) A. Alaska Current
    B. Brazilian Current

Printed by Libri Plureos GmbH in Hamburg,
Germany